A Book Lover's Holidays in the Open

A Book Lover's Holidays in the Open

Theodore Roosevelt

Ross & Perry, Inc.
Washington, D.C.

Copyright 1916, Charles Scribner's Sons
Reprinted by Ross & Perry, Inc. 2002
© Ross & Perry, Inc. 2002 on new material. All rights reserved.

Protected under the Berne Convention.

Printed in The United States of America

Ross & Perry, Inc. Publishers
216 G St., N.E.
Washington, D.C. 20002
Telephone (202) 675-8300
Facsimile (202) 675-8400
info@RossPerry.com

SAN 253-8555

Library of Congress Control Number: 2002100339
http://www.rossperry.com

ISBN 1-931839-57-3

Image on cover provided by Howie Garber/Wanderlustimages.com

The paper used in this publication meets the requirements for permanence
established by the American National Standard for Information Sciences
"Permanence of Paper for Printed Library Materials" (ANSI Z39.48-1984).

All rights reserved. No copyrighted part of this publication may be reproduced,
stored in a retrieval system, or transmitted, in any form or by any means,
electronic, photocopying, recording, or otherwise, without the prior written
permission of the publisher.

From a painting by Theodore B. Pitman in possession of Colonel Roosevelt.

On the brink of the Grand Canyon.

To

ARCHIE AND QUENTIN

FOREWORD

THE man should have youth and strength who seeks adventure in the wide, waste spaces of the earth, in the marshes, and among the vast mountain masses, in the northern forests, amid the steaming jungles of the tropics, or on the deserts of sand or of snow. He must long greatly for the lonely winds that blow across the wilderness, and for sunrise and sunset over the rim of the empty world. His heart must thrill for the saddle and not for the hearthstone. He must be helmsman and chief, the cragsman, the rifleman, the boat steerer. He must be the wielder of axe and of paddle, the rider of fiery horses, the master of the craft that leaps through white water. His eye must be true and quick, his hand steady and strong. His heart must never fail nor his head grow bewildered, whether he face brute and human foes, or the frowning strength of hostile nature, or the awful fear that grips those who are lost in trackless lands. Wearing toil and hardship shall be his; thirst and famine he shall face, and burning fever. Death shall come to greet him with poison-fang or poison-arrow, in shape of charging beast or of scaly things that lurk in lake and river; it shall lie in wait for him among untrodden forests, in the swirl of wild waters, and in the blast of snow blizzard or thunder-shattered hurricane.

Not many men can with wisdom make such a life their permanent and serious occupation. Those whose tasks lie along other lines can lead it for but a few years. For them it must normally come in the hardy vigor of their youth, before the beat of the blood has grown sluggish in their veins.

Nevertheless, older men also can find joy in such a life, although in their case it must be led only on the outskirts of adventure, and although the part they play therein must be that of the onlooker rather than that of the doer. The feats of prowess are for others. It is for other men to face the peril of unknown lands, to master unbroken horses, and to hold their own among their fellows with bodies of supple strength. But much, very much, remains for the man who has "warmed both hands before the fire of life," and who, although he loves the great cities, loves even more the fenceless grassland, and the forest-clad hills.

The grandest scenery of the world is his to look at if he chooses; and he can witness the strange ways of tribes who have survived into an alien age from an immemorial past, tribes whose priests dance in honor of the serpent and worship the spirits of the wolf and the bear. Far and wide, all the continents are open to him as they never were to any of his forefathers; the Nile and the Paraguay are easy of access, and the borderland between savagery and civilization; and the veil of the past has been lifted so that he can dimly see how, in time immeasurably remote, his ancestors — no less remote — led furtive lives among uncouth and terrible beasts, whose kind has perished utterly from the face of the earth. He will take books with him as he journeys; for the keenest enjoyment of the wilderness is reserved for him who enjoys also the garnered wisdom of the present and the past. He will take pleasure in the companionship of the men of the open; in South America, the daring and reckless horsemen who guard the herds of the grazing country, and the dark-skinned paddlers who guide their clumsy dugouts down the dangerous equatorial rivers; the white and red and half-breed hunters of the Rockies, and of the Canadian woodland; and in Africa the faithful black gun-bearers who have stood steadily at his elbow when the lion came on with coughing grunts, or when the huge mass of the charging elephant burst asunder the vine-tangled branches.

The beauty and charm of the wilderness are his for the asking, for the edges of the wilderness lie close beside the beaten roads of present travel. He can see the red splendor of desert sunsets, and the unearthly glory of the afterglow on the battlements of desolate mountains. In sapphire gulfs of ocean he can visit islets, above which the wings of myriads of sea-fowl make a kind of shifting cuneiform script in the air. He can ride along the brink of the stupendous cliff-walled canyon, where eagles soar below him, and cougars make their lairs on the ledges and harry the big-horned sheep. He can journey through the northern forests, the home of the giant moose, the forests of fragrant and murmuring life in summer, the iron-bound and melancholy forests of winter.

The joy of living is his who has the heart to demand it.

THEODORE ROOSEVELT.

SAGAMORE HILL, January 1, 1916.

CONTENTS

CHAPTER		PAGE
I.	A Cougar Hunt on the Rim of the Grand Canyon	1
II.	Across the Navajo Desert	29
III.	The Hopi Snake-Dance	63
IV.	The Ranchland of Argentina and Southern Brazil	98
V.	A Chilean Rondeo	117
VI.	Across the Andes and Northern Patagonia	130
VII.	Wild Hunting Companions	152
VIII.	Primitive Man; and the Horse, the Lion, and the Elephant	190
IX.	Books for Holidays in the Open	259
X.	Bird Reserves at the Mouth of the Mississippi	274
XI.	A Curious Experience	318
	Appendices:	
	A.	359
	B.	366

ILLUSTRATIONS

On the brink of the Grand Canyon . . . *Frontispiece*

Colonel Roosevelt and Arthur Lirette with antlers
of moose shot September 19, 1915
Facing page **348**

A BOOK-LOVER'S HOLIDAYS IN THE OPEN

CHAPTER I

A COUGAR HUNT ON THE RIM OF THE GRAND CANYON

ON July 14, 1913, our party gathered at the comfortable El Tovar Hotel, on the edge of the Grand Canyon of the Colorado, and therefore overlooking the most wonderful scenery in the world. The moon was full. Dim, vast, mysterious, the canyon lay in the shimmering radiance. To all else that is strange and beautiful in nature the Canyon stands as Karnak and Baalbec, seen by moonlight, stand to all other ruined temples and palaces of the bygone ages.

With me were my two younger sons, Archie and Quentin, aged nineteen and fifteen respectively, and a cousin of theirs, Nicholas, aged twenty. The cousin had driven our horses, and what outfit we did not ourselves carry, from southern Arizona to the north side of the canyon, and had then crossed the canyon to meet us. The youngest one of the three had not before been on such a trip as that we intended to take; but the two elder boys, for their good fortune, had formerly been at the Evans School in Mesa, Arizona, and among the by-products of their education was a practical and working familiarity with ranch life, with the round-up, and with travelling through the desert and on the mountains. Jesse Cummings, of Mesa, was along to act as cook, packer, and horse-wrangler, helped in all three branches by the two elder boys; he was a Kentuckian by birth, and a better man for our trip and a stancher friend could not have been found.

On the 15th we went down to the bottom of the canyon. There we were to have been met by our outfit with two men whom we had engaged; but they never turned up, and we should have been in a bad way had not Mr. Stevenson, of the Bar Z Cattle Company, come down the trail behind us, while the foreman of the Bar Z, Mr. Mansfield, appeared to meet him, on the opposite side of the rushing, muddy torrent of the Colorado. Mansfield worked us across on the trolley which spans the river; and then we joined in and worked Stevenson, and some friends he had with him, across. Among us all we had food enough for dinner and for a light breakfast, and we had our bedding. With characteristic cattleman's generosity, our new friends turned over to us two pack-mules, which could carry our bedding and the like, and two spare saddle-horses—both the mules and the spare saddle-horses having been brought down by Mansfield because of a lucky mistake as to the number of men he was to meet.

Mansfield was a representative of the best type of old-style ranch foreman. It is a hard climb out of the canyon on the north side, and Mansfield was bound that we should have an early start. He was up at half-past one in the morning; we breakfasted on a few spoonfuls of mush; packed the mules and saddled the horses; and then in the sultry darkness, which in spite of the moon filled the bottom of the stupendous gorge, we started up the Bright Angel trail. Cummings and the two elder boys walked; the rest of us were on horseback. The trail crossed and recrossed the rapid brook, and for rods at a time went up its bowlder-filled bed; groping and stumbling, we made our blind way along it; and over an hour passed before the first grayness of the dawn faintly lighted our footsteps.

At last we left the stream bed, and the trail

climbed the sheer slopes and zigzagged upward through the breaks in the cliff walls. At one place the Bar Z men showed us where one of their pack-animals had lost his footing and fallen down the mountainside a year previously. It was eight hours before we topped the rim and came out on the high, wooded, broken plateau which at this part of its course forms the northern barrier of the deep-sunk Colorado River. Three or four miles farther on we found the men who were to have met us; they were two days behindhand, so we told them we would not need them, and reclaimed what horses, provisions, and other outfit were ours. With Cummings and the two elder boys we were quite competent to take care of ourselves under all circumstances, and extra men, tents, and provisions merely represented a slight, and dispensable, increase in convenience and comfort.

As it turned out, there was no loss even of comfort. We went straight to the cabin of the game warden, Uncle Jim Owens; and he instantly accepted us as his guests, treated us as such, and accompanied us throughout our fortnight's stay north of the river. A kinder host and better companion in a wild country could not be found. Through him we hired a very

A COUGAR HUNT

good fellow, a mining prospector, who stayed with us until we crossed the Colorado at Lee's Ferry. He was originally a New York State man, who had grown up in Montana, and had prospected through the mountains from the Athabaska River to the Mexican boundary. Uncle Jim was a Texan, born at San Antonio, and raised in the Panhandle, on the Goodnight ranch. In his youth he had seen the thronging myriads of bison, and taken part in the rough life of the border, the life of the cow-men, the buffalo-hunters, and the Indian-fighters. He was by instinct a man of the right kind in all relations; and he early hailed with delight the growth of the movement among our people to put a stop to the senseless and wanton destruction of our wild life. Together with his — and my — friend Buffalo Jones he had worked for the preservation of the scattered bands of bison; he was keenly interested not only in the preservation of the forests but in the preservation of the game. He had been two years buffalo warden in the Yellowstone National Park. Then he had come to the Colorado National Forest Reserve and Game Reserve, where he had been game warden for over six years at the time of our trip. He has given zealous and efficient service to the people as a whole; for which, by the way, his salary has been an inadequate return. One important feature of his work is to keep down the larger beasts and birds of prey, the arch-enemies of the deer, mountain-sheep, and grouse; and the most formidable among these foes of the harmless wild life are the cougars. At the time of our visit he owned five hounds, which he had trained especially, as far as his manifold duties gave him the time, to the chase of cougars and bobcats. Coyotes were plentiful, and he shot these wherever the chance offered; but coyotes are best kept down by poison, and poison cannot be used where any man is keeping the hounds with which alone it is possible effectively to handle the cougars.

At this point the Colorado, in its deep gulf, bends south, then west, then north, and incloses on three sides the high plateau which is the heart of the forest and game reserve. It was on this plateau, locally known as Buckskin Mountain, that we spent the next fortnight. The altitude is from eight thousand to nearly ten thousand feet, and the climate is that of the far north. Spring does not come until June; the snow lies deep for seven months. We were there in midsummer, but the thermometer went down at night to 36, 34, and once

A COUGAR HUNT

to 33 degrees Fahrenheit; there was hoarfrost in the mornings. Sound was our sleep under our blankets, in the open, or under a shelf of rock, or beneath a tent, or most often under a thickly leaved tree. Throughout the day the air was cool and bracing.

Although we reached the plateau in mid-July, the spring was but just coming to an end. Silver-voiced Rocky Mountain hermit-thrushes chanted divinely from the deep woods. There were multitudes of flowers, of which, alas! I know only a very few, and these by their vernacular names; for as yet there is no such handbook for the flowers of the southern Rocky Mountains as, thanks to Mrs. Frances Dana, we have for those of the Eastern States, and, thanks to Miss Mary Elizabeth Parsons, for those of California. The sego lilies, looking like very handsome Eastern trilliums, were as plentiful as they were beautiful; and there were the striking Indian paint-brushes, fragrant purple locust blooms, the blossoms of that strange bush the plumed acacia, delicately beautiful white columbines, bluebells, great sheets of blue lupin, and the tall, crowded spikes of the brilliant red bell — and innumerable others. The rainfall is light and the ground porous; springs are few, and brooks wanting; but the trees are handsome. In a few places the forest is dense; in most places it is sufficiently open to allow a mountain-horse to twist in and out among the tree trunks at a smart canter. The tall yellow pines are everywhere; the erect spires of the mountain-spruce and of the blue-tipped Western balsam shoot up around their taller cousins, and the quaking asps, the aspens with their ever-quivering leaves and glimmering white boles, are scattered among and beneath the conifers, or stand in groves by themselves. Blue grouse were plentiful — having increased greatly, partly because of the war waged by Uncle Jim against their foes the great horned owls; and among the numerous birds were long-crested, dark-blue jays, pinyon-jays, doves, band-tailed pigeons, golden-winged flickers, chickadees, juncos, mountain-bluebirds, thistle-finches, and Louisiana tanagers. A very handsome cock tanager, the orange yellow of its plumage dashed with red on the head and throat, flew familiarly round Uncle Jim's cabin, and spent most of its time foraging in the grass. Once three birds flew by which I am convinced were the strange and interesting evening grosbeaks. Chipmunks and white-footed mice lived in the cabin, the former very bold and friendly; in fact, the chipmunks, of several species, were everywhere;

A COUGAR HUNT

and there were gophers or rock-squirrels, and small tree-squirrels, like the Eastern chickarees, and big tree-squirrels — the handsomest squirrels I have ever seen — with black bodies and bushy white tails. These last lived in the pines, were diurnal in their habits, and often foraged among the fallen cones on the ground; and they were strikingly conspicuous.

We met, and were most favorably impressed by, the forest supervisor, and some of his rangers. This forest and game reserve is thrown open to grazing, as with all similar reserves. Among the real settlers, the home-makers of sense and far-sightedness, there is a growing belief in the wisdom of the policy of the preservation of the national resources by the National Government. On small, permanent farms, the owner, if reasonably intelligent, will himself preserve his own patrimony; but everywhere the uncontrolled use in common of the public domain has meant reckless, and usually wanton, destruction. All the public domain that is used should be used under strictly supervised governmental lease; that is, the lease system should be applied everywhere substantially as it is now applied in the forest. In every case the small neighboring settlers, the actual home-makers, should be given priority of chance to lease the land in reasonable sized tracts. Continual efforts are made by demagogues and by unscrupulous agitators to excite hostility to the forest policy of the government; and needy men who are short-sighted and unscrupulous join in the cry, and play into the hands of the corrupt politicians who do the bidding of the big and selfish exploiters of the public domain. One device of these politicians is through their representatives in Congress to cut down the appropriation for the forest service; and in consequence the administrative heads of the service, in the effort to be economical, are sometimes driven to the expedient of trying to replace the permanently employed experts by short-term men, picked up at haphazard, and hired only for the summer season. This is all wrong: first, because the men thus hired give very inferior service; and, second, because the government should be a model employer, and should not set a vicious example in hiring men under conditions that tend to create a shifting class of laborers who suffer from all the evils of unsteady employment, varied by long seasons of idleness. At this time the best and most thoughtful farmers are endeavoring to devise means for doing away with the system of employing farm-hands in mass for a few months and then discharging them; and the government should not itself have recourse to this thoroughly pernicious system.

The preservation of game and of wild life generally — aside from the noxious species — on these reserves is of incalculable benefit to the people as a whole. As the game increases in these national refuges and nurseries it overflows into the surrounding country. Very wealthy men can have private game-preserves of their own. But the average man of small or moderate means can enjoy the vigorous pastime of the chase, and indeed can enjoy wild nature, only if there are good general laws, properly enforced, for the preservation of the game and wild life, and if, furthermore, there are big parks or reserves provided for the use of all our people, like those of the Yellowstone, the Yosemite, and the Colorado.

A small herd of bison has been brought to the reserve; it is slowly increasing. It is privately owned, one-third of the ownership being in Uncle Jim, who handles the herd. The government should immediately buy this herd. Everything should be done to increase the number of bison on the public reservations.

The chief game animal of the Colorado Canyon reserve is the Rocky Mountain blacktail, or mule, deer. The deer have increased greatly in numbers since the reserve was created, partly because of the stopping of hunting by men, and even more because of the killing off of the cougars. The high plateau is their summer range; in the winter the bitter cold and driving snow send them and the cattle, as well as the bands of wild horses, to the lower desert country. For some cause, perhaps the limestone soil, their antlers are unusually stout and large. We found the deer tame and plentiful, and as we rode or walked through the forest we continually came across them — now a doe with her fawn, now a party of does and fawns, or a single buck, or a party of bucks. The antlers were still in the velvet. Does would stand and watch us go by within fifty or a hundred yards, their big ears thrown forward; while the fawns stayed hid near by. Sometimes we roused the pretty spotted fawns, and watched them dart away, the embodiments of delicate grace. One buck, when a hound chased it, refused to run and promptly stood at bay; another buck jumped and capered, and also refused to run, as we passed at but a few yards' distance. One of the most beautiful sights I ever saw was on this trip. We were slowly riding through the open pine forest when we came on a party of seven bucks. Four were yearlings or two-year-olds; but three were mighty master bucks, and their velvet-clad antlers made them look as if they had rocking-chairs on their heads. Stately of port and bearing, they walked a few steps at a time, or stood at gaze on the carpet of brown needles strewn with cones; on their red coats the flecked and broken sun-rays played; and as we watched them, down the aisles of tall tree trunks the odorous breath of the pines blew in our faces.

The deadly enemies of the deer are the cougars. They had been very plentiful all over the table-land until Uncle Jim thinned them out, killing between two and three hundred. Usually their lairs are made in the well-nigh inaccessible ruggedness of the canyon itself. Those which dwelt in the open forest were soon killed off. Along the part of the canyon where we hunted there was usually an upper wall of sheer white cliffs; then came a very steep slope covered by a thick scrub of dwarf oak and locust, with an occasional pinyon or pine; and then another and deeper wall of vermilion cliffs. It was along this intermediate slope that the cougars usually passed the day. At night they came up through some gorge or break in the cliff and rambled through the forests and along the rim after the deer. They are the most successful of all still-hunters, killing deer much more easily than a wolf can; and those we killed were very fat.

Cougars are strange and interesting creatures. They are among the most successful and to their prey the most formidable beasts of rapine in the world. Yet when themselves attacked they are the least dangerous of all beasts of prey, except hyenas. Their every movement is so lithe and stealthy, they move with such sinuous and noiseless caution, and are such past masters in the art of concealment, that they are hardly ever seen unless roused by dogs. In the wilds they occasionally kill wapiti, and often bighorn sheep and white goats; but their favorite prey is the deer.

Among domestic animals, while they at times kill all, including, occasionally, horned cattle, they are especially destructive to horses. Among the first bands of horses brought to this plateau there were some of which the cougars killed every foal. The big males attacked full-grown horses. Uncle Jim had killed one big male which had killed a large draft-horse, and another which had killed two saddle-horses and a pack-mule, although the mule had a bell on its neck, which it was mistakenly supposed would keep the cougar away. We saw the

A COUGAR HUNT

skeleton of one of the saddle-horses. It was killed when snow was on the ground, and when Uncle Jim first saw the carcass the marks of the struggle were plain. The cougar sprang on its neck, holding the face with the claws of one paw, while his fangs tore at the back of the neck, just at the base of the skull; the other fore paw was on the other side of the neck, and the hind claws tore the withers and one shoulder and flank. The horse struggled thirty yards or so before he fell, and never rose again. The draft-horse was seized in similar fashion. It went but twenty yards before falling; then in the snow could be seen the marks where it had struggled madly on its side, plunging in a circle, and the marks of the hind feet of the cougar in an outside circle, while the fangs and fore talons of the great cat never ceased tearing the prey. In this case the fore claws so ripped and tore the neck and throat that it was doubtful whether they, and not the teeth, had not given the fatal wounds.

We came across the bodies of a number of deer that had been killed by cougars. Generally the remains were in such condition that we could not see how the killing had been done. In one or two cases the carcasses were sufficiently fresh for us to examine them carefully. One doe had claw marks on her face, but no fang marks on the head or neck; apparently the neck had been broken by her own plunging fall; then the cougar had bitten a hole in the flank and eaten part of one haunch; but it had not disembowelled its prey, as an African lion would have done. Another deer, a buck, was seized in similar manner; but the death-wound was inflicted with the teeth, in singular fashion, a great hole being torn into the chest, where the neck joins the shoulder. Evidently there is no settled and invariable method of killing. We saw no signs of any cougar being injured in the struggle; the prey was always seized suddenly and by surprise, and in such fashion that it could make no counter-attack.

Few African leopards would attack such quarry as the big male cougars do. Yet the leopard sometimes preys on man, and it is the boldest and most formidable of fighters when brought to bay. The cougar, on the contrary, is the least dangerous to man of all the big cats. There are authentic instances of its attacking man; but they are not merely rare but so wholly exceptional that in practise they can be entirely disregarded. There is no more need of being frightened when sleeping in, or wandering after nightfall through, a forest infested by

A COUGAR HUNT

cougars than if they were so many tom-cats. Moreover, when itself assailed by either dogs or men the cougar makes no aggressive fight. It will stay in a tree for hours, kept there by a single dog which it could kill at once if it had the heart — and this although if hungry it will itself attack and kill any dog, and on occasions even a big wolf. If the dogs — or men — come within a few feet, it will inflict formidable wounds with its claws and teeth, the former being used to hold the assailant while the latter inflict the fatal bite. But it fights purely on the defensive, whereas the leopard readily assumes the offensive and often charges, at headlong, racing speed, from a distance of fifty or sixty yards. It is absolutely safe to walk up to within ten yards of a cougar at bay, whether wounded or unwounded, and to shoot it at leisure.

Cougars are solitary beasts. When full-grown the females outnumber the males about three to one; and the sexes stay together for only a few days at mating-time. The female rears her kittens alone, usually in some cave; the male would be apt to kill them if he could get at them. The young are playful. Uncle Jim once brought back to his cabin a young cougar, two or three months old. At the time he had a hound puppy named Pot — he was an old dog, the most dependable in the pack, when we made our hunt. Pot had lost his mother; Uncle Jim was raising him on canned milk, and, as it was winter, kept him at night in a German sock. The young cougar speedily accepted Pot as a playmate, to be enjoyed and tyrannized over. The two would lap out of the same dish; but when the milk was nearly lapped up, the cougar would put one paw on Pot's face, and hold him firmly while it finished the dish itself. Then it would seize Pot in its fore paws and toss him up, catching him again; while Pot would occasionally howl dismally, for the young cougar had sharp little claws. Finally the cougar would tire of the play, and then it would take Pot by the back of the neck, carry him off, and put him down in his box by the German sock.

When we started on our cougar hunt there were seven of us, with six pack-animals. The latter included one mule, three donkeys — two of them, Ted and Possum, very wise donkeys — and two horses. The saddle-animals included two mules and five horses, one of which solemnly carried a cow-bell. It was a characteristic old-time Western outfit. We met with the customary misadventures of such a trip, chiefly

A COUGAR HUNT

in connection with our animals. At night they were turned loose to feed, most of them with hobbles, some of them with bells. Before dawn, two or three of the party — usually including one, and sometimes both, of the elder boys — were off on foot, through the chilly dew, to bring them in. Usually this was a matter of an hour or two; but once it took a day, and twice it took a half-day. Both breaking camp and making camp, with a pack-outfit, take time; and in our case each of the packers, including the two elder boys, used his own hitch — single-diamond, squaw hitch, cow-man's hitch, miner's hitch, Navajo hitch, as the case might be. As for cooking and washing dishes — why, I wish that the average tourist-sportsman, the city-hunter-with-a-guide, would once in a while have to cook and wash dishes for himself; it would enable him to grasp the reality of things. We were sometimes nearly drowned out by heavy rain-storms. We had good food; but the only fresh meat we had was the cougar meat. This was delicious; quite as good as venison. Yet men rarely eat cougar flesh.

Cougars should be hunted when snow is on the ground. It is difficult for hounds to trail them in hot weather, when there is no water and the ground is dry and hard. However, we had to do the best we could; and the frequent rains helped us. On most of the hunting days we rode along the rim of the canyon and through the woods, hour after hour, until the dogs grew tired, or their feet sore, so that we deemed it best to turn toward camp; having either struck no trail or else a trail so old that the hounds could not puzzle it out. I did not have a rifle, wishing the boys to do the shooting. The two elder boys had tossed up for the first shot, Nick winning. In cougar hunting the shot is usually much the least interesting and important part of the performance. The credit belongs to the hounds, and to the man who hunts the hounds. Uncle Jim hunted his hounds excellently. He had neither horn nor whip; instead, he threw pebbles, with much accuracy of aim, at any recalcitrant dog — and several showed a tendency to hunt deer or coyote. "They think they know best and needn't obey me unless I have a nose-bag full of rocks," observed Uncle Jim.

Twice we had lucky days. On the first occasion we all seven left camp by sunrise with the hounds. We began with an hour's chase after a bobcat, which dodged back and forth over and under the rim rock, and finally escaped along a ledge in the cliff wall. At about

A COUGAR HUNT

eleven we struck a cougar trail of the night before. It was a fine sight to see the hounds running it through the woods in full cry, while we loped after them. After one or two checks, they finally roused the cougar, a big male, from a grove of aspens at the head of a great gorge which broke through the cliffs into the canyon. Down the gorge went the cougar, and then along the slope between the white cliffs and the red; and after some delay in taking the wrong trail, the hounds followed him. The gorge was impassable for horses, and we rode along the rim, looking down into the depths, from which rose the chiming of the hounds. At last a change in the sound showed that they had him treed; and after a while we saw them far below under a pine, across the gorge, and on the upper edge of the vermilion cliff wall. Down we went to them, scrambling and sliding; down a break in the cliffs, round the head of the gorge just before it broke off into a side-canyon, through the thorny scrub which tore our hands and faces, along the slope where, if a man started rolling, he never would stop until life had left his body. Before we reached him the cougar leaped from the tree and tore off, with his big tail stretched straight as a bar behind him; but a cougar is a short-winded beast, and a couple of hundred yards on, the hounds put him up another tree. Thither we went.

It was a wild sight. The maddened hounds bayed at the foot of the pine. Above them, in the lower branches, stood the big horse-killing cat, the destroyer of the deer, the lord of stealthy murder, facing his doom with a heart both craven and cruel. Almost beneath him the vermilion cliffs fell sheer a thousand feet without a break. Behind him lay the Grand Canyon in its awful and desolate majesty.

Nicholas shot true. With his neck broken, the cougar fell from the tree, and the body was clutched by Uncle Jim and Archie before it could roll over the cliff — while I experienced a moment's lively doubt as to whether all three might not waltz into the abyss together. Cautiously we dragged him along the rim to another tree, where we skinned him. Then, after a hard pull out of the canyon, we rejoined the horses; rain came on; and, while the storm pelted against our slickers and down-drawn slouch-hats, we rode back to our water-drenched camp.

On our second day of success only three of us went out — Uncle Jim, Archie, and I. Unfortunately, Quentin's horse went lame that morning, and he had to stay with the pack-train.

A COUGAR HUNT

For two or three hours we rode through the woods and along the rim of the canyon. Then the hounds struck a cold trail and began to puzzle it out. They went slowly along to one of the deep, precipice-hemmed gorges which from time to time break the upper cliff wall of the canyon; and after some busy nose-work they plunged into its depths. We led our horses to the bottom, slipping, sliding, and pitching, and clambered, panting and gasping, up the other side. Then we galloped along the rim. Far below us we could at times hear the hounds. One of them was a bitch, with a squealing voice. The other dogs were under the first cliffs, working out a trail, which was evidently growing fresher. Much farther down we could hear the squealing of the bitch, apparently on another trail. However, the trails came together, and the shrill yelps of the bitch were drowned in the deeper-toned chorus of the other hounds, as the fierce intensity of the cry told that the game was at last roused. Soon they had the cougar treed. Like the first, it was in a pine at the foot of the steep slope, just above the vermilion cliff wall. We scrambled down to the beast, a big male, and Archie broke its neck; in such a position it was advisable to kill it outright, as, if it struggled at all, it was likely to slide over the edge of the cliff and fall a thousand feet sheer.

It was a long way down the slope, with its jungle of dwarf oak and locust, and the climb back, with the skin and flesh of the cougar, would be heart-breaking. So, as there was a break in the cliff line above, Uncle Jim suggested to Archie to try to lead down our riding animals while he, Uncle Jim, skinned the cougar. By the time the skin was off, Archie turned up with our two horses and Uncle Jim's mule — an animal which galloped as freely as a horse. Then the skin and flesh were packed behind his and Uncle Jim's saddles, and we started to lead the three animals up the steep, nearly sheer mountainside. We had our hands full. The horses and mule could barely make it. Finally the saddles of both the laden animals slipped, and Archie's horse in his fright nearly went over the cliff — it was a favorite horse of his, a black horse from the plains below, with good blood in it, but less at home climbing cliffs than were the mountain horses. On that slope anything that started rolling never stopped unless it went against one of the rare pine or pinyon trees. The horse plunged and reared; Archie clung to its head for dear life, trying to prevent it from turning down-hill, while Uncle

A COUGAR HUNT

Jim sought to undo the saddle and I clutched the bridle of his mule and of my horse and kept them quiet. Finally the frightened black horse sank on his knees with his head on Archie's lap; the saddle was taken off—and promptly rolled down-hill fifty or sixty yards before it fetched up against a pinyon; we repacked, and finally reached the top of the rim.

Meanwhile the hounds had again started, and we concluded that the bitch must have been on the trail of a different animal, after all. By the time we were ready to proceed they were out of hearing, and we completely lost track of them. So Uncle Jim started in the direction he deemed it probable they would take, and after a while we were joined by Pot. Evidently the dogs were tired and thirsty and had scattered. In about an hour, as we rode through the open pine forest across hills and valleys, Archie and I caught, very faintly, a far-off baying note. Uncle Jim could not hear it, but we rode toward the spot, and after a time caught the note again. Soon Pot heard it and trotted toward the sound. Then we came over a low hill crest, and when half-way down we saw a cougar crouched in a pine on the opposite slope, while one of the hounds, named Ranger, uttered at short intervals a husky bay as he kept his solitary vigil at the foot of the tree. Archie insisted that I should shoot, and thrust the rifle into my hand as we galloped down the incline. The cougar, a young and active female, leaped out of the tree and rushed off at a gait that for a moment left both dogs behind; and after her we tore at full speed through the woods and over rocks and logs. A few hundred yards farther on her bolt was shot, and the dogs, and we also, were at her heels. She went up a pine which had no branches for the lower thirty or forty feet. It was interesting to see her climb. Her two fore paws were placed on each side of the stem, and her hind paws against it, all the claws digging into the wood; her body was held as clear of the tree as if she had been walking on the ground, the legs being straight, and she walked or ran up the perpendicular stem with as much daylight between her body and the trunk as there was between her body and the earth when she was on the ground. As she faced us among the branches I could only get a clear shot into her chest where the neck joins the shoulder; down she came, but on the ground she jumped to her feet, ran fifty yards with the dogs at her heels, turned to bay in some fallen timber, and dropped dead.

A COUGAR HUNT

The last days before we left this beautiful holiday region we spent on the table-land called Greenland, which projects into the canyon east of Bright Angel. We were camped by the Dripping Springs, in singular and striking surroundings. A long valley leads south through the table-land; and just as it breaks into a sheer walled chasm which opens into one of the side loops of the great canyon, the trail turns into a natural gallery along the face of the cliff. For a couple of hundred yards a rock shelf a dozen feet wide runs under a rock overhang which often projects beyond it. The gallery is in some places twenty feet high; in other places a man on horseback must stoop his head as he rides. Then, at a point where the shelf broadens, the clear spring pools of living water, fed by constant dripping from above, lie on the inner side next to and under the rock wall. A little beyond these pools, with the chasm at our feet, and its opposite wall towering immediately in front of us, we threw down our bedding and made camp. Darkness fell; the stars were brilliant overhead; the fire of pitchy pine stumps flared; and in the light of the wavering flames the cliff walls and jutting rocks momentarily shone with ghastly clearness, and as instantly vanished in utter gloom.

From the southernmost point of this tableland the view of the canyon left the beholder solemn with the sense of awe. At high noon, under the unveiled sun, every tremendous detail leaped in glory to the sight; yet in hue and shape the change was unceasing from moment to moment. When clouds swept the heavens, vast shadows were cast; but so vast was the canyon that these shadows seemed but patches of gray and purple and umber. The dawn and the evening twilight were brooding mysteries over the dusk of the abyss; night shrouded its immensity, but did not hide it; and to none of the sons of men is it given to tell of the wonder and splendor of sunrise and sunset in the Grand Canyon of the Colorado.

CHAPTER II

ACROSS THE NAVAJO DESERT

WE dropped down from Buckskin Mountain, from the land of the pine and spruce and of cold, clear springs, into the grim desolation of the desert. We drove the pack-animals and loose horses, usually one of us taking the lead to keep the trail. The foreman of the Bar Z had lent us two horses for our trip, in true cattleman's spirit; another Bar Z man, who with his wife lived at Lee's Ferry, showed us every hospitality, and gave us fruit from his garden, and chickens; and two of the Bar Z riders helped Archie and Nick shoe one of our horses. It was a land of wide spaces and few people, but those few we met were so friendly and helpful that we shall not soon forget them.

At noon of the first day we had come down the mountainside, from the tall northern forest trees at the summit, through the scattered, sprawling pinyons and cedars of the side slopes, to the barren, treeless plain of sand and sage-brush and greasewood. At the foot of the mountain we stopped for a few minutes at an outlying cow-ranch. There was not a tree, not a bush more than knee-high, on the whole plain round about. The bare little ranch-house, of stone and timber, lay in the full glare of the sun; through the open door we saw the cluttered cooking-utensils and the rolls of untidy bedding. The foreman, rough and kindly, greeted us from the door; spare and lean, his eyes bloodshot and his face like roughened oak from the pitiless sun, wind, and sand of the desert. After we had dismounted, our shabby ponies moped at the hitching-post as we stood talking. In the big corral a mob of half-broken horses were gathered, and two dust-grimed, hard-faced cow-punchers, lithe as panthers, were engaged in breaking a couple of wild ones. All around, dotted with stunted sage-brush and greasewood, the desert stretched, blinding white in the sunlight; across its surface the dust clouds moved in pillars, and in the distance the heat-waves danced and wavered.

During the afternoon we shogged steadily across the plain. At one place, far off to one side, we saw a band of buffalo, and between them and us a herd of wild donkeys. Otherwise the only living things were snakes and lizards.

ACROSS THE NAVAJO DESERT

On the other side of the plain, two or three miles from a high wall of vermilion cliffs, we stopped for the night at a little stone rest-house, built as a station by a cow outfit. Here there were big corrals, and a pool of water piped down by the cow-men from a spring many miles distant. On the sand grew the usual desert plants, and on some of the ridges a sparse growth of grass, sufficient for the night feed of the hardy horses. The little stone house and the corrals stood bare and desolate on the empty plain. Soon after we reached them a sand-storm rose and blew so violently that we took refuge inside the house. Then the wind died down; and as the sun sank toward the horizon we sauntered off through the hot, still evening. There were many sidewinder rattlesnakes. We killed several of the gray, flat-headed, venomous things; as we slept on the ground outside the house, under the open sky, we were glad to kill as many as possible, for they sometimes crawl into a sleeper's blankets. Except this baleful life, there was little save the sand and the harsh, scanty vegetation. Across the lonely wastes the sun went down. The sharply channelled cliffs turned crimson in the dying light; all the heavens flamed ruby red, and faded to a hundred dim hues of opal, beryl and amber, pale turquoise and delicate emerald; and then night fell and darkness shrouded the desert.

Next morning the horse-wranglers, Nick and Quentin, were off before dawn to bring in the saddle and pack animals; the sun rose in burning glory, and through the breathless heat we drove the pack-train before us toward the crossing of the Colorado. Hour after hour we plodded ahead. The cliff line bent back at an angle, and we followed into the valley of the Colorado. The trail edged in toward the high cliffs as they gradually drew toward the river. At last it followed along the base of the frowning rock masses. Far off on our right lay the Colorado; on its opposite side the broad river valley was hemmed in by another line of cliffs, at whose foot we were to travel for two days after crossing the river.

The landscape had become one of incredible wildness, of tremendous and desolate majesty. No one could paint or describe it save one of the great masters of imaginative art or literature — a Turner or Browning or Poe. The sullen rock walls towered hundreds of feet aloft, with something about their grim savagery that suggested both the terrible and the grotesque. All life was absent, both from them and from the fantastic barrenness of the bowlder-strewn land at their bases. The ground was burned out or washed bare. In one place a little stream trickled forth at the bottom of a ravine, but even here no grass grew — only little clusters of a coarse weed with flaring white flowers that looked as if it throve on poisoned soil. In the still heat "we saw the silences move by and beckon." The cliffs were channelled into myriad forms — battlements, spires, pillars, buttressed towers, flying arches; they looked like the ruined castles and temples of the monstrous devil-deities of some vanished race. All were ruins — ruins vaster than those of any structures ever reared by the hands of men — as if some magic city, built by warlocks and sorcerers, had been wrecked by the wrath of the elder gods. Evil dwelt in the silent places; from battlement to lonely battlement fiends' voices might have raved; in the utter desolation of each empty valley the squat blind tower might have stood, and giants lolled at length to see the death of a soul at bay.

As the afternoon wore on, storm boded in the south. The day grew sombre; to the desolation of the blinding light succeeded the desolation of utter gloom. The echoes of the thunder rolled among the crags, and lightning jagged the darkness. The heavens burst, and the downpour drove in our faces; then through cloud rifts the sun's beams shone again and we looked on "the shining race of rain whose hair a great wind scattereth."

At Lee's Ferry, once the home of the dark leader of the Danites, the cliffs, a medley of bold colors and striking forms, come close to the river's brink on either side; but at this one point there is a break in the canyon walls and a ferry can be run. A stream flows into the river from the north. By it there is a house, and the miracle of water has done its work. Under irrigation, there are fields of corn and alfalfa, groves of fruit-trees, and gardens; a splash of fresh, cool green in the harsh waste.

South of the ferry we found two mule-wagons, sent for us by Mr. Hubbell, of Ganado, to whose thoughtful kindness we owed much. One was driven by a Mexican, Francisco Marquez; the other, the smaller one, by a Navajo Indian, Loko, who acted as cook; both were capital men, and we lived in much comfort while with them. A Navajo policeman accompanied us as guide, for we were now in the great Navajo reservation. A Navajo brought us a sheep for sale, and we held a feast.

For two days we drove southward through the desert country, along the foot of a range of red cliffs. In places the sand was heavy; in others the ground was hard, and the teams made good progress. There were little water-holes, usually more or less alkaline, ten or fifteen miles apart. At these the Navajos were watering their big flocks of sheep and goats, their horses and donkeys, and their few cattle. They are very interesting Indians. They live scattered out, each family by itself, or two or three families together; not in villages, like their neighbors the Hopis. They are pastoral Indians, but they are agriculturists also, as far as the desert permits. Here and there, where there was a little seepage of water, we saw their meagre fields of corn, beans, squashes, and melons. All were mounted; the men usually on horses, the women and children often on donkeys. They were clad in white man's garb; at least the men wore shirts and trousers and the women bodices and skirts; but the shirts were often green or red or saffron or bright blue; their long hair was knotted at the back of the head, and they usually wore moccasins. The well-to-do carried much jewelry of their own make. They wore earrings and necklaces of turquoise; turquoises were set in their many silver ornaments; and they wore buttons and bangles of silver, for they are cunning silversmiths, as well as weavers of the famous

Navajo blankets. Although they practise polygamy, and divorce is easy, their women are usually well treated; and we saw evidences of courtesy and consideration not too common even among civilized people. At one halt a woman on a donkey, with a little boy behind her, rode up to the wagon. We gave her and the boy food. Later when a Navajo man came up, she quietly handed him a couple of delicacies. So far there was nothing of note; but the man equally quietly and with a slight smile of evident gratitude and appreciation stretched out his hand; and for a moment they stood with clasped hands, both pleased, one with the courtesy, and the other with the way the courtesy had been received. Both were tattered beings on donkeys; but it made a pleasant picture.

These are as a whole good Indians — although some are very bad, and should be handled rigorously. Most of them work hard, and wring a reluctant living from the desert; often their houses are miles from water, and they use it sparingly. They live on a reservation in which many acres are necessary to support life; I do not believe that at present they ought to be allotted land in severalty, and their whole reservation should be kept for them, if only they can be brought forward fast enough in stock-raising and agriculture to use it; for with Indians and white men alike it is use which should determine occupancy of the soil. The Navajos have made progress of a real type, and stand far above mere savagery; and everything possible should be done to help them help themselves, to teach them English, and, above all, to teach them how to be better stock-raisers and food-growers — as well as smiths and weavers — in their desert home. The whites have treated these Indians well. They benefited by the coming of the Spaniards; they have benefited more by the coming of our own people. For the last quarter of a century the lawless individuals among them have done much more wrong (including murder) to the whites than has been done to them by lawless whites. The lawless Indians are the worst menace to the others among the Navajos and Utes; and very serious harm has been done by well-meaning Eastern philanthropists who have encouraged and protected these criminals. I have known some startling cases of this kind.

During the second day of our southward journey the Painted Desert, in gaudy desolation, lay far to our right; and we crossed tongues and patches of the queer formation, with its hard, bright colors. Red and purple, green and bluish, orange and gray and umber brown, the streaked and splashed clays and marls had been carved by wind and weather into a thousand outlandish forms. Funnel-shaped sandstorms moved across the waste. We climbed gradually upward to the top of the mesa. The yellow sand grew heavier and deeper. There were occasional short streams from springs; but they ran in deep gullies, with nothing to tell of their presence; never a tree near by and hardly a bush or a tuft of grass, unless planted and tended by man. We passed the stone walls of an abandoned trading-post. The desert had claimed its own. The ruins lay close to a low range of cliffs; the white sand, dazzling under the sun, had drifted everywhere; there was not a plant, not a green thing in sight — nothing but the parched and burning lifelessness of rock and sand. This northern Arizona desert was less attractive than the southern desert along the road to the Roosevelt Dam and near Mesa, for instance; for in the south the cactus growth is infinitely varied in size and in fantastic shape.

In the late afternoon we reached Tuba, with its Indian school and its trader's store. Tuba was once a Mormon settlement, the Mormons having been invited thither by the people of a

ACROSS THE NAVAJO DESERT

near-by Hopi village — which we visited — because the Hopis wished protection from hostile Indian foes. As usual, the Mormon settlers had planted and cared for many trees — cottonwoods, poplars, almond-trees, and flowering acacias — and the green shade was doubly attractive in that sandy desert. We were most hospitably received, especially by the school superintendent, and also by the trader. They showed us every courtesy. Mentioning the abandoned trading-post in the desert to the wife of the trader, she told us that it was there she had gone as a bride. The women who live in the outposts of civilization have brave souls!

We rested the horses for a day, and then started northward, toward the trading-station of John Wetherill, near Navajo Mountain and the Natural Bridge. The first day's travel was through heavy sand and very tiring to the teams. Late in the afternoon we came to an outlying trader's store, on a sandy hillside. In the plain below, where not a blade of grass grew, were two or three permanent pools; and toward these the flocks of the Navajos were hurrying, from every quarter, with their herdsmen. The sight was curiously suggestive of the sights I so often saw in Africa, when the Masai and Samburu herdsmen brought their flocks to water. On we went, not halting until nine in the evening.

All next day we travelled through a parched, monotonous landscape, now and then meeting Navajos with their flocks and herds, and passing by an occasional Navajo "hogan," or hovel-like house, with its rough corral near by. Toward evening we struck into Marsh Pass, and camped at the summit. Here we were again among the mountains; and the great gorge was wonderfully picturesque — well worth a visit from any landscape-lover, were there not so many sights still more wonderful in the immediate neighborhood. The lower rock masses were orange-hued, and above them rose red battlements of cliff; where the former broke into sheer sides there were old houses of the cliff-dwellers, carved in the living rock. The half-moon hung high overhead; the scene was wild and lovely, when we strolled away from the camp-fire among the scattered cedars and pinyons through the cool, still night.

Next morning we journeyed on, and in the forenoon we reached Kayentay, where John Wetherill, the guide and Indian trader, lives. We had been travelling over a bare table-land, through surroundings utterly desolate; and with startling suddenness, as we dropped over the edge, we came on the group of houses — the store, the attractive house of Mr. and Mrs. Wetherill, and several other buildings. Our new friends were the kindest and most hospitable of hosts, and their house was a delight to every sense: clean, comfortable, with its bath and running water, its rugs and books, its desks, cupboards, couches and chairs, and the excellent taste of its Navajo ornamentation. Here we parted with our two wagons, and again took to pack-trains; we had already grown attached to Francisco and Loko, and felt sorry to say good-by to them.

On August 10, under Wetherill's guidance, we started for the Natural Bridge, seven of us, all told, with five pack-horses. We travelled light, with no tentage, and when it rained at night we curled up in our bedding under our slickers. I was treated as "the Colonel," and did nothing but look after my own horse and bedding, and usually not even this much; but every one else in the outfit worked! On the two days spent in actually getting into and out of the very difficult country around the Bridge itself we cut down our luggage still further, taking the necessary food in the most portable form, and, as regards bedding, trusting, in cowboy fashion, to our slickers and horse blankets. But we were comfortable, and the work was just hard enough to keep us in fine trim.

We began by retracing our steps to the head of Marsh Pass and turning westward up Laguna Canyon. This was so named because it contained pools of water when, half a century ago, Kit Carson, the type of all that was best among the old-style mountain man and plainsman, traversed it during one of his successful Indian campaigns. The story of the American advance through the Southwest is filled with feats of heroism. Yet, taking into account the means of doing the work, even greater dangers were fronted, even more severe hardships endured, and even more striking triumphs achieved by the soldiers and priests who three centuries previously, during Spain's brief sunburst of glory, first broke through the portals of the thirst-guarded, Indian-haunted desert.

At noon we halted in a side-canyon, at the foot of a mighty cliff, where there were ruins of a big village of cliff-dwellers. The cliff was of the form so common in this type of rock formation. It was not merely sheer, but reentrant, making a huge, arched, shallow cave, several hundred feet high, and at least a hundred — perhaps a hundred and fifty — feet deep, the overhang being enormous. The stone houses of the village, which in all essentials was like a Hopi village of to-day, were plastered against the wall in stories, each resting on a narrow ledge. Long poles permitted one to climb from ledge to ledge, and gave access, through the roofs, to the more inaccessible houses. The immense size of the cave — or overhanging, re-entrant cliff, whichever one chooses to call it — dwarfed the houses, so that they looked like toy houses.

There were many similar, although smaller, villages and little clusters of houses among the cliffs of this tangle of canyons. Once the cliff-dwellers had lived in numbers in this neighborhood, sleeping in their rock aeries, and venturing into the valleys only to cultivate their small patches of irrigated land. Generations had passed since these old cliff-dwellers had been killed or expelled. Compared with the neighboring Indians, they had already made a long stride in cultural advance when the Spaniards arrived; but they were shrinking back before the advance of the more savage tribes. Their history should teach the lesson — taught by all history in thousands of cases, and now being taught before our eyes by the experience of China, but being taught to no purpose so far as concerns those ultra peace advocates whose heads are even softer than their hearts — that the industrious race of advanced culture and peaceful ideals is lost unless it retains the power not merely for defensive but for offensive action, when itself menaced by vigorous and aggressive foes.

That night, having ridden only some twenty-five miles, we camped in Bubbling Spring Valley. It would be hard to imagine a wilder or more beautiful spot; if in the Old World, the valley would surely be celebrated in song and story; here it is one among many others, all equally unknown. We camped by the bubbling spring of pure cold water from which it derives its name. The long, winding valley was carpeted with emerald green, varied by wide bands and ribbons of lilac, where the tall ranks of bee-blossoms, haunted by humming-birds, grew thickly, often for a quarter of a mile at a stretch. The valley was walled in by towering cliffs, a few of them sloping, most of them sheer-sided or with the tops overhanging; and there were isolated rock domes and pinnacles. As everywhere round about, the rocks were of many colors, and the colors varied from hour to hour, so that the hues of sunrise differed from those of noonday, and yet again from the long lights of sunset. The cliffs seemed orange and purple; and again

ACROSS THE NAVAJO DESERT 45

they seemed vermilion and umber; or in the white glare they were white and yellow and light red.

Our routine was that usual when travelling with a pack-train. By earliest dawn the men whose duties were to wrangle the horses and cook had scrambled out of their bedding; and the others soon followed suit. There is always much work with a pack-outfit, and there are almost always some animals which cause trouble when being packed. The sun was well up before we started; then we travelled until sunset, taking out a couple of hours to let the hobbled horses and mules rest and feed at noon.

On the second day out we camped not far from the foot of Navajo Mountain. We came across several Indians, both Navajos and Utes, guarding their flocks and herds; and we passed by several of their flimsy branch-built summer houses, and their mud, stone, and log winter houses; and by their roughly fenced fields of corn and melons watered by irrigation ditches. Wetherill hired two Indians, a Ute and a Navajo, to go with us, chiefly to relieve us of the labor of looking after our horses at night. They were pleasant-faced, silent men. They wore broad hats, shirts and waistcoats, trousers, and red handkerchiefs loosely knotted round their necks; except for their moccasins, a feather in each hat, and two or three silver ornaments, they were dressed like cowboys, and both picturesquely and appropriately. Their ornamented saddles were of Navajo make.

The second day's march was long. At one point we dropped into and climbed out of a sheer-sided canyon some twelve hundred feet deep. The trail, which zigzagged up and down the rocky walls, had been made by the Navajos. After we had led our horses down into the canyon, and were lunching by a spring, we were followed by several Indians driving large flocks of goats and sheep. They came down the trail at a good rate, many of them riding instead of leading their horses. One rather comely squaw attracted our attention. She was riding a weedy, limber-legged brood-mare, followed by a foal. The mare did not look as if it would be particularly strong even on the level; yet the well-dressed squaw, holding before her both her baby and her long sticks for blanket-weaving, and with behind her another child and a small roll of things which included a black umbrella, ambled down among the broken rocks with entire unconcern, and joked cheerily with us as she passed.

The night was lovely, and the moon, nearly full, softened the dry harshness of the land,

ACROSS THE NAVAJO DESERT 47

while Navajo Mountain loomed up under it. When we rose, we saw the pale dawn turn blood-red; and shortly after sunrise we started for our third and final day's journey to the Bridge. For some ten miles the track was an ordinary rough mountain trail. Then we left all our pack-animals except two little mules, and began the hard part of our trip. From this point on the trail was that followed by Wetherill on his various trips to the Bridge, and it can perhaps fairly be called dangerous in two or three places, at least for horses. Wetherill has been with every party that has visited the Bridge from the time of its discovery by white men four years ago. On that occasion he was with two parties, their guide being the Ute who was at this time with us. Mrs. Wetherill has made an extraordinarily sympathetic study of the Navajos and to a less extent of the Utes; she knows, and feelingly understands, their traditions and ways of thought, and speaks their tongue fluently; and it was she who first got from the Indians full knowledge of the Bridge.

The hard trail began with a twenty minutes' crossing of a big mountain dome of bare sheet rock. Over this we led our horses, up, down, and along the sloping sides, which fell away into cliffs that were scores and even hundreds of feet deep. One spot was rather ticklish. We led the horses down the rounded slope to where a crack or shelf six or eight inches broad appeared and went off level to the right for some fifty feet. For half a dozen feet before we dropped down to this shelf the slope was steep enough to make it difficult for both horses and men to keep their footing on the smooth rock; there was nothing whatever to hold on to, and a precipice lay underneath.

On we went, under the pitiless sun, through a contorted wilderness of scalped peaks and ranges, barren passes, and twisted valleys of sun-baked clay. We worked up and down steep hill slopes, and along tilted masses of sheet-rock ending in cliffs. At the foot of one of these lay the bleached skeleton of a horse. It was one which Wetherill had ridden on one of his trips to the Bridge. The horse lost his footing on the slippery slide rock, and went to his death over the cliff; Wetherill threw himself out of the saddle and just managed to escape. The last four miles were the worst of all for the horses. They led along the bottom of the Bridge canyon. It was covered with a torrent-strewn mass of smooth rocks, from pebbles to bowlders of a ton's weight. It was a marvel that the horses got down without breaking their

ACROSS THE NAVAJO DESERT 49

legs; and the poor beasts were nearly worn out.

Huge and bare the immense cliffs towered, on either hand, and in front and behind as the canyon turned right and left. They lifted straight above us for many hundreds of feet. The sunlight lingered on their tops; far below, we made our way like pygmies through the gloom of the great gorge. As we neared the Bridge the horse trail led up to one side, and along it the Indians drove the horses; we walked at the bottom of the canyon so as to see the Bridge first from below and realize its true size; for from above it is dwarfed by the immense mountain masses surrounding it.

At last we turned a corner, and the tremendous arch of the Bridge rose in front of us. It is surely one of the wonders of the world. It is a triumphal arch rather than a bridge, and spans the torrent bed in a majesty never shared by any arch ever reared by the mightiest conquerors among the nations of mankind. At this point there were deep pools in the rock bed of the canyon, with overhanging shelves under which grew beautiful ferns and hanging plants. Hot and tired, we greeted the chance for a bath, and as I floated on my back in the water the Bridge towered above me. Then we made camp. We built a blazing fire under one of the giant buttresses of the arch, and the leaping flame brought it momentarily into sudden relief. We white men talked and laughed by the fire, and the two silent Indians sat by and listened to us. The night was cloudless. The round moon rose under the arch and flooded the cliffs behind us with her radiance. After she passed behind the mountains the heavens were still brilliant with starlight, and whenever I waked I turned and gazed at the loom of the mighty arch against the clear night sky.

Next morning early we started on our toilsome return trip. The pony trail led under the arch. Along this the Ute drove our pack-mules, and as I followed him I noticed that the Navajo rode around outside. His creed bade him never pass under an arch, for the arch is the sign of the rainbow, the sign of the sun's course over the earth, and to the Navajo it is sacred. This great natural bridge, so recently "discovered" by white men, has for ages been known to the Indians. Near it, against the rock walls of the canyon, we saw the crumbling remains of some cliff-dwellings, and almost under it there is what appears to be the ruin of a very ancient shrine.

We travelled steadily at a good gait, and we

ACROSS THE NAVAJO DESERT 51

feasted on a sheep we bought from a band of Utes. Early on the afternoon of the sixth day of our absence we again rode our weary horses over the hill slope down to the store at Kayentay, and glad we were to see the comfortable ranch buildings.

Many Navajos were continually visiting the store. It seems a queer thing to say, but I really believe Kayentay would be an excellent place for a summer school of archæology and ethnology. There are many old cliff-dwellings, some of large size and peculiar interest, in the neighborhood; and the Navajos of this region themselves, not to mention the village-dwelling Hopis, are Indians who will repay the most careful study, whether of language, religion, or ordinary customs and culture. As always when I have seen Indians in their homes, in mass, I was struck by the wide cultural and intellectual difference among the different tribes, as well as among the different individuals of each tribe, and both by the great possibilities for their improvement and by the need of showing common sense even more than good intentions if this improvement is to be achieved. Some Indians can hardly be moved forward at all. Some can be moved forward both fast and far. To let them entirely alone usually means their ruin. To interfere with them foolishly, with whatever good intentions, and to try to move all of them forward in a mass, with a jump, means their ruin. A few individuals in every tribe, and most of the individuals in some tribes, can move very far forward at once; the non-reservation schools do excellently for these. Most of them need to be advanced by degrees; there must be a half-way house at which they can halt, or they may never reach their final destination and stand on a level with the white man.

The Navajos have made long strides in advance during the last fifty years, *thanks to the presence of the white men in their neighborhood.* Many decent men have helped them — soldiers, agents, missionaries, traders; and the help has quite as often been given unconsciously as consciously; and some of the most conscientious efforts to help them have flatly failed. The missionaries have made comparatively few converts; but many of the missionaries have added much to the influences telling for the gradual uplift of the tribe. Outside benevolent societies have done some good work at times, but have been mischievous influences when guided by ignorance and sentimentality — a notable instance on this Navajo reservation is given by

Mr. Leupp in his book "The Indian and His Problem." Agents and other government officials, when of the best type, have done most good, and when not of the right type have done most evil; and they have never done any good at all when they have been afraid of the Indians or have hesitated relentlessly to punish Indian wrong-doers, even if these wrong-doers were supported by some unwise missionaries or ill-advised Eastern benevolent societies. The traders of the right type have rendered genuine, and ill-appreciated, service, and their stores and houses are centres of civilizing influence.

Good work can be done, and has been done, at the schools. Wherever the effort is to jump the ordinary Indian too far ahead and yet send him back to the reservation, the result is usually failure. To be useful the steps for the ordinary boy or girl, in any save the most advanced tribes, must normally be gradual. Enough English should be taught to enable such a boy or girl to read, write, and cipher so as not to be cheated in ordinary commercial transactions. Outside of this the training should be industrial, and, among the Navajos, it should be *the kind of industrial training which shall avail in the home cabins and in tending flocks and herds and irrigated fields.* The Indian should be encouraged to build a better house; but the house must not be too different from his present dwelling, or he will, *as a rule*, neither build it nor live in it. The boy should be taught what will be of actual use to him among his fellows, and not what might be of use to a skilled mechanic in a big city, who can work only with first-class appliances; and the agency farmer should strive steadily to teach the young men out in the field how to better their stock and practically to increase the yield of their rough agriculture. The girl should be taught domestic science, not as it would be practised in a first-class hotel or a wealthy private home, but as she must practise it in a hut with no conveniences, and with intervals of sheep-herding. If the boy and girl are not so taught, their after lives will normally be worthless both to themselves and to others. If they are so taught, they will normally themselves rise and will be the most effective of home missionaries for their tribe.

In Horace Greeley's "Overland Journey," published more than half a century ago, there are words of sound wisdom on this subject. Said Greeley (I condense): "In future efforts to improve the condition of the Indians the women should be specially regarded and appealed to. A conscientious, humane, capable Christian trader, with a wife thoroughly skilled in household manufactures and handicrafts, each speaking the language of the tribe with whom they take up their residence, can do [incalculable] good. Let them keep and sell whatever articles are adapted to the Indians' needs . . . and maintain an industrial school for Indian women and children, which, though primarily industrial, should impart intellectual and religious instruction also, wisely adapted in character and season to the needs of the pupils. . . . Such an enterprise would *gradually*" [the italics here are mine] "mould a generation after its own spirit. . . . The Indian likes bread as well as the white; he must be taught to prefer the toil of producing it to the privation of lacking it." Mrs. Wetherill is doing, and striving to do, much more than Horace Greeley held up as an ideal. One of her hopes is to establish a "model hogan," an Indian home, both advanced and possible for the Navajos now to live up to — a half-way house on the road to higher civilization, a house in which, for instance, the Indian girl will be taught to wash in a tub with a pail of water heated at the fire; it is utterly useless to teach her to wash in a laundry with steam and cement bathtubs and expect her to apply this knowledge on a reservation. I wish some admirer of Horace Greeley and friend of the Indian would help Mrs. Wetherill establish her half-way house.

Mrs. Wetherill was not only versed in archæological lore concerning ruins and the like, she was also versed in the yet stranger and more interesting archæology of the Indian's own mind and soul. There have of recent years been some admirable books published on the phase of Indian life which is now, after so many tens of thousands of years, rapidly drawing to a close. There is the extraordinary, the monumental work of Mr. E. S. Curtis, whose photographs are not merely photographs, but pictures of the highest value; the capital volume by Miss Natalie Curtis; and others. If Mrs. Wetherill could be persuaded to write on the mythology of the Navajos, and also on their present-day psychology — by which somewhat magniloquent term I mean their present ways and habits of thought — she would render an invaluable service. She not only knows their language; she knows their minds; she has the keenest sympathy not only with their bodily needs, but with their mental and spiritual processes; and she is not in the least afraid of them or sentimental about them when

ACROSS THE NAVAJO DESERT 57

they do wrong. They trust her so fully that they will speak to her without reserve about those intimate things of the soul which they will never even hint at if they suspect want of sympathy or fear ridicule. She has collected some absorbingly interesting reproductions of the Navajo sand drawings, picture representations of the old mythological tales; they would be almost worthless unless she wrote out the interpretation, told her by the medicine-man, for the hieroglyphics themselves would be meaningless without such translation. According to their own creed, the Navajos are very devout, and pray continually to the gods of their belief. Some of these prayers are very beautiful; others differ but little from forms of mere devil-worship, of propitiation of the powers of possible evil. Mrs. Wetherill was good enough to write out for me, in the original and in English translation, a prayer of each type — a prayer to the God of the Dawn and the Goddess of Evening Light, and a prayer to the great Spirit Bear. They run as follows:

PRAYER TO THE DAWN

"Hi-yol-cank sil-kin Natany,
 Tee gee hozhone nas-shad,
 Sit-sigie hozhone nas-shad
 She-kayge hozhone nas-shad,

She-yage hozhone nas-shad,
She-kigee hozhone nas-shad,
She-now also hozhone nas-shad.

"San-naga, Toddetenie Huskie be-kay,
   hozhone nas-shad
Na-da-cleas, gekin, Natany,
Tes-gee hozhone nas-shad
She-kayge hozhone nas-shad,
She-kige hozhone nas-shad
She-yage hozhone nas-shad
She-now also hozhone nas-shad,

"Hozhone nas clee, hozhone nas clee,
Hozhone nas clee, hozhone nas clee."

PRAYER TO THE DAWN (TRANSLATION)

"Dawn, beautiful dawn, the Chief,
This day, let it be well with me as I go;
Let it be well before me as I go;
Let it be well behind me as I go;
Let it be well beneath me as I go;
Let it be well above me as I go;
Let all I see be well as I go.

"Everlasting, like unto the Pollen Boy;
Goddess of the Evening, the beautiful Chieftess,
This day, let it be well with me as I go;
Let it be well before me as I go;
Let it be well behind me as I go;
Let it be well beneath me as I go;
Let it be well above me as I go;
Let all I see be well as I go.

"Now all is well, now all is well,
Now all is well, now all is well."

ACROSS THE NAVAJO DESERT

(The Navajos believe in repeating a prayer, both in anticipatory and in realized form, four times, being firm in the faith that an adjuration four times repeated will bring the results they desire; the Pollen Boy is the God of Fertilization of the Flowers.)

PRAYER TO THE BIG BLACK BEAR

"Shush-et-so-dilth-kilth
Pash dilth-kilth ne-kay ba-she-che-un-de-de-talth;
Pash dilth-kilth ne-escla ba she chee un-de-de-talth;
Pash dilth-kilth ne-ea ba she chee un-de-de-talth;
Pash dilth-kilth ne-cha ba she chee un-de-de-talth;
Ba ne un-ne-ga ut-sen-el-clish; net saw now-o-tilth a
Sit saw now-o-tilth go-ud-dish-nilth;
Ba sit saw ne-egay go-ud-dish-nilth;
Ne change nis-salth dodo ne;
Ne change nis-salth do-ut-saw-daw;
Ne change nis-salth ta-de-tenie nus-cleango-ud-is-nilth;
   es-ze, es-ze, es-ze, es-ze."

PRAYER TO THE BIG BLACK BEAR (TRANSLATION)

"Big Black Bear,
With your black moccasins, like unto a knife, stand between me and danger;
With your black leggins, like unto a knife, stand between me and danger;
With your black shirt, like unto a knife, stand between me and danger,
With your black hat, like unto a knife, stand between me and danger;
With your charm send the lightning around you and around me;

By my charm tell the evil dream to leave me;
Let the evil dream not come true;
Give me medicine to dispel the evil dream;
The evil has missed me, the evil has missed me, the evil has missed me, the evil has missed me."

(The fourfold repetition of "the evil has missed me" is held to insure the accomplishment in the future of what the prayer asserts of the past. Instead of "hat" we could say "helmet," as the Navajos once wore a black buckskin helmet; and the knife was of black flint. Black was the war color. This prayer was to ward off the effect of a bad dream.)

On August 17, we left Wetherill's with our pack-train, for a three days' trip across the Black Mesa to Walpi, where we were to witness the snake-dance of the Hopis. The desert valley where Kayentay stands is bounded on the south by a high wall of cliffs, extending for scores of miles. Our first day's march took us up this; we led the saddle-horses and drove the pack-animals up a very rough Navajo trail which zigzagged to the top through a partial break in the continuous rock wall. From the summit we looked back over the desert, barren, desolate, and yet with a curious fascination of its own. In the middle distance rose a line of

ACROSS THE NAVAJO DESERT

low cliffs, deep red, well-nigh blood-red, in color. In the far distance isolated buttes lifted daringly against the horizon; prominent among them was the abrupt pinnacle known as El Capitan, a landmark for the whole region.

On the summit we were once more among pines, and we saw again the beautiful wild flowers and birds we had left on Buckskin Mountain. There were redbells and bluebells and the showy Indian paint-brushes; delicate white flowers and beautiful purple ones; rabbit-brush tipped with pale yellow, and the brighter yellow of the Navajo gorse; and innumerable others. I saw a Louisiana tanager; the pinyon jays were everywhere; ravens, true birds of the wilderness, croaked hoarsely.

From the cliff crest we travelled south through a wild and picturesque pass. The table-land was rugged and mountainous; but it sloped gradually to the south, and the mountains changed to rounded hills. It was a dry region, but with plenty of grama-grass, and much of it covered with an open forest of pinyon and cedar. After eight hours' steady jogging along Indian trails, and across country where there was no trail, we camped by some muddy pools of rain-water which lay at the bottom of a deep washout. Soon afterward a Navajo family passed camp; they were travelling in a wagon drawn by a mule and a horse, and the boys of the family were driving a big herd of sheep and goats. The incident merely illustrated the real progress the Indians are making, and how far they already are from pure savagery.

Next morning the red dawn and the flushed clouds that heralded the sunrise were very lovely. Only those who live and sleep in the open fully realize the beauty of dawn and moonlight and starlight. As we journeyed southward the land grew more arid; and the water was scarce and bad. In the afternoon we camped on a dry mud-flat, not far from a Navajo sheep-farmer, who soon visited us. Two Navajos were travelling with us; merry, pleasant fellows. One of them had a .22 Winchester rifle, with which he shot a couple of prairie-dogs — which he and his friend roasted whole for their supper, having previously shared ours.

Next day at noon we climbed the steep, narrow rock ridge on whose summit rise the three Hopi towns at one of which, Walpi, the snake-dance was to be held. The clustered rock villages stood in bold outline, on the cliff top, against the blue sky. In all America there is no more strikingly picturesque sight.

CHAPTER III

THE HOPI SNAKE-DANCE

ON our trip we not only traversed the domains of two totally different and very interesting and advanced Indian tribes, but we also met all sorts and conditions of white men. One of the latter, by the way, related an anecdote which delighted me because of its unexpected racial implications. The narrator was a Mormon, the son of an English immigrant. He had visited Belgium as a missionary. While there he went to a theatre to hear an American Negro minstrel troupe; and, happening to meet one of the minstrels in the street, he hailed him with "Halloo, Sam!" to which the pleased and astonished minstrel cordially responded: "Well, for de Lawd's sake! Who'd expect to see a white man in this country?"

I did not happen to run across any Mormons at the snake-dance; but it seemed to me that almost every other class of Americans was represented — tourists, traders, cattlemen, farmers, government officials, politicians, cowboys, scientists, philanthropists, all kinds of men and women. We were especially glad to meet the assistant commissioner of Indian affairs, Mr. Abbot, one of the most useful public servants in Uncle Sam's employ. Mr. Hubbell, whose courtesy toward us was unwearied, met us; and we owed our comfortable quarters to the kindness of the Indian agent and his assistant. As I rode in I was accosted by Miss Natalie Curtis, who has done so very much to give to Indian culture its proper position. Miss Curtis's purpose has been to preserve and perpetuate all the cultural development to which the Indian has already attained — in art, music, poetry, or manufacture — and, moreover, to endeavor to secure the further development and adaptation of this Indian culture so as to make it, what it can undoubtedly be made, an important constituent element in our national cultural development.

Among the others at the snake-dance was Geoffrey O'Hara, whom Secretary of the Interior Lane has wisely appointed instructor of native Indian music. Mr. O'Hara's purpose is to perpetuate and develop the wealth of Indian music and poetry — and ultimately the rhythmical dancing that goes with the music

THE HOPI SNAKE-DANCE

and poetry. The Indian children already know most of the poetry, with its peculiarly baffling rhythm. Mr. O'Hara wishes to appoint special Indian instructors of this music, carefully chosen, in the schools; as he said: "If the Navajo can bring with him into civilization the ability to preserve his striking and bewildering rhythm, he will have done in music what Thorpe, the Olympic champion, did in athletics." Miss Curtis and Mr. O'Hara represent the effort to perpetuate Indian art in the life of the Indian to-day, not only for his sake, but for our own. This side of Indian life is entirely unrevealed to most white men; and there is urgent need from the standpoint of the white man himself of a proper appreciation of native art. Such appreciation may mean much toward helping the development of an original American art for our whole people.

No white visitor to Walpi was quite as interesting as an Indian visitor, a Navajo who was the owner and chauffeur of the motor in which Mr. Hubbell had driven to Walpi. He was an excellent example of the Indian who ought to be given the chance to go to a non-reservation school — a class not perhaps as yet relatively very large, but which will grow steadily larger. He had gone to such a school;

and at the close of his course had entered the machine-shops of the Santa Fé and Northeastern Railway — I think that was the name of the road — staying there four years, joining the local union, going out with the other men when they struck, and having in all ways precisely the experience of the average skilled mechanic. Then he returned to the reservation, where he is now a prosperous merchant, running two stores; and he purchased his automobile as a matter of convenience and of economy in time, so as to get quickly from one store to the other, as they are far apart. He is not a Christian, nor is his wife; but his children have been baptized in the Catholic Church. Of course, such a prosperous career is exceptional for an Indian, as it would be exceptional for a white man; but there were Hopi Indians whom we met at the dance, both storekeepers and farmers, whose success had been almost as great. Among both the Navajos and Hopis the progress has been marked during the last thirty or forty years, and is more rapid now than ever before, and careers such as those just mentioned will in their essence be repeated again and again by members of both tribes in the near future. The Hopis are so far advanced that most of them can now fully profit by non-reservation

THE HOPI SNAKE-DANCE 67

schools. For large sections of the Navajos the advance must be slower. For these the agency school is the best school, and their industrial training should primarily be such as will fit them for work in their own homes, and for making these homes cleaner and better.

Of course, the advance in any given case is apt to be both fitful and one-sided — the marvel is that it is not more so. Moreover, the advance is sometimes taking place when there seems dishearteningly little evidence of it. I have never respected any men or women more than some of the missionaries and their wives — there were examples on the Navajo reservation — who bravely and uncomplainingly labor for righteousness, although knowing that the visible fruits of their labor will probably be gathered by others in a later generation. These missionaries may fail to make many converts at the moment, and yet they may unconsciously produce such an effect that the men and women who themselves remain heathen are rather pleased to have their children become Christians. I have in mind, as illustrating just what I mean, one missionary family on the Navajo reservation whom it was an inspiration to meet; and, by the way, the Christian Navajo interpreter at their mission, with his pretty wife and children, gave fine proof of what the right education can do for the Indian.

Among those at the snake-dance was a Franciscan priest, who has done much good work on the Navajo reservation. He has attained great influence with the Navajos because of his work for their practical betterment. He doesn't try to convert the adults; but he has worked with much success among the children. Like every competent judge I met, he strongly protested against opening or cutting down the Navajo reservation. I heartily agree with him. Such an act would be a cruel wrong, and would benefit only a few wealthy cattle and sheep men.

There has apparently been more missionary success among the adult Hopis than among the adult Navajos; at any rate, I came across a Baptist congregation of some thirty members, and from information given me I am convinced that these converts stood in all ways ahead of their heathen brethren. Exceptional qualities of courage, hard-headed common sense, sympathy, and understanding are needed by the missionary who is to do really first-class work; even more exceptional than are the qualities needed by the head of a white congregation under present conditions. The most marked successes have been won by men,

THE HOPI SNAKE-DANCE

themselves of lofty and broad-minded spirituality, who have respected the advances already made by the Indian toward a higher spiritual life, and instead of condemning these advances have made use of them in bringing his soul to a loftier level. One very important service rendered by the missionaries is their warfare on what is evil among the white men on the reservations; they are most potent allies in warring against drink and sexual immorality, two of the greatest curses with which the Indian has to contend. The missionary is always the foe of the white man of loose life, and of the white man who sells whiskey. Many of the missionaries, including all who do most good, are active in protecting the rights of each Indian to his land. Like the rest of us, the missionary needs to keep in mind the fact that the Indian criminal is on the whole more dangerous to the well-meaning Indian than any outsider can at present be; for there are as wide differences of character and conduct among Indians as among whites, and there is the same need in the one case as in the other of treating each individual according to his conduct — and of persuading the people of his own class and color thus to treat him.

Several times we walked up the precipitous cliff trails to the mesa top, and visited the three villages thereon. We were received with friendly courtesy — perhaps partly because we endeavored to show good manners ourselves, which, I am sorry to say, is not invariably the case with tourists. The houses were colored red or white; and the houses individually, and the villages as villages, compared favorably with the average dwelling or village in many of the southern portions of Mediterranean Europe. Contrary to what we had seen in the Hopi village near Tuba, most of the houses were scrupulously clean; although the condition of the streets — while not worse than in the Mediterranean villages above referred to — showed urgent need of a crusade for sanitation and elementary hygiene. The men and women were well dressed, in clothes quite as picturesque and quite as near our own garb as the dress of many European peasants of a good type; aside, of course, from the priests and young men who were preparing for the ceremonial dance, and who were clad, or unclad, according to the ancient ritual. There were several rooms in each house; and the furniture included stoves, sewing-machines, chairs, window-panes of glass, and sometimes window-curtains. There were wagons in one or two of the squares, for a wagon road has been built to one end of the

THE HOPI SNAKE-DANCE 71

mesa; and we saw donkeys laden with fagots or water — another south European analogy.

Altogether, the predominant impression made by the sight of the ordinary life — not the strange heathen ceremonies — was that of a reasonably advanced, and still advancing, semi-civilization; not savagery at all. There is big room for improvement; but so there is among whites; and while the improvement should be along the lines of gradual assimilation to the life of the best whites, it should unquestionably be so shaped as to preserve and develop the very real element of native culture possessed by these Indians — which, as I have already said, if thus preserved and developed, may in the end become an important contribution to American cultural life. Ultimately I hope the Indian will be absorbed into the white population, on a full equality; as was true, for instance, of the Indians who served in my own regiment, the Rough Riders; as is true on the Navajo reservation itself of two of the best men thereon, both in government employ, both partly of northern Indian blood, and both indistinguishable from the most upright and efficient of the men of pure white blood.

A visiting clergyman from the Episcopal Cathedral at Fond du Lac took me into one of the houses to look at the pottery. The grandmother of the house was the pottery-maker, and, entirely unhelped from without and with no incentive of material reward, but purely to gratify her own innate artistic feeling, she had developed the art of pottery-making to a very unusual degree; it was really beautiful pottery. On the walls, as in most of the other houses, were picture-cards and photographs, including those of her children and grandchildren, singly and grouped with their schoolmates. Two of her daughters and half a dozen grandchildren were present, and it was evident that the family life was gentle and attractive. The grandfather was not a Christian, but "he is one of the best old men I ever knew, and I must say that I admire and owe him much, if I am a parson," said my companion. The Hopis are monogamous, and the women are well treated; the man tills the fields and weaves, and may often be seen bringing in fire-wood; and the fondness of both father and mother for their children is very evident.

Many well-informed and well-meaning men are apt to protest against the effort to keep and develop what is best in the Indian's own historic life as incompatible with making him an American citizen, and speak of those of

THE HOPI SNAKE-DANCE · 73

opposite views as wishing to preserve the Indians only as national bric-à-brac. This is not so. We believe in fitting him for citizenship as rapidly as possible. But where he cannot be pushed ahead rapidly we believe in making progress slowly, and in all cases where it is possible we hope to keep for him and for us what was best in his old culture. As eminently practical men as Mr. Frissell, the head of Hampton Institute (an educational model for white, red, and black men alike), and Mr. Valentine, the late commissioner of Indian affairs, have agreed with Miss Curtis in drawing up a scheme for the payment from private sources of a number of high-grade, specially fitted educational experts, whose duty it should be to correlate all the agencies, public and private, that are working for Indian education, and also to make this education, not a mechanical impress from without, but a drawing out of the qualities that are within. The Indians themselves must be used in such education; many of their old men can speak as sincerely, as fervently, and as eloquently of duty as any white teacher, and these old men are the very teachers best fitted to perpetuate the Indian poetry and music. The effort should be to develop the existing art — whether in silver-making, pottery-making, blanket and basket weaving, or lace-knitting — and not to replace it by servile and mechanical copying. This is only to apply to the Indian a principle which ought to be recognized among all our people. A great art must be living, must spring from the soul of the people; if it represents merely a copying, an imitation, and if it is confined to a small caste, it cannot be great.

Of course all Indians should not be forced into the same mould. Some can be made farmers; others mechanics; yet others have the soul of the artist. Let us try to give each his chance to develop what is best in him. Moreover, let us be wary of interfering overmuch with either his work or his play. It is mere tyranny, for instance, to stop all Indian dances. Some which are obscene, or which are dangerous on other grounds, must be prohibited. Others should be permitted, and many of them encouraged. Nothing that tells for the joy of life, in any community, should be lightly touched.

A few Indians may be able to turn themselves into ordinary citizens in a dozen years. Give these exceptional Indians every chance; but remember that the majority must change gradually, and that it will take generations to make the change complete. Help them to

THE HOPI SNAKE-DANCE

make it in such fashion that when the change is accomplished we shall find that the original and valuable elements in the Indian culture have been retained, so that the new citizens come with full hands into the great field of American life, and contribute to that life something of marked value to all of us, something which it would be a misfortune to all of us to have destroyed.

As an example, take the case of these Hopi mesa towns, perched in such boldly picturesque fashion on high, sheer-walled rock ridges. Many good people wish to force the Hopis to desert these towns, and live in isolated families in nice tin-roofed houses on the plains below. I believe that this would be a mistake from the standpoint of the Indians — not to mention depriving our country of something as notable and as attractive as the castles that have helped make the Rhine beautiful and famous. Let the effort be to insist on cleanliness and sanitation in the villages as they are, and especially to train the Indians themselves to insist thereon; and to make it easier for them to get water. In insisting on cleanliness, remember that we preach a realizable ideal; our own ancestors lived in villages as filthy not three centuries ago. The breezy coolness of the rocky mesa top and the magnificent outlook would make it to me personally a far more attractive dwelling-place than the hot, dusty plains. Moreover, the present Hopi house, with its thick roof, is cooler and pleasanter than a tin-roofed house. I believe it would be far wiser gradually to develop the Hopi house itself, making it more commodious and convenient, rather than to abandon it and plant the Indian in a brand-new government-built house, precisely like some ten million other cheap houses. The Hopi architecture is a product of its own environment; it is as picturesque as anything of the kind which our art students travel to Spain in order to study. Therefore let us keep it. The Hopi architecture can be kept, adapted, and developed just as we have kept, adapted, and developed the Mission architecture of the Southwest — with the results seen in beautiful Leland Stanford University. The University of New Mexico is, most wisely, modelled on these pueblo buildings; and the architect, has done admirable work of the kind by adapting Indian architectural ideas in some of his California houses. The Hopi is himself already thus developing his house; as I have said, he has put in glass windows and larger doors; he is furnishing it; he is making it continually more livable. Give him a chance to utilize his own inherent sense of beauty in making over his own village for himself. Give him a chance to lead his own life as he ought to; and realize that he has something to teach us as well as to learn from us. The Hopi of the younger generation, at least in some of the towns, is changing rapidly; and it is safe to leave it to him to decide where he will build and keep his house.

I cannot so much as touch on the absorbingly interesting questions of the Hopi spiritual and religious life, and of the amount of deference that can properly be paid to one side of this life. The snake-dance and antelope-dance, which we had come to see, are not only interesting as relics of an almost inconceivably remote and savage past — analogous to the past wherein our own ancestors once dwelt — but also represent a mystic symbolism which has in it elements that are ennobling and not debasing. These dances are prayers or invocations for rain, the crowning blessing in this dry land. The rain is adored and invoked both as male and female; the gentle steady downpour is the female, the storm with lightning the male. The lightning-stick is "strong medicine," and is used in all these religious ceremonies. The snakes, the brothers of men, as are all living things in the Hopi creed, are besought to tell the beings of the underworld man's need of water.

As a former great chief at Washington I was admitted to the sacred room, or one-roomed house, the kiva, in which the chosen snake priests had for a fortnight been getting ready for the sacred dance. Very few white men have been thus admitted, and never unless it is known that they will treat with courtesy and respect what the Indians revere. Entrance to the house, which was sunk in the rock, was through a hole in the roof, down a ladder across whose top hung a cord from which fluttered three eagle plumes and dangled three small animal skins. Below was a room perhaps fifteen feet by twenty-five. One end of it, occupying perhaps a third of its length, was raised a foot above the rest, and the ladder led down to this raised part. Against the rear wall of this raised part or dais lay thirty odd rattlesnakes, most of them in a twined heap in one corner, but a dozen by themselves scattered along the wall. There was also a pot containing several striped ribbon-snakes, too lively to be left at large. Eight or ten priests, some old, some young, sat on the floor in the lower and

THE HOPI SNAKE-DANCE

larger two-thirds of the room, and greeted me with grave courtesy; they spread a blanket on the edge of the dais, and I sat down, with my back to the snakes and about eight feet from them; a little behind and to one side of me sat a priest with a kind of fan or brush made of two or three wing-plumes of an eagle, who kept quiet guard over his serpent wards. At the farther end of the room was the altar; the rude picture of a coyote was painted on the floor, and on the four sides of this coyote picture were paintings of snakes; on three sides it was hemmed in by lightning-sticks, or thunder-sticks, standing upright in little clay cups, and on the fourth side by eagle plumes held similarly erect. Some of the priests were smoking — for pleasure, not ceremonially — and they were working at parts of the ceremonial dress. One had a cast rattlesnake skin which he was chewing, to limber it up, just as Sioux squaws used to chew buckskin. Another was fixing a leather apron with pendent thongs; he stood up and tried it on. All were scantily clad, in breech-clouts or short kilts or loin flaps; their naked, copper-red bodies, lithe and sinewy, shone, and each had been splashed in two or three places with a blotch or streak of white paint. One spoke English and translated freely; I was careful not to betray too much curiosity or touch on any matter which they might be reluctant to discuss. The snakes behind me never rattled or showed any signs of anger; the translator volunteered the remark that they were peaceable because they had been given medicine — whatever that might mean, supposing the statement to be true according to the sense in which the words are accepted by plainsmen. But several of them were active in the sluggish rattlesnake fashion. One glided sinuously toward me; when he was a yard away, I pointed him out to the watcher with the eagle feathers; the watcher quietly extended the feathers and stroked and pushed the snake's head back, until it finally turned and crawled back to the wall. Half a dozen times different snakes thus crawled out toward me and were turned back, without their ever displaying a symptom of irritation. One snake got past the watcher and moved slowly past me about six inches away, whereupon the priest on my left leaned across me and checked its advance by throwing pinches of dust in its face until the watcher turned round with his feather sceptre. Every move was made without hurry and with quiet unconcern; neither snake nor man, at any time, showed a trace of worry or anger; all, human beings and reptiles,

THE HOPI SNAKE-DANCE

were in an atmosphere of quiet peacefulness. When I rose to say good-by, I thanked my hosts for their courtesy; they were pleased, and two or three shook hands with me.

On the afternoon of the following day, August 20, the antelope priests — the men of the antelope clan — held their dance. The snake priests took part. It was held in the middle of Walpi village, round a big, rugged column of rock, a dozen feet high, which juts out of the smooth surface. The antelope-dancers came in first, clad in kilts, with fox skins behind; otherwise naked, painted with white splashes and streaks, and their hair washed with the juice of the yucca root. Their leader's kilt was white; he wore a garland and anklets of cottonwood leaves, and sprinkled water from a sacred vessel to the four corners of heaven. Another leader carried the sacred bow and a bull-roarer, and they moved to its loud moaning sound. The snake priests were similarly clad, but their kirtles were of leather; eagle plumes were in their long hair, and under their knees they carried rattles made of tortoise-shell. In two lines they danced opposite each other, keeping time to the rhythm of their monotonous chanting.

On the top of the column were half a dozen Hopi young men, clad in ordinary white man's clothing. Archie joined these, and entered into conversation with them. They spoke English; they had been at non-reservation schools; they were doing well as farmers and citizens. One and all they asserted that, in order to prosper in after life, it was necessary for the Indian to get away to a non-reservation school; that merely to go to an agency school was not enough in any community which was on the highroad of progress; and that they intended to send their own children for a couple of years to an agency school and then to a non-reservation school. They looked at the ceremonial religious dances of their fathers precisely as the whites did; they were in effect Christians, although not connected with any specific church. They represented substantial success in the effort to raise the Indian to the level of the white man. In their case it was not necessary to push them toward forgetfulness of their past. They were travelling away from it naturally, and of their own accord. As their type becomes dominant the snake-dance and antelope-dance will disappear, the Hopi religious myths will become memories, and the Hopis will live in villages on the mesa tops, or scattered out on the plains, as their several inclinations point, just as if they were so many

THE HOPI SNAKE-DANCE 83

white men. It is to be hoped that the art, the music, the poetry of their elders will be preserved during the change coming over the younger generation.

On my return from this dance I met two of the best Indian agents in the entire service. The first was Mr. Parquette, a Wisconsin man, himself part Indian by blood. The other was Mr. Shelton, who has done more for the Navajos than any other living man. He has sternly put down the criminal element exactly as he has toiled for and raised the decent Indians and protected them against criminal whites; moreover, he has actually reformed these Indian criminals, so that they are now themselves decent people and his fast friends; while the mass of the Indians recognize him as their leader who has rendered them incalculable services. He has got the Indians themselves to put an absolute stop to gambling, whiskey-drinking, and sexual immorality. His annual agricultural fair is one of the features of Navajo life, and is of far-reaching educational value. Yet this exceptionally upright and efficient public servant, who has done such great and lasting good to the Indians, was for years the object of attack by certain Eastern philanthropic associations, simply because he warred against Indian criminals who were no more entitled to sympathy than the members of the Whyo gang in New York City. Messrs. Shelton and Parquette explained to me the cruel wrong that would be done to the Navajos if their reservation was thrown open or cut down. It is desert country. It cannot be utilized in small tracts, for in many parts the water is so scanty that hundreds, and in places even thousands, of acres must go to the support of any family. The Indians need it all; they are steadily improving as agriculturists and stock-growers; few small settlers could come in even if the reservation were thrown open; the movement to open it, and to ruin the Indians, is merely in the interest of a few needy adventurers and of a few wealthy men who wish to increase their already large fortunes, and who have much political influence.

Mr. Robinson, the superintendent of irrigation, in protesting against opening the reservation, dwelt upon the vital need of getting from Congress sufficient money to enable the engineers to develop water by digging wells, preserving springs, and making flood reservoirs. The lack of water is the curse of this desert reservation. The welfare of the Indians depends on the further development of the water-supply.

THE HOPI SNAKE-DANCE

That night fires flared from the villages on the top of the mesa. Before there was a hint of dawn we heard the voice of the crier summoning the runners to get ready for the snake-dance; and we rose and made our way to the mesa top. The "yellow line," as the Hopis call it, was in the east, and dawn was beautiful, as we stood on the summit and watched the women and children in their ceremonial finery, looking from the housetops and cliff edges for the return of the racers. On this occasion they dropped their civilized clothes. The children were painted and naked save for kilts; and they wore feathers and green corn leaves in their hair. The women wore the old-style clothing; many of them were in their white bridal dresses, which in this queer tribe are woven by the bridegroom and his male kinsfolk for the bride's trousseau. The returning racers ran at speed up the precipitous paths to the mesa, although it was the close of a six-mile run. Most of them, including the winner, wore only a breech-clout and were decked with feathers. I should like to have entered that easy-breathing winner in a Marathon contest! Many of the little boys ran the concluding mile or so with them; and the little girls made a pretty spectacle as they received the little boys much as the women and elder girls greeted the men. Then came the corn-scramble, or mock-fight over the corn; and then in each house a feast was set, especially for the children.

At noon, thanks to Mr. Hubbell, and to the fact that I was an ex-President, we were admitted to the sacred kiva — the one-roomed temple-house which I had already visited — while the snake priests performed the ceremony of washing the snakes. Very few white men have ever seen this ceremony. The sight was the most interesting of our entire trip.

There were twenty Indians in the kiva, all stripped to their breech-clouts; only about ten actually took part in handling the snakes, or in any of the ceremonies except the rhythmic chant, in which all joined. Eighty or a hundred snakes, half of them rattlers, the others bull-snakes or ribbon-snakes, lay singly or in tangled groups against the wall at the raised end of the room. They were quiet and in no way nervous or excited. Two men stood at this end of the room. Two more stood at the other end, where the altar was; there was some sand about the altar, and the eagle feathers we had previously seen there had been removed, but the upright thunder-sticks remained. The other Indians were squatted in the middle of the room,

THE HOPI SNAKE-DANCE

and half a dozen of them were in the immediate neighborhood of a very big, ornamented wooden bowl of water, placed on certain white-painted symbols on the floor. Two of these Indians held sacred rattles, and there was a small bowl of sacred meal beside them. There was some seemingly ceremonial pipe-smoking.

After some minutes of silence, one of the squatting priests, who seemed to be the leader, and who had already puffed smoke toward the bowl, began a low prayer, at the same time holding and manipulating in his fingers a pinch of the sacred meal. The others once and again during this prayer uttered in unison a single word or exclamation — a kind of selah or amen. At the end he threw the meal into the bowl of water; he had already put some in at the outset of the prayer. Then he began a rhythmic chant, in which all the others joined, the rattles being shaken and the hands moved in harmony with the rhythm. The chant consisted seemingly of a few words repeated over and over again. It was a strange scene, in the half-light of the ancient temple-room. The copper-red bodies of the priests swayed, and their strongly marked faces, hitherto changeless, gained a certain quiet intensity of emotion. The chanting grew in fervor; yet it remained curiously calm throughout (except for a moment at a time, about which I shall speak later). Then the two men who stood near the snakes stooped over, and each picked up a handful of them, these first handfuls being all rattlesnakes. It was done in tranquil, matter-of-fact fashion, and the snakes behaved with equally tranquil unconcern. All was quiet save for the chanting. The snakes were handed to two of the men squatting round the bowl, who received them as if they had been harmless, holding them by the middle of the body, or at least well away from the head. This was repeated until half a dozen of the squatting priests held each three or four poisonous serpents in his hands. The chanting continued, in strongly accented but monotonous rhythm, while the rattles were shaken, and the snakes moved up and down or shaken, in unison with it. Then suddenly the chant quickened and rose to a scream, and the snakes were all plunged into the great bowl of water, a writhing tangle of snakes and hands. Immediately afterward they were withdrawn, as suddenly as they had been plunged in, and were hurled half across the room, to the floor, on and around the altar. They were hurled from a distance of a dozen feet, with sufficient violence to overturn the erect thunder-sticks. That the snakes should have been quiet and inoffensive under the influence of the slow movements and atmosphere of calm that had hitherto obtained was understandable; but the unexpected violence of the bathing, and then of the way in which they were hurled to the floor, together with the sudden screaming intensity of the chant, ought to have upset the nerves of every snake there. However, it did not. The snakes woke to an interest in life, it is true, writhed themselves free of one another and of the upset lightning-sticks, and began to glide rapidly in every direction. But only one showed symptoms of anger, and these were not marked. The two standing Indians at this end of the room herded the snakes with their eagle feathers, gently brushing and stroking them back as they squirmed toward us, or toward the singing, sitting priests.

The process was repeated until all the snakes, venomous and non-venomous alike, had been suddenly bathed and then hurled on the floor, filling the other end of the room with a wriggling, somewhat excited serpent population, which was actively, but not in any way nervously, shepherded by the two Indians stationed for that purpose. These men were, like the others, clad only in a breech-clout, but they moved about among the snakes, barelegged and barefooted, with no touch of concern. One or two of the rattlers became vicious under the strain, and coiled and struck. I thought I saw one of the two shepherding watchers struck in the hand by a recalcitrant sidewinder which refused to be soothed by the feathers, and which he finally picked up; but, if so, the man gave no sign and his placidity remained unruffled. Most of the snakes showed no anger at all; it seemed to me extraordinary that they were not all of them maddened.

When the snakes had all been washed, the leading priest again prayed. Afterward he once more scattered meal in the bowl, in lines east, west, north, and south, and twice diagonally. The chant was renewed; it grew slower; the rattles were rattled more slowly; then the singing stopped and all was over.

At the end of the ceremony I thanked my hosts and asked if there was anything I could do to show my appreciation of the courtesy they had shown me. They asked if I could send them some cowry shells, which they use as decorations for the dance. I told them I would send them a sackful. They shook hands cordially with all of us, and we left. I have never seen a wilder or, in its way, more impres-

THE HOPI SNAKE-DANCE

sive spectacle than that of these chanting, swaying, red-skinned medicine-men, their lithe bodies naked, unconcernedly handling the death that glides and strikes, while they held their mystic worship in the gray twilight of the kiva. The ritual and the soul-needs it met, and the symbolism and the dark savagery, were all relics of an ages-vanished past, survivals of an elder world.

The snake-dance itself took place in the afternoon at five o'clock. There were many hundreds of onlookers, almost as many whites as Indians, and most of the Indian spectators were in white man's dress, in strong contrast to the dancers. The antelope priests entered first and ranged themselves by a tree-like bundle of cottonwood branches against the wall of buildings to one side of the open place where the dance takes place; the other side is the cliff edge. The snakes, in a bag, were stowed by the bundle of cottonwood branches. Young girls stood near the big pillar of stone with sacred meal to scatter at the foot of the pillar after the snakes had been thrown down there and taken away. Then the snake priests entered in their fringed leather kilts and eagle-plume head-dresses; fox skins hung at the backs of their girdles, their bodies were splashed and streaked with white, and on each of them the upper part of the face was painted black and the lower part white. Chanting, and stepping in rhythm to the chant, and on one particular stone slab stamping hard as a signal to the underworld, they circled the empty space and for some minutes danced opposite the line of antelope priests. Then, in couples, one of each couple seizing and carrying in his mouth a snake, they began to circle the space again. The leading couple consisted of one man who had his arm across the shoulder of another, while this second man held in his teeth, by the upper middle of its body, a rattlesnake four feet long, the flat, ace-of-clubs-shaped head and curving neck of the snake being almost against the man's face. Rattlesnakes, bull-snakes, ribbon-snakes, all were carried in the same way. One man carried at the same time two small sidewinder rattlesnakes in his mouth. After a while each snake was thrown on the rock and soon again picked up and held in the hand, while a new snake was held in the mouth. Finally, each man carried a bundle of snakes in his hand, all so held as to leave the head free, so that the snake could strike if it wished. Most of the snakes showed no anger or resentment. But occasionally one, usually a small sidewinder, half coiled or rattled when thrown down; and in picking these up much caution was shown, the Indian stroking the snake with his eagle feathers and trying to soothe it and get it to straighten out; and if it refused to be soothed, he did his best to grasp it just back of the head; and when he had it in his hand, he continued to stroke the body with the feathers, obviously to quiet it. But whether it were angry or not, he always in the end grasped and lifted it — besides keeping it from crawling among the spectators. Several times I saw the snakes strike at the men who were carrying them, and twice I was sure they struck home — once a man's wrist, once his finger. Neither man paid any attention or seemed to suffer in any way. I saw no man struck in the face; but several of my friends had at previous dances seen men so struck. In one case the man soon showed that he was in much pain, although he continued to dance, and he was badly sick for days; in the other cases no bad result whatever followed.

At last all the snakes were in the hands of the dancers. Then all were thrown at the foot of the natural stone pillar, and immediately, with a yell, the dancers leaped in, seized, each of them, several snakes, and rushed away, east, west, north, and south, dashing over the edge of the cliff and jumping like goats down the precipitous trails. At the foot of the cliff, or on the plain, they dropped the snakes, and then returned to purify themselves by drinking and washing from pails of dark sacred water — medicine water — brought by the women. It was a strange and most interesting ceremony all through.

I do not think any adequate explanation of the immunity of the dancers has been advanced. Perhaps there are several explanations. These desert rattlesnakes are not nearly as poisonous as the huge diamond-backs of Florida and Texas; their poison is rarely fatal. The dancers are sometimes bitten; usually they show no effects, but, as above said, in one instance the bitten man was very sick for several days. It has been said that the fangs are extracted; but even in this case the poison would be loose in the snake's mouth and might get in the skin through the wounds made by the other teeth; and I noticed that when any snake, usually a small sidewinder, showed anger and either rattled or coiled, much caution was shown in handling it, and every effort made to avoid being bitten. It is also asserted that the snakes show the quiet and placid indifference

THE HOPI SNAKE-DANCE 95

they do because they are drugged, and one priest told me they are given "medicine"; but I have no idea whether this is true. Nor do I know whether the priests themselves take medicine. I believe that one element in the matter is that the snake priests either naturally possess or develop the same calm power over these serpents that certain men have over bees; the latter power, the existence of which is so well known, has never received the attention and study it deserves. An occasional white man has such power with snakes. There was near my ranch on the Little Missouri, twenty-five years ago, a man who had this power. He was a rather shiftless, ignorant man, of a common frontier type, who failed at about everything, and I think he was himself surprised when he found that he could pick up and handle rattlesnakes with impunity. There was no deception about it. I would take him off on horseback, and when I found a rattler he would quietly pick it up by the thick part of the body and put it in a sack. He sometimes made movements with his hands before picking up a coiled rattler; but when he had several in a bag he would simply put his hand in, take hold of a snake anywhere, and draw it out. I can understand the snakes being soothed and quieted by the matter-of-fact calm and fearlessness of the priests for most of the time; but why the rattlers were not all maddened by the treatment they received at the washing in the kiva, and again when thrown on the dance rock, I cannot understand.

That night we motored across the desert with Mr. Hubbell to his house and store at Ganado, sixty miles away, and from Ganado we motored to Gallup, and our holiday was at an end. Mr. Hubbell is an Indian trader. His Ganado house, right out in the bare desert, is very comfortable and very attractive, and he treats all comers with an open-handed hospitality inherited from pioneer days. He has great influence among the Navajos, and his services to them have been of much value. Every ounce of his influence has been successfully exerted to put a stop to gambling and drinking; his business has been so managed as to be an important factor in the material and moral betterment of the Indians with whom he has dealt. And he has been the able champion of their rights wherever these rights have been menaced from any outside source.

Arizona and New Mexico hold a wealth of attraction for the archæologist, the anthropologist, and the lover of what is strange and

THE HOPI SNAKE-DANCE

striking and beautiful in nature. More and more they will attract visitors and students and holiday-makers. That part of northern Arizona which we traversed is of such extraordinary interest that it should be made more accessible by means of a government-built motor road from Gallup to the Grand Canyon; a road from which branch roads, as good as those of Switzerland, would gradually be built to such points as the Hopi villages and the neighborhood of the Natural Bridge.

CHAPTER IV

THE RANCHLAND OF ARGENTINA AND SOUTHERN BRAZIL

IN the fall of 1913 I enjoyed a glimpse of the ranch country of southern Brazil and of Argentina. It was only a glimpse; for I was bent on going northward into the vast wilderness of tropical South America. I had no time to halt in the grazing country of temperate South America, which is no longer a wilderness, but a land already feeling the sweep of the modern movement. It is a civilized land, already fairly well settled, which by leaps and bounds is becoming thickly settled; a region which at the present day is in essentials far more closely kin to the plains country, which in temperate North America stretches from Hudson Bay to the Gulf, than either land is kin to what each was even half a century ago. The main difference is that the great cow country, the plains country, of North America was peopled only by savages when the white pioneers entered it in the nineteenth century; whereas throughout temperate

RANCHLANDS 99

South America there were here and there oases of thin settlement, including even small, stagnant cities, already two or three centuries old. In these oases people wholly or partly of European blood had gradually developed a peculiar and backward, but real, semicivilization of their own. This quaint, distinctive social culture has been, or is now being, engulfed by the rising tide of intensely modern internationalized material development.

Among the many pleasant memories of my visit to Argentina, one of the most pleasant is that of a dinner at the house of the governor of the old provincial capital of Mendoza. Our distinguished host came of an old country family which for many centuries led the life of the great cattle-breeding ranch-owners, although his people were more and more turning their attention to agriculture, he himself being a successful farmer, as well as an invaluable public servant of advanced views. His father was at the dinner. He had retired as a general after forty-nine years' service in the Argentine army. The fine old fellow represented what was best in the Argentine type before the days of modern industrialism. A very vigorous and manly best it was, too. He wore the old Argentine uniform, which for his rank was the same as the uniform once worn by Napoleon's officers. He had served in the bloody Paraguayan War, when Argentina, Brazil, and Uruguay joined to overthrow the inconceivably murderous dictatorship of Lopez, and when the Paraguayans rallied with savage valor under the banner of the dictator, who tyrannized over them, but who nevertheless represented in their eyes the nation. This old general had served in many Indian wars, both in Patagonia and in the Grand Chaco, and had seen desperate fighting in the civil wars. He wore medals commemorating his services in the Paraguayan and Indian campaigns, but he would not wear any medals commemorating his services in the civil wars. Yet the only time he was wounded was in one of the battles in one of these civil wars. He was then shot twice and received a bayonet thrust, and was also stabbed with a lance. If he had not possessed a constitution of iron he would never have survived. Our people in the United States often speak of these South American wars with the same ignorant lack of appreciation that used to be shown by European military men in speaking of our own Civil War and other contests. This attitude is as foolish on our part in the one case as it was foolish on the part of the Europeans in question

RANCHLANDS

in the other case. The South American Indian fighting was of the same hazardous character, and the Indian campaigns were fraught with the same wearing fatigue, and marked by the same risk and wild adventure, as in the case of our own Indian campaigns. In the Argentine civil wars, and in the Paraguayan War, as in the wars which the Chileans have waged, the fighting was, on the whole, rather more desperate than in any contest between the civilized nations of Europe from the close of the Napoleonic struggles to the opening of the present gigantic contest. There is no more formidable fighting material in the world than is afforded by certain elements in the populations of some of these Latin-American countries. The general of whom I am speaking was himself a most interesting example of a vanishing type. Lovers of good literature should read the sketches of old-time Argentine life in Hudson's "El Ombu." When they have done so, they will understand the strength and the ruthlessness which produced leaders of the stamp of the scarred and war-hardened veteran who in full general's uniform met us at dinner at the house of his son, the governor of Mendoza.

The old-time conditions of gaucho civilization that produced these wild and formidable fighting men, who fought as they lived, on the backs of their horses, have vanished as utterly as our own Far West of the days of Kit Carson. The Argentine country life has changed as completely as the Argentine city life. They are gone, those long years during which the gaucho rode over unfenced plains after gaunt cattle, and warred against the scarcely wilder Indians with whom he vied in horsemanship and plainscraft and hardihood and from whom he borrowed that strange weapon, the bolas. Even the southern Andes of what was once Patagonia are unexplored only in the sense that the Rockies of Alberta are not yet completely explored. Much of the former ranch country is now wheatland, where the workmen of foreign, especially Italian, origin far outnumber the men of old Hispano-Indian stock. Great cattle-ranches remain; but they are handled substantially like great modern ranches in our own Southwest, and the blooded horses and high-grade cattle are kept in large, fenced pastures. In most places the gaucho has changed as our own cowboy has changed. He is as bold and good a horseman as ever; but it is only in out-of-the-way places that he retains all his old-time wild and individual picturesqueness. Elsewhere he is now merely an unusually capable ranch-hand. His employer has changed even more. The big handsome ranch-houses are fitted with every modern comfort and luxury, and the owners belong in all ways to the internationalized upper class of the world of to-day. The interest attaching to a visit to one of these civilized ranches is that which attaches to a visit to a fine modern stock-farm anywhere, whether in Hungary or Kentucky or Victoria.

But there is one vital point — *the* vital point — in which the men and women of these ranch-houses, like those of the South America that I visited generally, are striking examples to us of the English-speaking countries both of North America and Australia. The families are large. The women, charming and attractive, are good and fertile mothers in all classes of society. There are no symptoms of that artificially self-produced dwindling of population which is by far the most threatening symptom in the social life of the United States, Canada, and the Australian commonwealths. The nineteenth century saw a prodigious growth of the English-speaking, relative to the Spanish-speaking, population of the new worlds west of the Atlantic and in the Southern Pacific. The end of the twentieth century will see this completely reversed unless the present ominous tendencies as regards the birth-rate are reversed. A race is worthless and contemptible if its men cease to be willing and able to work hard and, at need, to fight hard, and if its women cease to breed freely. I am not speaking of pauper families with excessive numbers of ill-nourished and badly brought up children; I am well aware that, like most wise and good principles, this which I advocate can be carried to a mischievous excess; but it nevertheless remains true that voluntary sterility among married men and women of good life is, even more than military or physical cowardice in the ordinary man, the capital sin of civilization, whether in France or Scandinavia, New England or New Zealand. If the best classes do not reproduce themselves the nation will of course go down; for the real question is encouraging the fit, and discouraging the unfit, to survive. When the ordinary decent man does not understand that to marry the woman he loves, as early as he can, is the most desirable of all goals, the most successful of all forms of life entitled to be called really successful; when the ordinary woman does not understand that all other forms of life are but makeshift and starveling substitutes for the life of the happy wife, the mother of a fair-sized family of healthy children; then the state is rotten at heart. The loss of a healthy, vigorous, natural sexual instinct is fatal; and just as much so if the loss is by disuse and atrophy as if it is by abuse and perversion. Whether the man, in the exercise of one form of selfishness, leads a life of easy self-indulgence and celibate profligacy; or whether in the exercise of a colder but no less repulsive selfishness, he sacrifices what is highest to some form of mere material achievement in accord with the base proverb that "he travels farthest who travels alone"; or whether the sacrifice is made in the name of the warped and diseased conscience of asceticism; the result is equally evil. So, likewise, with the woman. In many modern novels there is portrayed a type of cold, selfish, sexless woman who plumes herself on being "respectable," but who is really a rather less desirable member of society than a prostitute. Unfortunately the portrayal is true to life. The woman who shrinks from motherhood is as low a creature as a man of the professional pacificist, or poltroon, type, who shirks his duty as a soldier. The only full life for man or woman is led by those men and women who together, with hearts both gentle and valiant, face lives of love and duty, who see their children rise up to call them blessed and who leave behind them their seed to inherit the earth. Dealing with averages, it is the bare truth to say that no celibate life approaches such a life in point of usefulness, no matter what the motive for the celibacy — religious, philanthropic, political, or professional. The mother comes ahead of the nun — and also of the settlement or hospital worker; and if either man or woman must treat a profession as a substitute for, instead of as an addition to or basis for, marriage, then by all means the profession or other "career" should be abandoned. It is of course not possible to lay down universal rules. There must be exceptions. But the rule must be as above given. In a community which is at peace there may be a few women or a few men who for good reasons do not marry, and who do excellent work nevertheless; just as in a community which is at war, there may be a few men who for good reasons do not go out as soldiers. But if the average woman does not marry and become the mother of enough healthy children to permit the increase of the race; and if the average man does not, above all other things, wish to marry in time of peace, and to do his full duty in war if the need arises, then the race is decadent, and should be swept aside to make room for one that is better. Only that nation has a future whose sons and daughters recognize and obey the primary laws of their racial being.

In these essentials Argentina, Chile, Uruguay, and Brazil have far more to teach than to learn from the English-speaking countries which are so proud of their abounding material prosperity and of their wide-spread, but superficial, popular education and intelligence. In this same material prosperity, and in many other matters, Argentina much resembles our own country. Brazil is travelling a similar path, although much more slowly; and although its climate is not so good, its natural resources are vaster and will in the present century undergo an extraordinary development. Very much of the Brazilian country from São Paulo to the Uruguayan frontier is essentially like Argentina. The city life and the ranch life are advancing in much the same fashion; although of course there are sharp differences in culture and habits of thought and life between the great Spanish-speaking and great Portuguese-speaking republics which are such close, and not wholly friendly, neighbors.

One point of similarity is the number of immigrants in each country. In our journey southward from São Paulo we found both towns and stretches of ranchland in which Germans, Italians, and Catholic, Orthodox, or Uniate Slavs, were important, and sometimes preponderant, elements of the population. There were German Lutheran churches and also congregations of native Protestants started by American missionaries; for Brazil, like Argentina and the United States, enjoys genuine religious liberty.

This rich and beautiful country of southern Brazil is part of the last great stretch of country — south-temperate America — which remains in either temperate zone open to white settlement on a large scale; the last great stretch of scantily peopled land with a good climate and fertile soil to which white immigration can go in mass.

Of part of tropical Brazil I have written elsewhere, and I allude to it elsewhere in this book. Here I am speaking not of the tropical but of the temperate country.

Portions of temperate Brazil are open prairie, portions are forest. The climate is never very hot, nor is there ever severe cold. The colonists with whom I conversed had not found the insects specially troublesome; not much more, and in places rather less, troublesome than in Louisiana and Texas. There was no more sickness than in the early days in the West. The general effect in the forest country, while of course the species of plants are entirely different, reminds the observer of the Louisiana and Mississippi cane-brake lands and the country along the Nueces. The activities of the settlers in the open country are substantially those with which I was familiar thirty years ago in the cattle country of the West. In the forests one is reminded more of early days on the Ohio, the Yazoo, and the Red River of the South.

Certainly this is a country with a wonderful future. It offers fine opportunities for settlers who desire with the labor of their own hands to make homes for themselves and their children. This does not mean that all people who go there will prosper, or that success will come save at the price of labor and effort, of risk and hardship. If any Americans have forgotten how our own West in the pioneer days appealed to an observer who was friendly, but who had not the faintest glimmering of the pioneer spirit, let them read "Martin Chuzzlewit." Dickens represented the numerous men who foolishly hope to enjoy pioneer triumphs and yet escape pioneer risks and hardships and the unlovely and wearing toil which is the essential prerequisite to the triumph; and every one should remember that in a new country, which opens a chance of success to the settler, there always goes with this the chance of heart-breaking failure. Brazil offers remarkable openings for settlers who have the toughness of the born pioneer, and for certain business men and engineers who have the mixture of daring enterprise and sound common sense needed by those who push the industrial development of new countries. Both classes have great opportunities, and both need to be perpetually on their guard against the swindlers and the crack-brained enthusiasts who are always sure to turn up in connection with any country of large developmental possibilities. On the frontier, more than anywhere else, a man needs to be able to rely on himself and to remember that on every frontier there are innumerable failures.

No man can be guaranteed success. Men who are not prepared for labor and effort and rough living, for persistence and self-denial, are out of place in a new country; and foolish people who will probably fail anywhere are more certain to fail badly in a new country than anywhere else. During the whole period of the marvellous growth of the United States there has been a constant and uninterrupted stream

RANCHLANDS

of failure going side by side with the larger stream of success. Unless there is revolutionary disorder and anarchy, the future holds for southern Brazil much what half a century ago the future held for large portions of our country lying west of the Mississippi.

In southern Brazil the forest landscape through which we passed was very beautiful. The most conspicuous tree in the forest was the flat-topped pine, the shaft of which rose like that of a royal palm. The branches spread out at the top just where the palm-leaves spread out on the palm, only instead of drooping they curved upward like the branches of a candelabra. There were many other trees in the forests which I could not recognize or place. Some of them looked like our Southern live-oaks. Then there were palms, and multitudes of big tree-ferns. In places where these tree-ferns grew thickly among the tall, strange candelabra pines, with palms scattered here and there, and other queer ancient tropical plants, the landscape looked as if it had come out of the carboniferous period — at least as the carboniferous period was represented in the attractive popular geologies of my youth. There were flowers in the woods, of brilliant and varied hue, although we saw but few orchids;

and in the glades or spots of open prairie there were immense patches of lilac and blue blossoms. The flowering trees were wonderful. On some the blooms were blue, on others yellow. The most beautiful of all flamed brilliant scarlet. The trees that bore them, when scattered over hillsides that sloped steeply to the brink of some rushing river, made splashes of burning red against the wet and vivid green of the subtropical foliage. As we got farther south I was told that there were occasional sharp frosts, but that the low temperature never lasted for more than an hour or so. In answer to a question as to how these rare, short frosts affected such plants as palms and tree-ferns, it was explained to me that the frosts prevented coffee being grown, but that they had no effect on the palms, and, rather curiously, no effect on the tree-ferns if they were under big forest trees, but that if they were in the open the fronds were killed, the trees themselves not being injured, and new fronds taking the place of the old ones.

, In the open prairie country of the state of Parana we stopped at Morungava to visit the ranch of the Brazil Land, Cattle, and Packing Company. Our host, the head of this company, Murdo Mackenzie, for many years one of

RANCHLANDS

the best-known cattlemen in our own Western cow country, was an old friend of mine. During my term as President he was, on the whole, the most influential of the Western cattle-growers. He was a leader of the far-seeing and enlightened element. He was a most powerful supporter of the government in the fight for the conservation of our natural resources, for the utilization without waste of our forests and pastures, for honest treatment of everybody, and for the shaping of governmental policy primarily in the interest of the small settler, the home-maker.

We rode first to Mackenzie's home ranch, about a mile from the railway, and then to an outlying set of ranch buildings ten miles off. At the home ranch were the American foreman and his American wife and their children. The buildings and the food and the whole life were typical of all that was best in the old-time "Far West," in the days when I knew it as a cattle country. We were given a most delicious and purely American lunch, including all the fresh milk we could drink; and the foreman himself piloted us over the immense stretches of rolling country, and in every action showed himself the born cattleman, the born and trained stockman. Half of the employees were men from the Western ranches, from Montana, Colorado, Texas, or elsewhere; and they and the stock and the vast, pleasant, open-air country were enough to make any man feel at home who had ever lived in the West. The children round the ranch-house were already speaking fluent Portuguese!

There were Indians in the neighborhood; but we saw none, for they are very shy and dwell in the timber. Although nominally Christian, and somewhat under the influence of the priests, they are otherwise entirely outside of governmental control. At first Mackenzie's cattle were sometimes killed by the wild, furtive creatures; but he stopped this by a mixture of firmness and fair treatment.

It was a beautiful country, well watered, with good grass and much timber. I was assured by both the men on the ranch and their wives that the climate was better than that of our own Western cattle country, for the heat is not as extreme as during summer in the southern part of our country, and the winters are mild, with only occasional touches of frost. Much care has to be shown in dealing with the ticks and certain other insect plagues, but not materially more than in some of our own Southern regions. While we were at the outlying ranch we saw the cattle being dipped in familiar ranch fashion.

Cattle, horses, and hogs all thrive. All the native stock offers material on which to improve. The company is carefully breeding upward, following precisely the same course which in Texas, for instance, has effected a complete substitution of graded beef and dairy cattle for the old longhorns. The native cattle are very distinctly better than the old Texan cattle — the native Mexican cattle. The Durham and Hereford bulls introduced from the States will in a very few years completely change the character of the herds. Good cows are kept in sufficient numbers to insure a constant supply of the breeding bulls. In the same way Berkshire boars are being crossed with the native pigs, and blooded stallions with the native mares. In short, everything is being done exactly as on our advanced and successful ranches at home. The country is still largely vacant, and opportunities for development will be almost limitless for at least another generation.

Aside from the extreme interest of seeing the ranch itself, the twenty-mile ride was most enjoyable. The country was like our own plains near the foothills of the Rockies, except that there was more water and a greater variety of timber. The most striking trees were the occasional peculiar flat-top pines, and there were also other and very beautiful pines through which the wind sang mournfully; and there were many flowers. In one place we saw a small prairie deer, and in galloping we had to keep a lookout for armadillo burrows, just as we keep a lookout for prairie-dog holes in the West. The birds were strange and interesting, some of them with beautiful voices. Out on the plains were screamers, noisy birds, as big as African bustards. One sparrow sang loudly, at midday, round the corrals where we dismounted for lunch. He was a confiding, pretty little fellow, with head markings somewhat like those of our white-crowned and white-throated sparrows. He sang better than the former, and not as well as the latter.

The horses were good, and we thoroughly enjoyed our afternoon canter back to the home ranch, when the shadows had begun to lengthen. We loped across the rolling grass-land and by the groves of strange trees, through the brilliant weather. Under us the horses thrilled with life; it was a country of vast horizons; we felt the promise of the future of the land across which we rode.

CHAPTER V

A CHILEAN RONDEO

ON November 21, 1913, we crossed the Andes into Chile by rail. The railway led up the pass which, used from time immemorial by the Indians, afterward marked the course of traffic for their Spanish successors, and was traversed by the army of San Martin in the hazardous march that enabled him to strike the decisive blows in the war for South American independence. The valleys were gray and barren, the sides of the towering mountains were bare, the landscape was one of desolate grandeur. To the north the stupendous peak of Aconquija rose in its snows.

On the Chilean side, as we descended, we passed a lovely lake, and went through wonderful narrow gorges; and farther down were trees, and huge cactus, and flowers of many colors. Then we reached the lower valleys and the plains; and the change was like magic. Suddenly we were in a rich fairy-land of teeming plenty and beauty, a land of fertile fields and shady groves, a land of grain and, above all, of many kinds of luscious fruits.

As in the Argentine and Brazil, every courtesy and hospitality was shown us in Chile. We enjoyed every experience throughout our stay. One of the pleasantest and most interesting days we passed was at a great ranch, a great cattle-farm and country place twenty-five or thirty miles from Santiago. It was some fifteen miles from the railway station. The road led through a rich, fertile country largely under tillage, but also largely consisting of great fenced pastures.

The owners of the ranch, our kind and courteous hosts, had summoned all the riders of the neighborhood to attend the *rondeo* (round-up and sports), and several hundred, perhaps a thousand, came. With the growth of cultivation of the soil and the introduction of improved methods of stock-breeding in Chile, the old rude life of the wild cow-herders is passing rapidly away. But in many places it remains in modified form, and the country folk whose business is pastoral form a striking and distinctive class. These countrymen live their lives in the saddle. All these men, whose industries are connected with cattle, are known as *huasos*. They are kin to the Argentine

A CHILEAN RONDEO

gauchos, and more remotely to our own cowboys.

As we neared the ranch, slipping down broad, dusty, tree-bordered roads beside which irrigation streams ran, we began to come across the *huasos* gathering for the sports. They rode singly and by twos and threes, or in parties of fifteen or twenty. They were on native Chilean horses — stocky, well-built beasts, hardy and enduring, and on the whole docile. Almost all the men wore the light *manta*, less heavy than the *serapi*, but like it in shape, the head of the rider being thrust through a hole in the middle. It would seem as though it might interfere with the free use of their arms, but it does not, and at the subsequent cattle sports many of the participants never took off their *mantas*. The riders wore straw hats of various types, but none of them with the sugar-loaf cones of the Mexicans. Their long spurs bore huge rowels. The *mantas* were not only picturesque, but gave the company a look of diversified and gaudy brilliancy, for they were of all possible colors, green, red, brown, and blue, solid and patterned. The saddles were far forward, and the shoe-shaped wooden stirrups were elaborately carved.

The men were fine-looking fellows, some with smooth faces or mustaches, some with beards, some of them light, most of them dark. They rode their horses with the utter ease found only in those who are born to the saddle. Now and then there were family parties, mother and children, all, down to the smallest, riding their own horses or perhaps all going in a wagon. Once or twice we passed horsemen who were coming out of the yards of their tumble-down houses, women and children crowding round. Generally the women had something in the dress that reminded one more or less of our Southwestern semicivilized Indians, and the strain of Indian blood in both men and women was evident. Some of the men were poorly clad, others had paid much attention to their get-up and looked like very efficient dandies; but in its essentials the dress was always the same.

When we reached the ranch we first drove to a mass of buildings, which included the barns, branding-pens, corrals, and the like. It was here that the horsemen had gathered, and one of the pens was filled with an uneasy mass of cattle. Not far from this pen was a big hitching rail or bar, very stout, consisting of tree trunks at least a foot in diameter, the total length of the rail being forty or fifty feet. Beside it was a very large and stout corral.

A CHILEAN RONDEO

The inside of this corral was well padded with poles, making a somewhat springy wall, a feature I have never seen in any corrals in our own ranch country, but essential where the horses are trained to jam the cattle against the corral side.

Most of the sports took place inside this big corral. Gates led into it from opposite ends. Some thirty or forty feet in front of one of the gates, and just about that distance from the middle of the corral, was a short, crescent-shaped fence which served to keep the stock that had yet to be worked separate from those that had been worked. Proceedings were begun by some thirty riders and a mob of cattle coming through one of the doors of the corral. A glance at the cattle was enough to show that the old days of the wild ranches had passed. These were not longhorns, staring, vicious creatures, shy and fleet as deer; they were graded stock, domestic in their ways, and rather reluctant to run. Among the riders, however, there was not the slightest falling off from the old dash and skill, and their very air, as they rode quietly in, and the way they sat every sudden, quick move of their horses showed their complete ease and self-confidence.

In addition to the *huasos*, the peasants-on-horseback, the riders included several of the gentry, the great landed proprietors. These took part in the sports, precisely as in our own land men of the corresponding class follow the hounds or play polo. Two of the most skilful and daring riders, who always worked together, were a wealthy neighboring ranchman and his son.

The first feat began by two of the horsemen, acting together, cutting out an animal from the bunch. This was done with skill and precision, but differed in no way from the work I used formerly to see and take part in on the Little Missouri. What followed, however, was totally different. The animal was raced by the two men out from the herd and from behind the little semicircular fence, and was taken at full speed round the edge of the great corral past the closed gate on the other side, and almost back to the starting-point. One horseman rode behind the animal, a little on its inner side. The other rode outside it, the horse's head abreast of the steer's flank. As they galloped the riders uttered strange, long-drawn cries, evidently of Indian origin. Round the corral rushed the steer, and, after it passed the door on the opposite side and began to return toward its starting-point and saw the other cattle ahead, it put on speed. Then the outside rider raced forward and at the same moment wheeled inward, pinning the steer behind the horns and either by the neck or shoulder against the rough, yielding boughs with which the corral was lined. Instantly the other horseman pressed the steer's hind quarters outward, so that it found itself not only checked, but turned in the opposite direction. Again it was urged into a gallop, the calling horsemen following and repeating their performance. The steer was thus turned three times. After the third turning the gate which it had passed was opened and it trotted out.

A dozen times different pairs of riders performed the feat with different steers. It was a fine exhibition of daring prowess and of good training in both the horses and the riders. Of course, if it had not been for the lining of the inner fence with limber poles the steer would have been killed or crippled — we saw one of them injured, as it was. The horse, which entered heartily into the spirit of the chase, had to crash straight into the fence, nailing the steer and bringing it to a standstill in the midst of its headlong gallop. Once or twice at the critical moment the rider was not able to charge quickly enough; and when the steer was caught too far back it usually made its escape and rejoined the huddle of cattle from which it had been cut out. The men were riders of such skill that shaking them in their seats was impossible, no matter how quickly the horse turned or how violent the shocks were; nor was a single horse hurt in the rough play. It was a wild scene, and an exhibition of prowess well worth witnessing.

Other exhibitions of horsemanship followed, including the old feat of riding a bull. The bull, a vicious one, was left alone in the ring, and his temper soon showed signs of extreme shortness as he pawed the dirt, tossing it above his shoulders. Watching the chance when the bull's attention was fixed elsewhere, a man ran in and got to the little fence before the bull could charge him. Then, while the bull was still angrily endeavoring to get at the man, the corral gate opposite was thrown open and six or eight horsemen entered, riding with quiet unconcern. The bull was obviously not in the least afraid of the footman, whereas he had a certain feeling of respect for the horsemen. Two of the latter approached him. One got his rope over the bull's horns, and the other then dexterously roped the hind legs. The footman rushed in and seized the tail, and the

A CHILEAN RONDEO

bull was speedily on his side. Then a lean, slab-sided, rather frowzy-looking man, outwardly differing in no essential respect from the professional bronco-buster of the Southwest, slipped from the spectators' seats into the ring. A saddle was girthed tight on the bull, and a rope ring placed round his broad chest so as to give the rider something by which to hang. The lassos upon him were cast loose, and he rose, snorting with rage and terror. If he had thrown the man, the horsemen would have had to work with instantaneous swiftness to save his life. But all the bull's furious bucking and jumping could not unseat the rider. The horsemen began to tease the animal, flapping red blankets in his face, and luring him to charges which they easily evaded. Finally they threw him again, took off his saddle and turned him loose, and at the same time some steers were driven into the corral to serve as company for him. A couple of the horsemen took him out of the bunch and raced him round the corral, turning him when they wished by pressing him against the pole corral lining, thus repeating the game that had already been played with so many of the steers. In his case it was, of course, more dangerous. But they showed complete mastery, and the horses had not the slightest fear, nailing him flat against the wall with their chests, and spinning him round when they struck him on occasions when he was trying to make up his mind to resist.

Meanwhile the bull-rider passed his hat among the spectators, who tossed silver pieces into it — thus marking the fundamental difference between the life we were witnessing and our own Western ranch life. In Chile, with its aristocratic social structure, there is a wide gulf between the gentry and the ranch-hands; whereas in the democratic life of our own cow country the ranch-owner has, more often than not, at one time been himself a ranch-hand.

After the sports in the corral were finished eight or ten of the *huasos* appeared on big horses at the bar of which I have spoken, and took part in a sport which was entirely new to me. Two champions would appear side by side or half-facing each other, at the bar. Each would turn his horse's head until it hung over the bar as they half-fronted each other, on the same side of the bar. The object was for each man to try to push his opponent away from the bar and then shove past him, usually carrying his opponent with him. Sometimes it was a contest of man against man. Sometimes each would have two or three backers. No one could touch any other man's horse, and each drove his animal right against his opponent. The two men fronting each other at the bar kept their horses head-on against the bar; the others strove each to get his horse's head between the body of one of his opponents and the head of that opponent's horse. They then remained in a knot for some minutes, the riders cheering the horses with their strange, wild, Indian-like cries, while the horses pushed and strained. Usually there was almost no progress on either side at first. It would look as though not an inch was gained. Gradually, however, the horses on one side or the other got an inch or two or three inches advantage of position by straining and shoving. Suddenly the right vantage-point was attained. There was an outburst of furious shouting from the riders. The horses of one side with straining quarters thrust their way through the press, whirling round or half upsetting their opponents, and rushed down alongside the bar. Why the men's legs were not broken I could not say. On this occasion all the men were good-natured. But it was a rough sport, and I could well credit the statement that, if there were bad blood to gratify, the chances were excellent for a fight.

After the sports we motored down to a great pasture on one side of a lake, beyond which rose lofty mountains. Then we returned to the ranch-house itself — a huge, white, single-storied house with a great courtyard in the middle and wings extending toward the stable, the saddle-rooms, and the like. It was a house of charm and distinction; the low building — or rather group of buildings, with galleries and colonnades connecting them — being in the old native style, an outgrowth of the life and the land. After a siesta our hosts led us out across a wide garden brilliant and fragrant with flowers, to the deep, cool shade of a row of lofty trees, where stood a long table spread with white linen and laden with silver and glass; and here, we were served with a delicious and elaborate breakfast — the Chilean breakfast, that of Latin Europe, for in most ways the life of South America is a development of that of Latin Europe, and much more closely kin to it than it is to the life of the English-speaking peoples north of the Rio Grande.

In the afternoon we drove back to the railroad. At one point of our drive we were joined by a rider who had taken part in the morning's sports. He galloped at full speed beside the rushing motor-car, waving his hat to us and shouting good-by. He was a tall, powerfully built, middle-aged man, with fine, clean-cut features; his brightly colored mantle streamed in the wind, and he sat in the saddle with utter ease while his horse tore over the ground alongside us. He was a noble figure, and his farewell to us was our last glimpse of the wild, old-time *huaso* life.

CHAPTER VI

ACROSS THE ANDES AND NORTHERN PATAGONIA

AS the great chain of the Andes stretches southward its altitude grows less, and the mountain wall is here and there broken by passes. When the time came for me to leave Chile I determined to cross the Andes by the easiest and most accessible and one of the most beautiful of these comparatively low passes. At the other end of the pass, on the Argentine or Patagonian side, we were to be met by motor-cars, sent thither by my considerate hosts, the governmental authorities of Argentina.

From Santiago we went south by rail to Puerto Varas. The railway passed through the wide, rolling agricultural country of central Chile, a country of farms and prosperous towns. As we went southward we found ourselves in a land which was new in the sense that our own West is new. Middle and southern Chile were in the hands of the Indians but a short while since. We were met by fine-looking represen-

ACROSS THE ANDES

tatives of these Araucanian Indians, all of them now peaceable farmers and stock-growers, at a town of twenty or thirty thousand people where there was not a single white man to be found a quarter of a century ago. Our party included, among others, Major Shipton, U. S. A., the military aide to our legation at Buenos Ayres, my son Kermit, and several kind Chilean friends.

We reached our destination, Puerto Varas, early in the morning. It stands on the shore of a lovely lake. There has been a considerable German settlement in middle and southern Chile, and, as everywhere, the Germans have made capital colonists. At Puerto Varas there are two villages, mainly of Germans, one Protestant and the other Catholic. We were made welcome and given breakfast in an inn which, with its signs and pictures, might have come from the Fatherland. Among the guests at the breakfast, in addition to the native Chilean Intendente, were three or four normal-school teachers, all of them Germans — and evidently uncommonly good teachers, too. There were school-children, there were citizens of every kind. Many of the Germans born abroad could speak nothing but German. The children, however, spoke Spanish, and in some cases nothing but Spanish. Here, as so often in the addresses made to me, special stress was laid upon the fact that my country represented the cause of civil and religious liberty, of the absolute equality of treatment of all men without regard to creed, and of social and industrial justice; in short, the cause of orderly liberty in body, soul, and mind, in things intellectual and spiritual no less than in things industrial and political; the liberty that guarantees to each free, bold spirit the right to search for truth without any check from political or ecclesiastical tyranny, and that also guarantees to the weak their bodily rights as against any man who would exploit or oppress them.

We left Puerto Varas by steamer on the lake to begin our four days' trip across the Andes and through northern Patagonia, which was to end when we struck the Argentine Railway at Neuquen. This break in the Andes makes an easy road, for the pass at its summit is but three thousand feet high. The route followed leads between high mountains and across lake after lake, and the scenery is as beautiful as any in the world.

The first lake was surrounded by a rugged, forest-clad mountain wilderness, broken here and there by settlers' clearings. Wonderful mountains rose near by; one was a snow-clad volcano with a broken cone which not many years ago was in violent eruption. Another, even more beautiful, was a lofty peak of virginal snow. At the farther end of the lake we lunched at a clean little hotel. Then we took horses and rode for a dozen miles to another lake, called Esmeralda or Los Santos. Surely there can be no more beautiful lake anywhere than this! All around it are high mountains, many of them volcanoes. One of these mountains to the north, Punti Agudo, rises in sheer cliffs to its soaring summit, so steep that snow will hardly lie on its sides. Another to the southwest, called Tronador, the Thunderer, is capped with vast fields of perpetual snow, from which the glaciers creep down to the valleys. It gains its name of thunderer from the tremendous roaring of the shattered ice masses when they fall. Out of a huge cave in one of its glaciers a river rushes, full grown at birth. At the eastern end of this lake stands a thoroughly comfortable hotel, which we reached at sunset. Behind us in the evening lights, against the sunset, under the still air, the lake was very beautiful. The peaks were golden in the dying sunlight, and over them hung the crescent moon.

Next morning, before sunrise, we were riding eastward through the valley. For two or three miles the ride suggested that through the Yosemite, because of the abruptness with which the high mountain walls rose on either hand, while the valley was flat, with glades and woods alternating on its surface. Then we got into thick forest. The trees were for the most part giant beeches, but with some conifers, including a rather small species of sequoia. Here and there, in the glades and open spaces, there were masses of many-hued wild flowers; conspicuous among them were the fuchsias.

A dozen miles on we stopped at another little inn. Here we said good-by to the kind Chilean friends who had accompanied us thus far, and were greeted by no less kind Argentine friends, including Colonel Reybaud of the Argentine army, and Doctor Moreno, the noted Argentine scientist, explorer, and educator. Then we climbed through a wooded pass between two mountains. Its summit, near which lies the boundary-line between Chile and Argentina, is somewhere in the neighborhood of three thousand feet high; and this is the extreme height over which at this point it is necessary to go in traversing what is elsewhere the mighty mountain wall of the Andes. Here we met a

ACROSS THE ANDES 135

tame guanaco (a kind of llama) in the road; it strolled up to us, smelled the noses of the horses, which were rather afraid of it, and then walked on by us. From the summit of the pass the ground fell rapidly to a wonderfully beautiful little lake of lovely green water. This little gem is hemmed in by sheer-sided mountains, densely timbered save where the cliffs rise too boldly for even the hardiest trees to take root. As with all these lakes, there are many beautiful waterfalls. The rapid mountain brooks fling themselves over precipices which are sometimes so high that the water reaches the foot in sheets of wavering mist. Everywhere in the background rise the snow peaks.

We crossed this little lake in a steam-launch, and on the other side found the quaintest wooden railway, with a couple of rough handcars, each dragged by an ox. In going downhill the ox is put behind the car, which he holds back with a rope tied to his horns. We piled our baggage on one car, three or four members of the party got on the other, and the rest of us walked for the two miles or so before we reached the last lake we were to traverse — Nahuel Huapi. Here there happened one of those incidents which show how the world is shrinking. Three travellers, evidently Englishmen, were at the landing. One of them came up to me and introduced himself, saying: "You won't remember me; when I last saw you, you were romping with little Prince Sigurd, in Buckingham Palace at the time of the King's funeral; I was in attendance on (naming an august lady); my name is Herschel, Lord Herschel." I recalled the incident at once. On returning from my African trip I had passed through western Europe, and had been most courteously received. In one palace the son and heir — whom I have called Sigurd, which was not his name — was a dear little fellow, very manly and also very friendly; and he reminded me so of my own children when they were small that I was unable to resist the temptation of romping with him, just as I had romped with them. A month later, when as special ambassador I was attending King Edward's funeral, I called at Buckingham Palace to pay my respects, and was taken in to see the august lady above alluded to. The visit lasted nearly an hour, and toward the end I heard little squeaks and sounds in the hall outside, for which I could not account. Finally I was dismissed, and, on opening the door, there was little Sigurd, with his nurse, waiting for me. He had heard that I was in the palace, and had refused to go down to dinner until he had had a play with me; and he was patiently and expectantly waiting outside the door for me to appear. I seized him, tossed him up, while he shouted gleefully, caught him, and rolled him on the floor, quite forgetting that any one was looking on; and then, in the midst of the romp, happening to look up, I saw the lady on whom I had been calling, watching the play with much interest, with her equally interested two brothers, both of them sovereigns, and her lords-in-waiting; she had come out to see what the little boy's laughter meant. I straightened up, whereupon the little boy's face fell, and he anxiously inquired: "But you're not going to stop the play, are you?" Of all this my new-found friend reminded me. If was a far cry in space and in surroundings, from where he and I had first met to the Andes that border Patagonia. He was a man of knowledge and experience, and the half-hour I spent with him was most pleasant.

At Nahuel Huapi we were met by a little lake steamer, on which we spent the next four hours. The lake is of bold and irregular outline, with many deep bays, and with mountain walls standing as promontories between the bays. For a couple of hours the scenery was as beautiful as it had been during any part of the two days, especially when we looked back at the mass of snow-shrouded peaks. Then the lake opened, the shores became clear of woods, the mountains lower, and near the eastern end, where there were only low rolling hills, we came to the little village of Bariloche.

Bariloche is a real frontier village. Forty years previously Doctor Moreno had been captured by Indians at this very spot, had escaped from them, and after days of extraordinary hardship had reached safety. He showed us a strange, giant pine-tree, of a kind different from any of our northern cone-bearers, near which the Indians had camped while he was prisoner with them. He had persuaded the settlers to have this tree preserved, and it is still protected, though slowly dying of old age. The town is nearly four hundred miles from a railway, and the people are of the vigorous, enterprising frontier type. It was like one of our frontier towns in the old-time West as regards the diversity in ethnic type and nationality among the citizens. The little houses stood well away from one another on the broad, rough, faintly marked streets. In one we might see a Spanish family, in another blond Germans or Swiss,

ACROSS THE ANDES

in yet another a family of gaucho stock looking more Indian than white. All worked and lived on a footing of equality, and all showed the effect of the wide-spread educational effort of the Argentine Government; an effort as marked as in our own country, although in the Argentine it is made by the nation instead of by the several states. We visited the little public school. The two women teachers were, one of Argentine descent, the other the daughter of an English father and an Argentine mother — the girl herself spoke English only with difficulty. They told us that the Germans had a school of their own, but that the Swiss and the other immigrants sent their children to the government school with the children of the native Argentines. Afterward I visited the German school, where I was welcomed by a dozen of the German immigrants — men of the same stamp as those whom I had so often seen, and whom I so much admired and liked, in our own Western country. I was rather amused to see in this school, together with a picture of the Kaiser, a very large picture of Martin Luther, although about a third of the Germans were Catholics; their feelings as Germans seemed in this instance to have overcome any religious differences, and Martin Luther was simply accepted as one of the great Germans whose memory they wished to impress on the minds of their children. In this school there was a good little library, all the books being, of course, German; it was the only library in the town.

That night we had a very pleasant dinner. Our host was a German. Of the two ladies who did the honors of the table, one was a Belgian, the wife of the only doctor in Bariloche, and the other a Russian. In our own party, aside from the four of us from the United States, there were Colonel Reybaud, of the Argentine army, my aide, and a first-class soldier; Doctor Moreno, who was as devoted a friend as if he had been my aide; and three other Argentine gentlemen — the head of the Interior Department, the governor of Neuquen, and the head of the Indian Service. Among the other guests was a man originally from County Meath, and a tall, blond, red-bearded Venetian, a carpenter by trade. After a while we got talking of books, and it was fairly startling to see the way that polyglot assemblage brightened when the subject was introduced, and the extraordinary variety of its taste in good literature. The men began eagerly to speak about and quote from their favorite authors — Cervantes, Lope de Vega, Camoëns, Molière, Shakespeare, Virgil, and the Greek dramatists. Our host quoted from the "Nibelungenlied" and from Homer, and at least two-thirds of the men at the table seemed to have dozens of authors at their tongues' ends. But it was the Italian carpenter who capped the climax, for when we touched on Dante he became almost inspired and repeated passage after passage, the majesty and sonorous cadence of the lines thrilling him so that his listeners were almost as much moved as he was. We sat thus for an hour — an unexpected type of *Kaffee Klatsch* for such an outpost of civilization.

Next morning at five we were off for our four-hundred-mile drive across the Patagonian wastes to the railway at Neuquen. We had been through a stretch of scenery as lovely as can be found anywhere in the world — a stretch that in parts suggested the Swiss lakes and mountains, and in other parts Yellowstone Park or the Yosemite or the mountains near Puget Sound. In a couple of years the Argentines will have pushed their railway system to Bariloche, and then all tourists who come to South America should make a point of visiting this wonderfully beautiful region. Doubtless in the end it will be developed for travellers much as other regions of great scenic attraction are developed. Thanks to Doctor Moreno, the Argentine end of it is already a national park; I trust the Chilean end soon will be.

We left Bariloche in three motor-cars, knowing that we had a couple of hard days ahead of us. After skirting the lake for a mile or two we struck inland over flats and through valleys. We had to cross a rapid river at a riffle where the motor-cars were just able to make it. The road consisted only of the ruts made by the passage of the great bullock carts, and often we had to go alongside it, or leave it entirely where at some crossing of a small stream the ground looked too boggy for us to venture in with the motor-cars. Three times in making such a crossing one of the cars bogged down, and we had hard work in getting out. In one case it caused us two hours' labor in building a stone causeway under and in front of the wheels — repeating what I had helped do not many months before in Arizona, when we struck a place where a cloudburst had taken away the bridge across a stream and a good part of the road that led up to it on either side.

In another place the leading car got into heavy sand and was unable to move. A party of gauchos came loping up, and two of them tied their ropes to the car and pulled it backward onto firm ground. These gauchos were a most picturesque set. They were riding good horses, strong and hardy and wild, and the men were consummate horsemen, utterly indifferent to the sudden leaps and twists of the nervous beasts they rode. Each wore a broad, silver-studded belt, with a long knife thrust into it. Some had their trousers in boots, others wore baggy breeches gathered in at the ankle. The saddles, unlike our cow saddles, had no horns, and the rope when in use was attached to the girth ring. The stirrups were the queerest of all. Often they were heavy flat disks, the terminal part of the stirrup-leather being represented by a narrow metal, or stiff leather, bar a foot in length. A slit was cut in the heavy flat disk big enough to admit the toe of the foot, and with this type of stirrup, which to me would have been almost as unsatisfactory as no stirrup at all, they sat their bucking or jumping horses with complete indifference.

It was gaucho land through which we were travelling. Every man in it was born to the saddle. We saw tiny boys not only riding but performing all the duties of full-grown men in guiding loose herds or pack-animals. No less characteristic than these daredevil horsemen were the lines of great two-wheeled carts, each dragged by five mules, three in the lead, with two wheelers, or else perhaps drawn by four or six oxen. For the most part these carts were carrying wool or hides. Occasionally we came on great pastures surrounded by wire fences. Elsewhere the stony, desolate land lay as it had lain from time immemorial. We saw many flocks of sheep, and many herds of horses, among which piebald horses were unusually plentiful. There were a good many cattle, too, and on two or three occasions we saw flocks of goats. It was a wild, rough country, and in such a country life is hard for both man and beast. Everywhere along the trail were the skeletons and dried carcasses of cattle, and occasionally horses. Yet there were almost no carrion birds, no ravens or crows, no small vultures, although once very high up in the air we saw a great condor. Indeed, wild life was not plentiful, although we saw ostriches — the South American rhea — and there was an occasional guanaco, or wild llama. Foxes were certainly abundant, because at the squalid little country stores there were hundreds of their skins and also many skunk skins.

Now and then we passed ranch-houses. There might be two or three fairly close together, then again we might travel for twenty miles without a sign of a habitation or a human being. In one place there was a cluster of buildings and a little schoolhouse. We stopped to shake hands with the teacher. Some of the ranch-houses were cleanly built and neatly kept, shade-trees being planted round about — the only trees we saw during the entire motor journey. Other houses were slovenly huts of mud and thatch, with a brush corral near by. Around the houses of this type the bare dirt surface was filthy and unkempt, and covered with a litter of the skulls and bones of sheep and oxen, fragments of skin and hide, and odds and ends of all kinds, foul to every sense.

Every now and then along the road we came to a solitary little store. If it was very poor and squalid, it was called a *pulpería;* if it was large, it was called an *almacén*. Inside there was a rough floor of dirt or boards, and a counter ran round it. At one end of the counter was the bar, at which drinks were sold. Over the rest of the counter the business of the store proper was done. Hats, blankets, horse-gear, rude articles of clothing, and the like were on the shelves or hung from rings in the ceiling. Sometimes we saw gauchos drinking at these bars — rough, wild-looking men, some of them more than three parts Indian, others blond, hairy creatures with the northern blood showing obviously. Although they are dangerous men when angered, they are generally polite, and we, of course, had no trouble with them. Hides, fox skins, and the like are brought by them for sale or for barter.

Order is kept by the mounted territorial police, an excellent body, much like the Canadian mounted police and the Pennsylvania constabulary. These men are alert and soldierly, with fine horses, well-kept arms, and smart uniforms. Many of them were obviously mainly, and most of them were partly, of Indian blood. I think that Indian blood is on the whole a distinct addition to the race stock when the ancestral Indian tribe is of the right kind. The acting president of the Argentine during my visit, the vice-president, a very able and forceful man, wealthy, well educated, a thorough statesman and man of the world, and a delightful companion, had a strong strain of Indian blood in him.

The ordinary people we met used "Indian" and "Christian" as opposite terms, having cultural rather than theological or racial significance, this being customary in the border regions of temperate South America. In one place

ACROSS THE ANDES 147

where we stopped four Indians came in to see us. The chief or head man looked like a thorough Indian. He might have been a Sioux or a Comanche. One of his companions was apparently a half-breed, showing strong Indian features, however. A third had a full beard, and, though he certainly did not look quite like a white man, no less certainly he did not look like an Indian. The fourth was considerably more white than Indian. He had a long beard, being dressed, as were the others, in shabby white man's garb. He looked much more like one of the poorer class of Boers than like any Indian I have ever seen. I noticed this man talking to two of the mounted police. They were smart, well-set-up men, thoroughly identified with the rest of the population, and regarding themselves and being regarded by others as on the same level with their fellow citizens. Yet they were obviously far more Indian in blood than was the unkempt, bearded white man to whom they were talking, and whom they and their fellows spoke of as an Indian, while they spoke of themselves, and were spoken of by others, as "Christians." "Indian" was the term reserved for the Indians who were still pagans and who still kept up a certain tribal relation. Whenever an Indian adopted Christianity in the excessively primitive form known to the gauchos, came out to live with the whites, and followed the ordinary occupations, he seemed to be promptly accepted as a white man, no different from any one else. The Indians, by the way, now have property, and are well treated. Nevertheless, the pure stock is dying out, and those that survive are being absorbed in the rest of the population.

The various accidents we met with during the forenoon delayed us, and we did not take breakfast — or, as we at home would call it, lunch — until about three o'clock in the afternoon. We had then halted at a big group of buildings which included a store and a government telegraph office. The store was a long, whitewashed, one-story house, the bedrooms in the rear, and all kinds of outbuildings round about. In some corrals near by a thousand sheep were being sheared. Breakfast had been long deferred, and we were hungry. But it was a feast when it did come, for two young sheep or big lambs were roasted whole before a fire in the open, and were then set before us; the open-air cook was evidently of almost pure Indian blood.

On we went with the cars, with no further

ACROSS THE ANDES 149

accidents and no trouble except once in crossing a sand belt. The landscape was parched and barren. Yet its look of almost inconceivable desolation was not entirely warranted, for in the flats and valleys water could evidently be obtained a few feet below the surface, and where it was pumped up anything could be grown on the soil.

But, unless thus artificially supplied, water was too scarce to permit any luxuriance of growth. Here and there were stretches of fairly good grass, but on the whole the country was covered with dry scrub a foot or two high, rising in clumps out of the earth or gravel or sand. The hills were stony and bare, sometimes with flat, sheer-sided tops, and the herds of half-wild horses and of cattle and sheep, and the even wilder riders we met, and the squalid little ranch-houses, all combined to give the landscape a peculiar touch.

As evening drew on, the harsh, raw sunlight softened. The hills assumed a myriad tints as the sun sank. The long gloaming followed. The young moon hung overhead, well toward the west, and just on the edge of the horizon the Southern Cross stood upside down. Then clouds gathered, boding a storm. The night grew black, and on we went through the darkness, the motormen clutching the steering-wheels and peering anxiously forward as they strove to make out the ruts and faint road-marks in the shifting glare of the headlights. The play of the lightning and the rolling of the thunder came near and nearer. We were evidently in for a storm, which would probably have brought us to a complete halt, and we looked out for a house to stop at. At 10.15 we caught a glimpse of a long white building on one side of the road. It was one of the stores of which I have spoken. With some effort we roused the people, and after arranging the motor-cars we went inside. They were good people. They got us eggs and coffee, and, as we had a cold pig, we fared well. Then we lay down on the floor of the store and on the counters and slept for four hours.

At three I waked the sleepers with the cry that in bygone days on the Western cattle plains had so often roused me from the heavy slumber of the men of the round-up. It was the short November night of high southern latitudes. Dawn came early. We started as soon as the faint gray enabled us to see the road. The stars paled and vanished. The sunrise was glorious. We came out from among the hills on to vast barren plains. Hour after hour,

ACROSS THE ANDES

all day long, we drove at speed over them. The sun set in red and angry splendor amid gathering clouds. When we reached the Rio Negro the light was dying from the sky, and a heavy storm was rolling toward us. The guardians of the rope ferry feared to try the river, with the storm rising through the black night; but we forced them to put off, and we reached the other shore just before the wind smote us, and the rushing rain drove in our faces.

CHAPTER VII

WILD HUNTING COMPANIONS

IN the days when I lived and worked on a cattle-ranch, on the Little Missouri, I usually hunted alone; and, if not, my companion was one of the cow-hands, unless I was taking out a guest from the East. On some of my regular hunting trips in the Rockies I went with one or more of my ranch-hands — who were valued friends and fellow workers. On others of these trips I went with men who were either temporarily, like John Willis, or permanently, like Tazewell Woody and John Goff, professional guides and hunters. In Africa I sometimes hunted with some of the settlers, and often alone or with my son Kermit; but even more frequently with either Cunninghame or Tarlton, the former for many years a professional elephant hunter, and the latter by choice and preference a lion hunter. Both of them, I think I may say, became permanently my friends as the result of the trip.

Often, however, my companions were not white men, but either half-breeds and people of mixed blood or else wild natives of the wild lands over which the great game roamed. To some of these men I became really attached. Not a few of them showed a courage and loyalty and devotion to duty which would have put to shame very many civilized men. Almost all of them at times did or said things that were very interesting because of the glimpses they gave into souls that really belong to a totally different age from that in which I and my friends of civilized lands are living.

December, 1913, and January, 1914, I spent in the remote interior of Brazil, on and near various rivers which form the headwaters of the mighty Paraguay. It is still a frontier country; the province is known as the Matto Grosso, the province of the great wooded wilderness. Yet it has a civilized and Christian history which runs back for over a century. It is on the eve of striking material development, and, nevertheless, it is still primitive with a primitiveness half that of a belated Europe, half that of a savagery struggling over the border-line into an exceedingly simple civilization. Out of these diverse and conflicting elements, and with a century of comparative isolation behind it, the land has produced a far more distinctive and peculiar life than our own frontier communities ever had the chance to develop. It would be difficult to find in any country more charming and better-bred men than some of the gentlemen, the great ranchmen and the political and social leaders in city life, whose generous hospitality made me their debtor. But the ordinary folk, and especially the Caboclos, the peasantry, although with many sterling qualities, were of a type wholly different from anything to be found either in Europe or in temperate North America.

The land is largely composed of the pantanals, the flat, wide-stretching marshes through which the Paraguay and its affluents wind. Where the land is low it is covered with papyrus and water-grass; if a few feet higher, with open palm forest. It offers fine pasturage for the herds of cattle. In addition there are mountains and belts of tropic jungle and forest, and to the north rises the sandy central table-land of Brazil. There are no railroads, and no highroads of any length for wheeled vehicles. The rivers are the highways. Native boats, with palm-thatch houses and cooking-ovens of red earth on the decks, drift down them and are poled or towed up them. A few light-draft steamers, running every week or fortnight, connect the widely scattered little cities. They

WILD HUNTING COMPANIONS 155

are quaint, picturesque little cities, without a wheeled vehicle except the water-carts. The one-story houses enclose open courtyards. The walls are thick, and the windows and doors very high, so as to let whatever coolness the night air carries fan the sleepers in their hammocks. In the bigger houses there are beds in the guest-chambers; but the hammock is really the bed; and in the inns the bedrooms have rings in the walls from which the traveller hangs the hammock he has brought with him. After nightfall the men sit at little tables under the trees in the public squares or outside the taverns, and through the open doors and windows of the houses, in the mysterious darkness, are the half-seen figures of girls and women; and stringed instruments tinkle in the still tropic night.

When Portugal still ruled Brazil, the first of these cities was founded, toward the end of the eighteenth century. At that time it could only be reached by a long voyage of peril and hardship up the Amazon and the Madeira, and then by mule back. No place in the world is now so remote from civilization as this little capital of the "Great Wilderness" then was; but its life was fervent under the torrid sky. Governors, generals, priests were there, slaveowners and gold seekers; killers of men and lovers of women. There was a palace and a cathedral and a fort, adorned with paintings and carvings. All are in ruins now; the rank vegetation of the tropics, beautiful and lethal, has covered them and twisted them asunder; for the strange little one-time capital city is dead, and those that dwelt therein have left it.

The next comers followed a route that led from the opposite direction, the south. These were the Paolistas. At São Paulo, almost under the Tropic of Cancer, the Portuguese conquerors married with the women of the native Indians, and made, first slaves, and then soldiers, of men from many Indian tribes. They all became welded together into one people, speaking Portuguese, but largely, and probably mainly, Indian by blood; and being of various martial stocks, with the morals of the viking age, they grew into a community of freebooters whose raiding expeditions, carried on with the utmost energy, daring, and ruthlessness, spread terror far and wide. Early in the nineteenth century these hardy horsemen and boatmen, searching for gold, land, and slaves, penetrated to the headwaters of the Paraguay, and with their advent began the first rude change from

WILD HUNTING COMPANIONS 157

mere savagery to that which held within it the germ of civilization.

Two or three of the ranches at which we stopped were provided with elaborate and even handsome ranch-houses and other buildings. One of them was owned by a wealthy and cultivated native proprietor. It was fitted with much stately luxury, and some comfort. Two others were owned by foreign corporations. Among the higher employees were men from Europe and the United States, and also "orientáls," as the men of Uruguay are always called — Uruguay being the "banda oriental," or eastern shore, of the Plate. These orientáls were as pure white as the Europeans and North Americans, and were of a high grade. The ordinary cow-hands on these two ranches were mostly Paraguayans, men of almost pure Indian blood, speaking the Guarani tongue, which is the real home language of the peculiar and interesting little republic which takes its name from the great river. These particular ranches were on the borders of the Bolivian country, and along this frontier the conditions as regards order and international law are much what they were on the border between England and Scotland in the sixteenth century. The man who cannot protect his own life by his own fierce and wary prowess cannot exist under such conditions, and the cow-hands must be men recklessly ready to fight for their cattle. The Paraguayans of the class who sought employment in the western interior of Brazil bore a fighting, and somewhat murderous, reputation. They were a daredevil set, and under men of masterful type they did hard and dangerous work for their employers.

The ordinary ranches where we stopped were of a different type. The houses were of one story, with thick, white walls. The few rooms were furnished only with rough tables and benches and rings for the hammocks. The unglazed windows were fitted with solid wooden shutters. Outbuildings stood near by; one perhaps for a kitchen; sheds for skinning or for the few stores; cabins in which the ranch-hands lived with their families. Palm-trees, or bananas with huge, ragged leaves, or trees unlike any familiar to our experience, might stand near by, close to the big cow corrals. On the poorer ranches the houses were nothing but log skeletons thatched with palm-leaves.

On these ranches the "camaradas," the cow-hands, in whose company we hunted, were all native Brazilians, of the same type as the men whom subsequently we took with us on our voyage of exploration down the Rio da Dúvida to the Amazon. It was a simple, primitive existence. All the industry was connected with the cattle or with cultivating the tropical vegetables and fruits of the garden. Two-wheeled ox-carts, each wheel taller than a man, carried hides and smoked flesh to the river landing where native boats, or now and then light-draft steamers, were moored. After sunset the life went on outdoors, unless it rained, until bedtime. As it grew dusk the doorways and the unglazed windows, standing open, showed only empty darkness within. The cooking was done in pots, at small fires outside. Now and then some one played a guitar or banjo; or sang strange songs, light-hearted songs of dances, melancholy songs of love or of death, songs about the feats of men and of bulls, and of famous horses; but always with something queer and barbaric as if they came from a time and a life immeasurably remote. Always the darkness shrouded from us the hot, furtive life we knew it held.

These poor country folk were on the whole a kindly, courteous race; it was pleasant to have them known as "camaradas" by the men of the upper class. They represented every shade of mixture among the three strains of

Portuguese, Indian, and negro, and no color-line was drawn by the pure bloods of any of the three races. Whatever their blood, they lived alike and dressed alike. There were very curious customs among many of them, customs which were probably dying out, but which must surely have been imported from utter savagery, although they were all Christians and all spoke Portuguese. As an instance, a number of them, from out-of-the-way places, but including at least one man who was of practically pure white blood, had the edges of their front teeth filed so as to make them semicircular.

When we hunted we would leave our camp, or the ranch-house where we had slept, before dawn. The hot sun flamed red above the marshes or sent long shafts of crimson light between the palm trunks. It might be evening before we returned. The heat of the day would be spent in the shade near a pond, and often our dusky companions would then get into long conversations with us. These camaradas usually rode little stallions, but sometimes one would be mounted on a trotting ox, which was guided by a string through the nostrils. Half-starved dogs followed behind. The men carried spears, rarely firearms. Their hats and clothes, their saddles and bridles seemed on the point of fall-

WILD HUNTING COMPANIONS 161

ing to pieces. On their bare feet they wore rusty spurs, and the stirrups were iron rings, in which they thrust the big toe, and the toe next it. But no antic of the half-broken horse and no difficulty in the jungle trail made the slightest impression on them. They were only fairly good hunters and trailers, and when in thick forest Kermit with his compass could find his way better than they could. A few of them hunted the jaguar and also the cashada, the big peccary which goes in herds and is aggressive and truculent; but most of them let the dangerous big cat and the dangerous little hogs severely alone, and hunted only the tapir, deer, and capybara. The rare jaguars that become man-eaters, the occasional giant anacondas, the deadly poisonous snakes, and the cashadas, were all the subjects of superstitious tales. They were shy about telling these stories to persons who might laugh, but if assured of sympathy would occasionally unbend. Then they would describe how man-eating jaguars were warlocks, able to enslave the souls of those they slew; so that each murdered man thenceforth served the dreadful beast that had eaten him, guarded him from danger, and guided him to fresh victims; or they would tell a ghost-story I never quite understood, about a seemingly harmless ghost, white and without any arms, which in the night-time rode the biggest peccary of the herd. In these tales the giant ant-eater always appeared as a comic character, a figure of fun, although with a somewhat grim ability to take care of himself; it was he who would meet drunken men and embrace them with his unpleasant claws and then hurry them home.

The camaradas whom we took with us on our exploring trip were mostly drawn from among these country folk of the ranches, although two or three came from the coast towns. The two best hunters were Antonio the Pareçis, a fullblood Pareçis Indian, and Antonio Correa, an intelligent, daredevil mulatto, probably with also a dash of Indian blood. The latter, like several other of our men, had lived among the wild Indians and had adopted some of their traits, including one exceedingly odd matter of dress. Antonio the Pareçis, a kindly, faithful, stupid soul, had abandoned his tribe, come into the settlements, and married a dark mulattress — the queer result being that according to the custom of the country their children would be regarded as civilized and therefore white. Antonio Correa was one of the two best and most trustworthy men on the trip; uncomplaining, hardworking, and undaunted in time of peril.

WILD HUNTING COMPANIONS 163

When, during our descent of the unknown river, we reached the first rubber man's house he expressed with curious eloquence the feeling we all had at hearing around us again the voices of men and women, and knowing that the chance of utter disaster was over; instead of camping at night in the midst of dangerous rapids, while every hour of the day carried its menace, and there always loomed ahead the danger of death in any one of a dozen possible ways, from famine to fever and dysentery, and from drowning to battle with Indians. When we reached the first rubber-gatherer's store the delicacy which all our men most eagerly coveted was condensed milk, and to my amused horror they solemnly proceeded each to eat a canful of the sweet and sticky luxury.

Of all my wilder hunting companions those to whom I became most attached — although some of them were the wildest of all — were those Kermit and I had with us in Africa for eleven months. Disregarding a very problematical Christian, these were either Mohammedans or heathens. However, after having been in our employ a little while, and after having adopted the fez, jersey, and short trousers — and, as a matter of pure pride and symbolism, boots — they all regarded themselves as of an elevated social status, and openly looked down on the unregenerated "shenzis" or natives who were still in the kirtle-of-banana-leaves cultural stage. They represented many different tribes. Some of them were file-toothed cannibals. Many of them had come from long distances; for — as philanthropists will do well to note — being even a porter in a white man's service in British East Africa or Uganda or the Soudan, meant an amount of pay and a comfort of living and (although this, I think, was subordinate in their minds) a justness of treatment which they could by no possibility achieve in their own homes under native conditions. As for the personal attendants, the gun-bearers, tent-boys, and saises, as well as the head men and askaris, or soldiers, they felt as far above the porters as the latter did above the shenzis. The common tongue was Swahili, a negro-Arab dialect, originally spoken by the descendants, mainly negro in blood, of the Arab conquerors, traders, and slave-raiders of Zanzibar. This is a lingo found over much of central Africa. But only a few of our men were Swahilis by blood.

Of course, most of them were like children, with a grasshopper inability for continuity of thought and realization of the future. They would often act with an inconsequence that

WILD HUNTING COMPANIONS 165

was really puzzling. Dog-like fidelity, persevered in for months, would be ended by a fit of resentment at something unknown, or by a sheer volatility which made them abandon their jobs when it was even more to their detriment than to ours. But they had certain fixed standards of honor; the porter would not abandon his load, the gun-bearer would not abandon his master when in danger from a charging beast — although, unless a first-class man, he might at that critical moment need discipline to restrain his nervous excitability. They appreciated justice, but they were neither happy nor well behaved unless they were under authority; weakness toward them was even more ruinous than harshness and overseverity.

The personal attendants of Kermit and myself established a kind of "chief petty officers' mess" in the caravan. Not only his own boys, but mine, really cared more for Kermit than they did for me. This was partly because he spoke Swahili; partly because he could see game, follow its tracks, and walk as I could not; and partly because he exercised more strict control over his men and yet more thought and care in giving them their pleasures and rewards. I was apt to become amused and therefore too lenient in dealing with grasshopper-like failings

— which was bad for the grasshoppers themselves; and, moreover, I was apt to announce to a man who had deserved well that he should receive so many rupees at the end of the trip, which to him seemed a prophecy about the somewhat remote future, whereas Kermit gave less, but gave it in more immediate form, such as sugar or tea, and rupees to be expended in the first Indian or Swahili trader's store we met; on which occasions I would see Kermit head a solemn procession of both his followers and mine to the store, where he would superintend their purchases, not only helping them to make up vacillating minds but seeing that they were not cheated.

An exception was my head tent-boy, Ali. He had a good deal of Arab blood in him, he spoke a little English, he was really intelligent, he was an innately loyal soul, and he was keenly alive to the honor of being the foremost attendant of the head of the expedition. He was distinctly an autocrat to the second tent-boy, whose tenure was apt to be short, and he regarded Somalis with professional rivalry and distrust. He always did his work excellently, and during the eleven months he was with me I never had to correct or rebuke him, and whenever I had a bout of fever he was devotion itself. Once, while at a friend's house, his Somali stole some silver from me, after which Ali always kept my silver himself with scrupulous honesty. I still now and then get a letter from him, but as the letters are sent through some professional Hindoo scribe they are of value chiefly as tokens of affection. The last one, written in acknowledgment of a gift sent him, contained a rather long letter in Swahili, a translation into Arabic, and then a would-be translation into English, which, however, went no further than the cumulative repetition of all the expressions of ceremonious regard known to the scribe.

My head gun-bearer, named Hartebeest — Kongoni — also did his work so well that I never had to reprove him; he was cool and game, a good tracker and tireless walker. But the second gun-bearer, Gouvimali, although a cheerful and willing soul, tended to get rattled when near dangerous animals. Unless his master is really in the grip of an animal, the worst sin a gun-bearer can commit, next to running away, is to shoot the gun he is carrying; for, if the master is fit to hunt dangerous game at all, it is he who must do the killing, and, if in a tight place, he must be able to count with absolute certainty on the gun-bearer's handing him a loaded rifle when his own has been fired. On one occasion I was covering a rhino which Kermit was trying to photograph. The beast was very close and seemed about to begin hostilities. Gouvimali became very much excited and raised his rifle to shoot. I overheard Kongoni chide him, and I spoke to him sharply, but he still kept the rifle at his shoulder; whereupon I slapped his face just before shooting the rhino. This prevented his firing and brought him to his senses, but was not a sufficient punishment. The really dreadful punishment would have been to send him back to the ranks of the porters. But I wished to give him another chance; so next morning I instructed Ali that he was to be my interpreter, and that Gouvimali was to be brought up for justice before my tent. To make it impressive, Kongoni and the second tent-boy were summoned to attend, which they did with pleased anticipation. But they were not alone. All of Kermit's attendants rushed gleefully over, including his two first-class gun-bearers, his camera-bearer, the wild 'Nmwezi ex-cannibal whom he had turned into a devoted and excellent tent-boy, and the cheerful Kikuyu savage who had taken naturally to being sais for his and my little mules. The sympathies of all of them were ostentatiously against the culprit, and they were prepared for the virtuous enjoyment characteristic of the orthodox sure-of-their-salvation at a heresy trial.

Court opened with me in my camp-chair in front of the tent. Ali stood beside me, erect with gratified horror, and eager to show that he was not merely an interpreter but a prosecutor and assistant judge. Abject Gouvimali stood in front, with head hanging. The others ranged themselves in a semicircle, and filled the function of a Greek chorus. The proceedings were as follows:

I (with frowning majesty): "Tell Gouvimali he knows that I have treated him very, very well; besides his wages, I have given him tea and sugar and tobacco and a red blanket."

Ali translates with the thunderous eloquence of Cicero against Verres; Verres writhes.

Chorus (with hands raised at the thought of such magnificent generosity): "Oh, *what* a good Bwana!"

I (reproachfully): "Whenever I shot a lion or an elephant I gave him some silver rupees."

Ali translates this with a voice shaken by emotion over the human baseness that could forget such gifts.

Chorus (in ecstatic contemplation of my virtue): "Oh, *what* a generous Bwana!"

I (leaning forward toward the accused): "And yet he started to shoot at a rhinoceros the Bwana Merodadi [Dandy Master, the Master who was a dandy to shoot and ride and get game] was photographing."

Ali fairly hisses this statement; malefactor shudders.

Chorus (almost bereft of speech at the revelation of a depravity of which they had never hitherto dreamed): "Hau! W-a-u!!"

I (severe, but melancholy): "You didn't stop until I had to slap your face."

Chorus (with unctuous relish): "The Bwana ought to have beaten you!"

I: "Do you wish to become a porter again? There's a Kavirondo porter very anxious to get your job!" (Deceitfully concealing a vagueness of recollection about this aspirant, who had been pronounced worthless.)

Malefactor (overcome by suggestion of the semimythical Kavirondo rival): "Oh, Bwana, have me beaten, but keep me as gun-bearer!"

I (with regal beneficence): "Well, I'll fine you ten rupees; and if you make another break, out you go; and you're to do all Kongoni's gun-cleaning for a week." (Kongoni, endeavoring to look both austere and disinterested, pokes malefactor in back.)

Chorus (disappointed of a tragedy, but fundamentally kind-hearted): "What a merciful Bwana! And now Gouvimali will always be careful! Good Gouvimali!"

On another occasion, on the White Nile, I one day took with me, to show me game, two natives of a village near our camp. I shot a roan antelope. It was mortally wounded; one of the natives, the "shenzis," saw it fall but said nothing and slipped away to get the horns and meat for himself. Later, Kongoni became suspicious, and very acutely — for he was not only a master of hunting craft but also pos-

WILD HUNTING COMPANIONS 171

sessed a sympathetic insight into the shenzi mind — led us to the spot and caught the offender, and a party of the villagers, red-handed. Kongoni and Gouvimali pounced on the faithless guide, while the others scattered; and the sais, unable to resist having something to do with the fray, handed the led mule to a small naked boy, rushed forward, gave the captive a thump, and then returned to his mule. The offender was brought to camp and put under guard — evidently horribly afraid we would eat him instead of the now far-gone roan. Next day Kermit got home from his hunt before I did. When I reached camp I found Kermit sitting with a book and his pipe under a great tree, in his camp-chair. The captive was tied with a string to the huge tree trunk. He sat on the ground and uttered hollow groans whenever he thought they would be effective. At nightfall we released him, keeping his knife, which we required him to redeem with a chicken; and when he returned with the chicken we bade him give it to Kongoni, to whom we owed the discovery of the roan.

In some of the wilder and more lonely camps these body-servants were my only companions, together with some shenzi porters; at others Kermit was with me, also with his tail of devoted personal attendants. Where the game swarmed and no human beings existed for many leagues round about we built circular fences of thorns to keep out beasts of prey. The porters, chanting a monotonous refrain, brought in wood to keep the watch-fires going all night. Supper was cooked and eaten. Then we sat and listened to the fierce and eager life that went on in the darkness outside. Hoofs thundered now and then, there were snortings and gruntings, occasional bellowings or roarings, or angry whinings, of fear or of cruel hunger or of savage love-making; ever there was a skipping and running of beasts unseen; for out there in the darkness a game as old as the world was being played, a game without any rules, where the forfeit was death.

Generally the wild creatures were not so close even at these lonely camps, and we did not have to guard against attack, although there were always sentries and watch-fires, and we always slept with our loaded rifles beside us. After dinner the tent-boys and gun-bearers would talk and laugh, or tell stories, or listen while one of their number, Kermit's first gun-bearer, a huge, absolutely honest, coal-black negro from south of the Victorian Lake, strummed on an odd little native harp; and

WILD HUNTING COMPANIONS 173

one of them might improvise a song. It was usually a very simple song; perhaps about something Kermit or I had done during the day, and of how we lived far away in an unknown land across vast oceans but had come to Africa with wonderful rifles to kill lions and elephants. Once the song was merely an expression of gratified approval of the quality of the meat of an eland I had shot during the day. Once we listened to a really humorous song describing the disapproval of the women about something their husbands had done, the shrill scolding of the women being mimicked with much effect. Some of the songs dealt with traditions and experiences which I did not understand, and which were probably far more interesting than any that I did understand.

My gun-bearers accompanied me whenever I visited the native villages of the different tribes. These tribes differed widely from one another in almost every respect. In Uganda my men stood behind me when some dignified and formally polite chief or great noble came to visit me; clothed in white, and perhaps dragged in a rickshaw or riding a mule with silver trappings, while his drummer beat on the huge native drum the distinctive clan tune which, when he walked abroad, bade all take notice just who the noble was, distinguishing him from all the other great lords, each of whom also had his own especial tune. My men strode at my back when I approached the rest-houses that were made ready for me, as we walked from one to the other of the two Nyanzas; palm-thatched rest-houses before which the musicians of the local chiefs received me with drum-beat, and the hollow booming of bamboos, and rattling of gourds, and the clashing of metal on metal, and the twanging of instruments of many strings. They accompanied me to the rings of square huts, plastered with cow-dung, where the Masai herdsmen dwelt, guarding their cattle, goats, and wire-haired sheep; and to the nomad camps of the camel-owning Samburu, on thorn-covered flats from which we looked southward toward the mighty equatorial snow peak of Kenia. They stood with me to gaze at the midnight dances of the Kikuyu. They followed me among the villages of beehive huts in the lands of the naked savages along the upper Nile.

Ali always, no matter how untoward the surroundings, had things ready and comfortable for me at night when I came in. My gunbearers trudged behind me all day long over the plains where the heat haze danced, or through

WILD HUNTING COMPANIONS 175

the marshes, or in the twilight of the tropic forests. After dark they always guided me back to camp if there were any landmarks; but, curiously enough, if we had to steer by the stars, I had to do the guiding. They were always alert for game. They were fine trackers. They never complained. They were always at my elbows when we had to deal with some dangerous beast. It is small wonder I became attached to them. All of Kermit's and my personal attendants went with us to Cairo, whence we shipped them back to Zanzibar. They earnestly besought us to take them to America. Cairo, of course, both enchanted and cowed them. What they most enjoyed while there was when Kermit took them all out in taxis to the zoo. They were children of the wilderness; their brains were in a whirl because of the big city; it made them feel at home to see the wild things they knew, and it interested them greatly to see the other wild things which were so different from what they knew.

In the old days, on the great plains and in the Rockies, I went out occasionally with Indians or half-breeds; Kermit went after mountain-sheep in the desert with a couple of Mexican packers; and Archie, Quentin, and I, while in Arizona, travelled on one occasion with a Mexican wagon-driver and a Navajo cook (both good men), and once or twice for a day or two at a time with Navajos or Utes to act as guides or horse-herders. On a hunting trip after white goat and deer in the Canadian Rockies Archie went with a guide who turned out to be from Arizona, and who almost fell on Archie's neck with joy at meeting a compatriot from the Southwest. He was the son of a Texas ranger and a Cherokee mother, was one of a family of twenty-four children — all native American families are not dying out, thank heaven! — and was a first-class rifle-shot and hunter.

The Indians with whom I hunted were hardy, quick to see game, and good at approaching it, but were not good shots, and as trackers and readers of sign did not compare with the 'Ndorobo of the east African forests. I always became good friends with them, and when they became assured that I was sympathetic and would not laugh at them they finally grew to talk freely to me, and tell me stories and legends of goblins and ghost-beasts and of the ancient days when animals talked like men. Most of what they said I could not understand, for I did not speak their tongues; and they talked without restraint only when I sat quiet and did not interrupt them. Occasionally one who spoke English, or a half-breed, and in one case a French-Canadian who had lived long with them, translated the stories to me. They were fairy-tales and folk-tales — I do not know the proper terminology. Where they dealt with the action of either men or gods they were as free from moral implication as if they came out of the Book of Judges; and throughout there was a certain inconsequence, an apparent absence of motive in what was done, and an equal absence of any feeling for the need of explanation. They were people still in the hunting stage, to whom hunting lore meant much, and many of the tales were of supernatural beasts. On the actions of these unearthly creatures might depend the success of the chase of their earthly relatives; or it might be necessary to placate them to avoid evil; or their deeds might be either beneficent or menacing without reference to what men did, whether in praise or prayer. Such beings of the other world were the spirit-bear of the Navajos; and the ghost-wolf of the Pawnees, to whom one of my troopers before Santiago, an educated, full-blood Pawnee, once suddenly alluded; and the spirit-buffaloes of whom the Sioux and the Mandans told endless stories, who came up from somewhere underground in the far north, who at night played games like those of human warriors in the daytime, who were malicious and might steal men and women, but who might also bring to the Indians the vast herds whose presence meant plenty and whose absence starvation. Almost everywhere the coyote appeared as a sharp, tricky hero, in adventures having to do with beasts and men and magic things. He played the part of Br' Rabbit in Uncle Remus.

Now and then a ghost-tale would have in it an element of horror. The northern Indians dwell in or on the borders of the vast and melancholy boreal forests, where the winter-time always brings with it the threat of famine, where any accident to the solitary wanderer may mean his death, and may mean also that his body will never be found. In the awful loneliness of that forest there are stretches as wide as many a kingdom of Europe to which for decades at a time no man ever goes. In the summer there is sunlit life in the forest; flowers bloom, birds sing, and the wind sighs through the budding branches. In the winter there is iron desolation; the bitter blasts sweep from the north, the driven ice dust sears the face, the snow lies far above a tall man's height, in their icy beds the rivers lie fixed like shining steel. It is

WILD HUNTING COMPANIONS 179

a sombre land, where death ever lurks behind the traveller. To the Indian its recesses are haunted by dread beings malevolent to man. Around the camp-fires, when the frosts of fall were heavy, I have heard the Indians talk of the oncoming winter and of things seen at twilight and sensed after nightfall by the trapper or belated wayfarer when the cold that gripped the body began also to grip the heart. They told of the windigoes which leaped and flew through the frozen air, and left huge footprints on the snow, and drove to madness and death men by lonely camp-fires. They told of the snow-walkers; how once a moose hunter, on webbed snow-shoes, bound campward in the late afternoon saw a dim figure walking afar off on the crust of the snow parallel to him among the tree trunks; how as the afternoon waned the figure came gradually nearer, until he saw that it was shrouded in some garment which wrapped even its head; how in the gray dusk that followed the sunset it came always closer, until he could see that what should have been its face was like the snout of a wolf, and that through a crack left bare by the shroud its eyes burned evil, baleful; how his heart was palsied with the awful terror of the unknown, of the dead that was not dead; and how suddenly he came on two other men, and the thing that had dogged him turned and vanished, and they could find no footprints on the snow.

More often the story would be nothing but a story, perhaps about birds or beasts. Once I heard a Kootenai tell such a story; but he said he had heard it very far north, and that it was not a Kootenai story. It explained why the loon has small wings and why the partridges in the north turn white in winter.

It happened very long ago. In those days there was no winter and the loon had ordinary wings and flew around like a raven. One midday the partridges were having tea on a sandpoint in a lake where there were small willows and blueberry bushes. The loon wished to take tea with them, but they crowed and chuckled and they would not let him. So he began to call in a very loud voice a long call, almost like the baying of a wolf; you can hear it now on the lakes. He called and he called, longer and louder. He was calling the spirit who dwells in the north, so far that no man has ever known where it is. The spirit was asleep. But the loon's medicine was very strong and he called until the spirit woke up. The spirit sent the North Wind down — he *was* the North Wind — and the snow came, and summer passed

WILD HUNTING COMPANIONS 181

away. The partridges no longer crowed and chuckled. Some of them flew away south. The others turned white; you can see them now very far north, but in the south only on the mountains. Then the loon began to laugh, for he was very glad and proud. He laughed louder and louder; you can hear him now on the lakes. But the spirit was very angry because the loon had called him. He began to blow on the lake and he began to blow on the loon. The lake began to freeze and the loon began to dive, longer and longer. But his wings began to grow smaller. So with great difficulty, before his wings were too small, he rose and his wings beat very rapidly and he flew away south. That is why winter came and why the loon dives so well and does not fly if he can help it.

In the cane-brakes on both sides of the lower Mississippi I have hunted bear in company with the hard-riding, straight-shooting planters of the country lying behind the levees — and a gamer, more open-handedly hospitable set of men can nowhere be found. What would, abroad, be called the hunt servants were all negroes from the Black Belt, in which we were doing our hunting. These negroes of the Black Belt have never had the opportunity to develop beyond a low cultural stage. Most of those with us were kindly, hard-working men, expert in their profession. One, who handled the hounds of two Mississippi planters, was a man in many respects of really high and fine character; although in certain other respects his moral standards were too nearly those of some of the Old Testament patriarchs to be quite suitable for the present century. These black hunters possessed an extensive and on the whole accurate knowledge of the habits of the wild creatures, and yet mingled with this knowledge was a mass of firmly held nonsense about hoop-snakes, snakes with poisonous stings in their tails, and the like. Most, although not all, of them were very superstitious and easily frightened if alone at night. Their ghost-stories were sometimes to me quite senseless; I did not know enough of the workings of their minds to understand what they meant. Those stories that were understandable usually had in them something of the grotesque and the inadequate. By daylight the black hunters would themselves laugh at their own fears; and even at night, when fully believing what they were telling, they would seriously insert details that struck us as too comic for grave acceptance. The story that most insistently lingers in my mind will explain my meaning.

Back in the swamp among cypress ponds was an abandoned plantation which had the reputation of being haunted. The "big house," the planter's house, had been dismantled but was still standing in fair condition. In the neighborhood there was a powerful negro scapegrace much given to boasting that he feared no ghost; and the local judge finally offered him five dollars if he would go alone after nightfall to the house in question and stay there until sunrise. The negro accepted with the stipulation that he was to be allowed to light a lamp that had been left in the house. The storyteller, who was as black as a shoe and a good man in the swamp after bear, told the tale as follows. I cannot pretend, however, to give his exact expressions.

"Jake started after sunset. The moon was a little more than half full, and it was a sure-enough lonely walk through the cypress woods along the abandoned, overgrown road. The branches kept waving and the moonlight flickered on the ground, and Jake couldn't see anything clearly and yet could see a good deal, and strange noises came from the swamp on both sides. He was glad to get to the clearing, but it was overgrown, too. The house shone white in the moonlight, but the staring, open windows were black, and all inside was coal-black beyond the moonlight, and he didn't know whether it was empty or whether he most wished it was or wasn't empty. But he went inside and lit the lamp and put it on a table and sat down beside it. Nothing happened for a long time except that he kept hearing queer things in the swamp and sometimes something went across the clearing. At last a clock struck twelve, *but he knew there wasn't any clock in the house*. Just as soon as it had finished striking, a monstrous big black cat walked into the room and jumped on the table and wropped his tail three times round the lamp-chimney and said: 'Nigger, you and I is the onliest things in this house!' And Jake said: 'Mr. Black Cat, in one second *you'll* be the onliest thing in this house,' and he went through the window. He run hard down the road, and pretty soon there was a crashing in the underbrush and a big buck, with horns on him like a rocking-chair, came up alongside and said: 'Well, nigger, you must be losing your wind,' and he answered mighty polite: 'Mr. Buck, I ain't even begun to catch my wind,' and he sure left that buck behind. And he ran and he ran until he did lose his wind, and he sat down on a log. And there was a patter of footsteps behind and somebody came up the road

WILD HUNTING COMPANIONS 185

and sat down on the log too. It was a white man, and he carried his head in his hand. The head spoke: 'Well, nigger, you surely can run!' and Jake he answered: 'Mr. White Man, you ain't never *seen* me run,' and then he *did* run. And he came to the judge's and he beat on the door and called out: 'Judge, I'se come back; and, Judge, I don't *want* that five dollars!'"

The planter in connection with whose hounds the negro worked told me that this was a ghost-story that for a year had been told everywhere among the colored folk, but about all kinds of houses and people, and that the narrator didn't really believe it; but that, nevertheless, he believed enough of it to be afraid of empty houses after dark, and moreover that he had been frightened into leaving a swamp planter's pigs entirely alone by the planter's playing ghost and calling out to him at nightfall as he, the negro, was travelling a lonely road with possible innocence of motive.

Strongly contrasted with such more than half comic or grotesque ghost-stories was one told me once, not by a hunting companion but by a polished and cultivated Tahitian gentleman, a guest of Henry Adams in Washington. His creed was the creed of his present surroundings; but back of the beyond in his mind lurked old tales, and old faiths glowed with a moment's flame at certain hours under certain conditions. One evening some of those present were talking of inexplicable things that had happened on the shifting borders between life and death, between the known and the unknown; and of vampires and werewolves and the ghosts of things long gone. Suddenly the Tahitian told of an experience of his mother's when she was an imperious queen in the far-off Polynesian island. She had directed her people to build a bridge across the mouth of a stream. After dark something came out of the water and killed one of the men, and the others returned to her, saying that the spirit which dwelt in the stream was evil and would kill all of them if they persevered in their work. She answered that her own family spirit, the familiar or ghost of the family, was very strong and would protect her people if she were present. Next day, accordingly, she went down in person to superintend the building of the bridge. She took with her two little tame pigs—pet pigs. All went well until evening came. Then suddenly a chill gust of wind blew from the river mouth, and in a moment the workmen fled, screaming that the spirit of the water was upon them. Almost immediately afterward there was a hubbub of a

WILD HUNTING COMPANIONS 187

totally different kind; and after listening a moment the queen spoke, telling that her spirit had arrived, had overcome the other spirit, and was chasing him. In another moment one of her girls called out that the little pigs were dead. The queen put out her hand and touched them; they were quite cold. The defeated spirit was hiding in them! But as she felt them they began to grow warm and come to life. Her familiar had followed the evil ghost into his hiding-place in the pigs, had chased him out, and slew him as he fled to the water. There was no further interruption to the building of the bridge.

The touch about the defeated spirit hiding in the pet pigs, which thereupon grew cold, and being chased out by his antagonist was thoroughly Polynesian. It was most interesting to see the cultivated man of the world suddenly go back to superstitions that marked the childhood of the race; and then he told tales of the shark god, and of many other gods, and of devils and magicians.

However, there is no lack of similar beliefs among our own people. Long ago I knew an old market gunner of eastern Long Island who shot ducks and bay-birds for a living. There was a deserted farmhouse on the edge of the marsh, handy to the shooting-grounds, which he would not enter. He insisted that once he had gone there on a gray, bitter November afternoon to escape the rain which was driving in sheets. He lit a fire in the kitchen and started to dry his soaked clothes. Suddenly, out of the storm, somebody fumbled at the latch of the door. It opened and a little old woman in gray entered. She did not look at him, and yet a chill seemed to fall on him. Nevertheless he rose and followed her as she went out into the hall. She went up the steep, narrow stairway. He went after her. She went up the still steeper little flight that went to the garret. But when he followed there was no one there. He came downstairs, put on his clothes, took up his heavy fowling-gun, and just as evening fell he started for the mainland along a road which at one point became a causeway. When he reached the causeway the light was dim; but a figure walked alongside the road on the reeds, not bending the tops; and it was a man with his throat cut from ear to ear.

However, to tell of the crooked beliefs of the men of our own race, who dwell beside the great waters or journey across the world's waste spaces, is aside from what I have to say of the wild hunting companions whose world was peopled by ghosts as real to their minds as the men and beasts with whom they were brought in touch during their daily lives.

CHAPTER VIII

PRIMEVAL MAN; AND THE HORSE, THE LION, AND THE ELEPHANT

TO say that progress goes on and has gone on at unequal speed in different continents, so far as human society is concerned, is so self-evident as to be trite. Yet, after all, we hardly visualize even this fact to ourselves; and we laymen, at least, often either disregard or else frankly forget the further fact that this statement is equally true as regards the prehistory of mankind and as regards the paleontological history of the great beasts with which he has been associated on the different continents during the last two or three hundred thousand years. In history, a given century may on one continent mean what on another continent was meant by a century that came a thousand years before or a thousand years later. In prehistory and paleontology there is the same geographical difference as regards the rapidity of development in time.

PRIMEVAL MAN 191

The Soudan under the Mahdi at the end of the nineteenth century was in religious, industrial, and social life, in fact in everything except mere time, part of the evil Mohammedan world of the seventh century. It had no relation to the contemporary body politic of humanity except that of being a plague-spot. The Tasmanians, Bushmen, and Esquimaux of the eighteenth century had nothing in common with the Europeans of their day. Their kinship, physical and cultural, was with certain races of Palæolithic Europeans and Asiatics fifty or a hundred thousand years back.

In just the same way the fierce wild life of parts of Africa to-day has nothing in common with what we now see in Europe and the Americas. Yet in its general aspect, and in many of its most striking details, it reproduces the life that once was, in Europe and in both the Americas, in what paleontologists call the Pleistocene age. By Pleistocene is meant that period — of incalculable length as we speak of historic time, but a mere moment if we speak of geologic time — which witnessed in Europe and Asia the slow change of the brute-like and but partly human predecessors of man into beings who were culturally on a level with the lower forms of the savages that still exist, and some of whom were physically, as far as we can see, abreast of the more advanced races of to-day.

Surely, this phase in the vast epic of life development on this planet offers a fascinating study. The history of man himself is by far the most absorbing of all histories, and it cannot be understood without some knowledge of his prehistory. Moreover, the history of the rest of the animal world also yields a drama of intense and vivid interest to all scholars gifted with imagination. The two histories — the prehistory of humanity and the history of the culminating phase of non-human mammalian life — were interwoven during the dim ages when man was slowly groping upward from the bestial to the half-divine.

It was my good fortune throughout one year of my life to roam, rifle in hand, over the empty, sunlit African wastes, and at night to camp by palm and thorn-tree on the banks of the African rivers. Day after day I watched the thronging herds of wild creatures and the sly, furtive human life of the wilderness. Often and often, as I so watched, my thoughts went back through measureless time to the ages when the western lands, where my people now dwell, and the northern lands of the eastern world, where their remote forefathers once dwelt, were filled with

PRIMEVAL MAN

just such a wild life. In those days these farback ancestors of ours led the same lives of suspicion and vigilant cunning among the beasts of the forest and plain that are now led by the wildest African savages. In that immemorial past the beasts conditioned the lives of men, as they conditioned the lives of one another; for the chief factors in man's existence were then the living things upon which he preyed and the fearsome creatures which sometimes made prey of him. Ages were to pass before his mastery grew to such a point that the fanged things he once had feared, and the hoofed things success in the chase of which had once meant to him life or death, became negligible factors in his existence.

Some of the naked or half skin-clad savages whom I met and with whom I hunted were still leading precisely the life of these ages-dead forebears of ours. More than once I spent days in heavy forests at the foot of equatorial mountains in company with small parties of 'Ndorobo hunters. They were men of the deep woods, as stealthy and wary as any of the woodland creatures. In each case they knew and trusted my companion — who was in one instance a settler, a famous lion hunter, and in the other a noted professional elephant hunter. Yet even so their trust did not extend to letting a stranger like himself see their women and children, who had retreated into some forest fastness from which we were kept aloof. The men wore each a small fur cape over the shoulders. Otherwise they were absolutely naked. Each carried a pouch, and a spear. The spear head was of iron, obtained from some of the settled tribes. Except this iron spear head, not one of their few belongings differed from what it doubtless was long prior to the age of metals. They carried bows, strung with zebra gut, and arrows of which the wooden tips were poisoned. In one place Kermit found where a party of them had dwelt in a cave, evidently for many weeks; there were bones and scraps of skin without and within; and inside were beds of grass, and fire-sticks, and a walled-off enclosure of branches in which their dogs had been penned. Elsewhere we came on one or two camping-places with rude brush shelters. Each little party consisted of a family, or perhaps temporarily of two or three families. They did not cultivate the earth; they owned a few dogs; and they lived on honey and game. They killed monkeys and hyraxes, occasionally forest hog and bongo — a beautifully striped forest antelope as big as a Jersey cow — and now and then elephant, rhino, and buffalo, and, on the open plains at the edge of the forest, zebra. The zebra was a favorite food; but they could only get at it when it left the open plains and came among the bushes or to drink at the river. Two of these wild hunters showed me the bones of an elephant they had killed in a pit a long time previously; and the head man of those we had with us on another trip bore the scars of frightful wounds inflicted by an angered buffalo. Hyenas at times haunted the neighborhood, and after nightfall might attempt to carry off a child or even a sleeping man. Very rarely the hunters killed a leopard, and sometimes a leopard pounced on one of them. The lion they feared greatly, but it did not enter the woods, and they were in danger from it only if they ventured on the plain. The head man above mentioned told us that once, when desperate with hunger, his little tribe, or family group, had found a buffalo killed by a lion, and had attacked and slain the lion, and then feasted on both it and the buffalo. But on another occasion a lion had turned the tables and killed two of their number. The father of one of my guides had been killed by baboons; he had attacked a young one with a club, and the old males tore him to pieces with their huge dog teeth. Death to the head of a family in encounter with an elephant or rhino might mean literal starvation to the weaker members. They were able to exist at all only because they had developed their senses and powers to a degree that placed them level with the creatures they dreaded or preyed upon. They climbed the huge trees almost as well as the big black-and-white monkey. I had with me gun-bearers from the hunting tribes of the plains, men accustomed to the chase, but brought up in villages where there was tillage and where goats and cattle were raised. These gun-bearers of mine were good trackers and at home in the ordinary wilderness. But compared to these true wild men of the forest they might almost as well have been town-bred. The 'Ndorobo trackers would take me straight to some particular tree or spot of ground, through miles of dense, steaming woodland every rood of which looked like every other, returning with unerring precision to a goal which my gun-bearers would have been as helpless to find again as I was myself; and they interpreted trails and signs and footprint-scrapes which we either hardly saw or else misread.

Doubtless the ancestors, or some of the ancestors, of these men had lived in the land,

PRIMEVAL MAN

just as they themselves now did, for untold generations before the soil-tillers and cattle-owners came into it. They had shrunk from the advent of the latter, and as a rule were found only in isolated tracts which were useless for tillage or pasturage, the dense forest forming their habitual dwelling-place and retreat of safety. From the best hunting-grounds, those where the great game teemed, they had been driven; yet these hunting-grounds were often untenanted by human beings for much of the year, being visited only at certain seasons by the cattle-owning nomads.

Often these hunting-grounds offered sights of wonder and enchantment. Day after day I rode across them without seeing, from dawn to sundown, a human being save the faithful black followers, hawk-eyed and steel-thewed, who trudged behind me. Sometimes the plains were seas of wind-rippled grass. Sometimes they were dotted with clumps of low thorn-trees or broken by barren, boldly outlined hills. Our camp might be pitched by a muddy pool, with only stunted thorns near by; or on the edge of a shrunken river, under the dense shade of some great, brilliantly green fig-tree; or in a grove of huge, flat-topped acacias with yellow trunks and foliage like the most delicate lace;

or where the long fronds of palms moved with a ceaseless, dry rustle in the evening breeze. At the drinking-holes, in pond or river, as the afternoon waned, or occasionally after nightfall when the moon was bright, I sometimes lay to see the game filing down to drink.

On these rides, I continually passed through, and while lying in ambush I often saw, a wealth of wild life, in numbers and variety such as the western world, and the cold-temperate regions of the Old World, have not seen for many, many thousands of years. How many kinds of beasts there were! Giraffes stared at us over the tops of the stunted thorn-trees. In the dawn we saw hyenas shambling homeward after their night's prowl. Wart-hogs as hideous as nightmares ploughed along with their fore knees on the ground as they rooted it up. Sleek oryx with horns like rapiers galloped off with even, gliding gait. Shaggy wildebeests curvetted and plunged with a ferocity both ludicrous and sinister; elands as heavy as prize cattle trotted away with shaking dewlaps. Ungainly hartebeests, and topi whose skins had the sheen of satin, ran with smooth speed. The lyre-horned waterbucks had the stately port of wapiti bulls. Rhinoceros, foolish, mighty, and uncouth, stood half asleep in the bright

PRIMEVAL MAN

sunlight. Buffalo sought the shade of the thorn-trees, their bodies black and their great horn-bosses glinting white. Hippos snorted and gambolled in the water. Dominant always, wherever we saw them, were the lion and the elephant; and the favorite prey of the lion was the zebra, the striped wild horse of the African wastes.

Of course, these many different creatures were not all to be seen at any one time or in any one place. But again and again there were so many of them that we felt as if we were passing through a gigantic zoological garden. Often the line of our burden-bearing carriers had to be shifted from its point of march, to avoid a rhinoceros which stared at us with dull and truculent curiosity; while the zebra herds filed off with barking cries across the sunlit plain, and delicate gazelles, dainty as wood-sprites, fled like shadows, and hartebeests gazed toward us with long, homely faces; or we stopped to watch a herd of elephants, cows and calves, browsing among the thorns, their curling trunks raised now and then to test the wind, or perhaps one big ear lifted and then slapped back against the body.

One day at noon, in the Sotik country of East Africa, we stopped to skin a hyena which

I had shot for the Smithsonian. As we skinned it the game of the neighborhood gathered to look on. The spectators included wildebeest, hartebeest, gazelle, topi, a zebra, and a rhinoceros — the hook-lipped kind. Late that afternoon I shot a lioness; the successive reports of the rifle and the grunting roars of the lioness, put to flight a mixed herd of zebra and hartebeest which had hitherto been unconcernedly grazing not far off to one side of the scene of action.

On another day as I journeyed along the valley of the Guaso Nyero — first at the head of the safari, as it travelled through the green forest of the river-bed, and then with only my gun-bearers, through the hot, waterless, sun-scorched country back from the river — I saw rhino, giraffe, buffalo, eland, oryx, waterbuck, impalla, big gazelle, and gerenuk or giraffe-gazelle. After camping, toward evening, I walked up-stream, away from the tents, until I came to a spot where the river ran through a wild, rugged ravine. On the hither side I found the carcass — little more than the skeleton — of a zebra which had been killed by a couple of lions as it came to drink the previous night. It was evidently a favorite drinking-place, for broad game trails led down to the river at this point from both banks. As I sat and watched, a herd of zebra approached cautiously from the opposite side. There were in it representatives of two species of these gaudily marked wild horses or wild asses, the common zebra and the much, bigger northern zebra with longer ears and more numerous and narrower stripes. The herd advanced, avoiding cover as much as possible, continually halting, once wheeling and galloping back, ever seeking with eye and nostril some token of the presence of their maned and tawny foe. At last the leader walked down through a break in the bank to the river. The others crowded close behind, jostling one another as they sank their muzzles in the water. For a moment fear left them, and they satisfied their thirst, and those that were through first then stood while the rearmost drank greedily. But as soon as one of them began to move back to the shore the others became uneasy and followed, and the whole herd broke into a gallop and tore off for a couple of hundred yards. Looking at them it was easy enough to bring before one's eyes the tragedy of the preceding night; the herd nearing the water, wary, but not wary enough, the panic flight as the lion dashed among them, the struggling and the neighing screams of the victim before the great teeth found the life they sought. The herd I watched was not assailed; it cantered off; oryx and waterbuck came down to drink and also cantered off. The carcass of the murdered zebra, little but bones and shreds of red sinew and scraps of skin, lay not far from me. Footprints showed where the lions had drunk after eating. As the long afternoon lights waned, a hyena, abroad earlier than usual, began to call somewhere in the distance. The lonely gorge was rather an eerie place as darkness fell, and I strode toward camp, alone, keeping a sharp lookout round about; and as I walked and watched in a present that might be dangerous, my thoughts went back through the immeasurable ages to a past that was always dangerous; to the days when our hairy and low-browed forefathers, under northern skies, fingered their stone-headed axes as they lay among the rocks in just such a ravine as that I had quitted, and gazed with mingled greed and terror as the cave-lion struck down his prey and scattered the herds of wild horses for whose flesh they themselves hungered.

Once in East Africa I stalked a hook-lipped rhino, a big bull with good horns. I wished its skin and skeleton for the Smithsonian. When a hundred and fifty yards off I stopped for a moment by an ant-hill and looked around over the wide plain. There were in sight a couple of giraffes, some solitary old wildebeest bulls, showing black against the bleached yellow grass, and herds of hartebeest, topi, big and little gazelle, and zebra. On another occasion, when with Kermit, we inspected three rhinos at close quarters, came to the conclusion that none of them would make good specimens, and backed off cautiously a couple of hundred yards to a big ant-hill. From this point, there were in sight all the kinds of game mentioned above except the giraffe and little gazelle, and in addition there were ostrich and wart-hog.

One night when we were camped on the western bank of the upper White Nile we heard a mighty chorus. Lions roared and elephants trumpeted, and in the papyrus beds, beneath the low bluff on which our tents stood, hippopotamus bellowed and blew like the exhaust-pipes of huge steam-engines. Next day I hunted the giant square-mouth rhinoceros, killing a cow and a bull, and taking their skins and the skeleton of one for the Smithsonian. On the walk out, and but a mile or two from camp, we had passed a small herd of elephants; and on our return we found them in the same place, still resting, with many white cow-herons perched on their backs. From where I stood looking at them hartebeest, kob, waterbuck, and oribi were also all in sight.

I could mention day after day such as these, when we saw myriads of game, often of many kinds. One afternoon of heat and sunlight on the parched Kapiti plains, teeming with wild life, I followed a lion, on horseback. During the gallop he ran for several minutes almost in the middle of a mixed herd of hartebeest and zebra. When he came to bay, I walked in on him. In the background the barren hills, "like giants at a hunting lay." Bands of hartebeests and of showy zebras, joined by grotesquely capering wildebeests and by lovely, long-horned gazelles, stood round in a wide, irregular ring, to see their two foes fight to the death. Another day, at burning noon, in a waste of sparsely scattered, withered thorn-trees, west of Redjaf on the upper Nile, I killed a magnificent giant eland bull; and during the hunt I saw elephant, giraffe, buffalo, straw-colored Nile hartebeest, and roan antelope, as big as horses, with shining coats which melted in ghostly fashion into the shimmering heat haze of the dry landscape.

In short, for months my companions and I travelled and hunted in the Pleistocene. Man and beasts alike were of types our own world

PRIMEVAL MAN

knew only in an incalculably remote past. My gun-bearers were really men such as those of later Palæolithic times. Now and then I spent days with hunters whose lives were led under conditions that the people of my race had not faced for ages; probably not since before, certainly not since immediately after, the close of the last glacial epoch. The number and variety of the great game, the terror inspired by some of the beasts of prey, the bulk and majesty of some of the beasts of the chase, were such as are unknown in the rest of the modern world; and nothing like them has been seen in the western and northern world since the Pleistocene.

Many of these great and beautiful beasts were of kinds which either have developed in Africa itself, and have never wandered to the other continents, or else had disappeared from these other continents before man appeared upon the earth. But three of the most characteristic of these beasts, the lion, the elephant, and the horse, were spread over almost the whole of this planet at the time when man as man had fairly begun his hunting. These three beasts then abounded in Europe and in Asia, in North America, and in South America. In each of these continents they were among the dominant types of a fauna as rich, varied, and impressive as only that of Africa is to-day.

When I speak of "elephant," "lion," and "horse" I am speaking of the beasts themselves, not their names in our vernacular. As regards two of these three animals, the horse and the big horse-killing cat, we have no common names to include the various species; whereas in the remaining case we have such a common name to include the two widely separate existing species, although we use different names to designate two well-known fossil species. We speak of both the Indian and the African proboscidians as elephants, although we style "mammoth" the recently extinct hairy elephant of the north, which was more closely related to the Asiatic elephant than the latter is to its African cousin, and although we use the word "mastodon" to denote a more primitive type of elephant also recently extinct in America. We have no such common term either for the various big cats or for the various horses. Yet the African and Asiatic elephants are far more widely separated from one another than the lion is from the tiger, or even from the jaguar. They are far more widely separated than horses, asses, and zebras are from one another. As regards both the horses and the big cats which have

PRIMEVAL MAN 207

always preyed so largely on horses, the differences are almost exclusively in color and in features of purely external anatomy. From the skull and skeleton it is not possible to determine with certainty the lion from the tiger, and both come very close to the big spotted cats; while the skulls of the horse, the ass, and the common zebra are with difficulty to be discriminated except by size — although the skull of the big northernmost African zebra is totally distinct.

In consequence, when we speak of extinct horses it is often impossible to guarantee that they were not asses or zebras; and when we speak of the great extinct cats of Europe and North America as lions, we know that it is possible that in life they may have looked more like tigers. Therefore it must be understood that I use the words horse and lion as terms of convenience and in a broad sense so as to avoid circumlocution. I use them in exactly the way in which "elephant" is always used to include the two totally distinct species now living in India and Africa. By "lion" I mean any one of the big extinct cats, true cats, which in their cranial and skeletal characters are almost or quite identical with living lions and tigers and closely related to living jaguars. By "horse"

I mean any existing species of horse, ass, or zebra, and any one of the numerous similar extinct species which may have belonged to any one of these three types, or have been intermediate between any two of them, or perhaps have been somewhat different from all of them. As thus used, the words horse, lion, and elephant are scientifically of nearly equivalent value.

The only region in which these three animals were not found during Pleistocene times was Australia, which was given over wholly to a relatively insignificant and undeveloped fauna of marsupials and into which it is probable that man did not intrude until at a late period. Everywhere else, from Patagonia to the Cape of Good Hope, including regions now faunistically as utterly unlike as Peru, California, Alaska, Siberia, Asia Minor, France, and Algiers, they abounded, many different and peculiar species being found. The Pleistocene gradually became part of the Age of Man; but at first it was emphatically the Age of the Horse, the Lion, and the Elephant, and the two ages overlapped for a very long period. The lion was primitive man's most deadly foe, as to this day is the case in parts of Africa. He feared the lion, and avoided him, and warred upon him, until gradually he got a little the upper

PRIMEVAL MAN

hand of him. The elephant greatly impressed the imagination of this primitive man, and it still greatly impresses it; as will be seen by any one who studies the carvings and pictures of our ancestors of the glacial and postglacial epochs, or who at the present day listens to the talk of his black gun-bearers round an African camp-fire. The horse was and is a quarry as eagerly followed by primitive man as by the lion himself. Ages elapsed before the horse, and finally even "my lord the elephant" were tamed by man, as man developed something that could properly be called a culture. The savages who, when England was merely a peninsula of continental Europe, dwelt by the banks of the mighty rivers which have since shrunk into the present Rhine and Seine, looked on the mammoth and the coarse-headed wild horse of their day as furnishing the flesh their stomachs craved, precisely as the savages of the Nile and the Zambesi now look on the African elephant and the zebra.

This Age of Primitive Man, this Age of the Horse, the Lion, and the Elephant, like all other historical or geological "ages," lasted longer in some places than in others, and, instead of having sharply defined limits, merged gradually into the preceding and succeeding ages. Moreover — in exact analogy with other divisions of time, all of which, however useful, are essentially artificial — we must constantly remember that the perspective changes utterly with the point of view. All paleontological terms of time are necessarily terms chiefly of convenience, which have and express a real intrinsic value, but which cannot be sharply defined. Miocene, Pliocene, Pleistocene, and Recent are such terms. They are arbitrarily chosen bits of terminology to express successive stages of the world's growth, and therefore successive and varying faunas. They are not equivalent in time to one another; the more remote the age from our own the greater is the length of time we include therein. "Recent" denotes a short period of time compared to "Pleistocene," and "Pleistocene" a short period compared to "Pliocene." If there are on this earth intelligent beings at a time in the future as remote from our day as our day is from the Pliocene, they will certainly consider "Recent" and "Pleistocene" as one short period. All the beast faunas and all the human cultures from the eras of the chinless Heidelberg and Piltdown men to our own time will seem in that remote perspective practically contemporaneous. Similarly, when we try to grasp life as lived even in such, geologically, near-by time as any portion of the Pleistocene, we cannot be sure of the exact time-parallelism of closely related faunas in different parts of the world, nor can we, in many cases, tell whether certain species were really contemporaneous or whether they were successive. Of the general paleontological facts, of the general aspects of the various faunas in various parts of the world, during some roughly indicated period of geologic time, we may be reasonably sure. But when we speak with more minuteness, we speak doubtfully, and at any moment new discoveries may unsettle theories by upsetting what we have supposed to be facts.

In considering what is in this chapter set forth these conditions must be kept in mind. When I speak of what I have myself seen or of the tools, carvings, and skeletons dug from the ground by competent observers, I speak of facts; but as yet the explanations of these facts must be accepted only as hypotheses, at least in part. Just as the elephant, wild horse, and lion exist in Africa to-day, and have disappeared from Europe and the two Americas thousands or tens of thousands of years ago, so it may well be that they had died out in North America ages before they had disappeared from the other end of the western hemisphere. Again, in North America, it is as yet quite impossible to be sure as to the exact succession, or contemporaneity of all of the many extinct species of horse and elephant. It is with our present knowledge equally impossible to be sure of the exact time relations between any given North American fauna and the Eurasiatic fauna most closely resembling it. Moreover, as yet we have only the vaguest idea of the duration of even modern geologic time; good observers vary as to whether a given period covers hundreds of thousands or only tens of thousands of years.

This does not impair the value of the general picture which we can make in our minds. It is not essentially different from what is the case in history. If we speak of the Græco-Roman world from the days of Aristides to those of Marcus Aurelius, we outline a historical period which has a real unity, and of which all the parts are bound together by real ties and real resemblances. Nevertheless, there were sharp differences in the successive cultures of this period; even the two centuries which intervened, say, between Miltiades and Demetrius Poliorketes, or between Marius and Trajan, showed such differences. Dealing roughly with the period as a whole, it would not be necessary

PRIMEVAL MAN 213

to try to draw all the distinctions and make all the qualifications that would be essential to minutely accurate treatment; such treatment would merely mar the outlines of a general sketch. The same thing is, of course, true of an outline sketch of what our present knowledge shows of man's most wide-spread beast associates, when he had begun, in forms not very different from those of the lower savages to-day, to spread over the world's surface.

Therefore it is necessary to remember that in dealing even with such a recent chapter of paleontological discovery as that concerned with early man and the great four-footed creatures that were his contemporaries, our general picture can rarely pretend to more than general accuracy. It is only in prehistoric and protohistoric Europe that the early career of "homo sapiens" and his immediate predecessors has been worked out in sufficient detail to give even the roughest idea of its successive stages, and of the varying groups of great beasts with which at the different stages man was associated. This is because the record has been better preserved, and more closely studied in Europe than elsewhere; for it seems fairly certain that it is in Eurasia, in the palæarctic realm, that there took place the development of the more or less ape-like predecessors of man and then of man himself. It is in Eurasia that all of the remains of man's immediate predecessors have been found — from the Javan pithecanthropus which can only doubtfully be called human, to the Piltdown and Heidelberg men, who were undoubtedly human, but who were so much closer than any existing savage to the beasts that (unless our present imperfect knowledge proves erroneous) they can hardly be deemed specifically identical with modern homo sapiens. Even the more modern Neanderthal men are probably not ancestral to our own stock. It is in Europe, following on these predecessors of existing man, that we find the skeletons, the weapons and tools, and the carvings of existing man in his earliest stages; and mingled with his remains those of the strange and mighty beasts which dwelt beside him in the land. Probably these European forefathers of existing man came from a stock which had previously gone through its early human and prehuman stages in Asia. But we only know what happened in Europe. There was a slow, halting, and interrupted but on the whole steady development in physical type — sometimes the type itself gradually changing, while sometimes it was displaced by a wholly different type

PRIMEVAL MAN 215

of wholly different blood. Roughly parallel with this was a corresponding development in cultural type. Probably from the earliest times, and certainly in late times, development or change in physical type was often wholly unrelated to development or change in culture. Sometimes the cultural change was an autochthonous development. Sometimes it was due to a more or less complete change in blood, owing to the immigration of a strong alien type of humanity. Sometimes it was due to the adoption of an alien culture.

Many good observers nowadays, judging from the facts at present accessible, are inclined to think that the American Indian stocks were the first human stocks that peopled the western hemisphere, that they are by blood nearest of kin to certain race-elements still existing in northeastern Asia — representing the only inhabitants of northeastern Asia when man first penetrated from there to northwestern America — and that more remotely they may be kin to certain late Palæolithic men of Europe. But much of the American Indian culture was essentially a Neolithic culture, seemingly from the beginning. In places — Peru, Maya-land, the Mexican plateau — it at times developed into a civilization equally extraordinary for its achievements and for its shortcomings and evanescence; but it never developed a metal epoch corresponding to, say, the bronze age of the Mediterranean, and although the small camel, the llama, was tamed in South America, in North America, the ox, sheep, white goat, and reindeer were never made servants of man, as befell so many corresponding beasts of Eurasia.

In this last respect the American Indians stayed almost on the level of the African tribes, whose native civilization was otherwise far less advanced. The African buffalo is as readily tamed as its Asiatic brother; the zebra was as susceptible of taming as the early wild horse and ass; the eland is probably of all big ruminants the one that most readily lends itself to domestication. But none of them was tamed until tribes owning animals which had been tamed for ages appeared in Africa; and then the already-tamed animals were accepted in their stead. The asses, cattle, sheep, and goats of Asia are now the domestic animals of the negroes and of the whites in Africa, merely because it is easier, more profitable, and more convenient to deal with animals already accustomed for ages to the yoke of domestic servitude than to again go through the labor incident to changing a wild into a tame beast.

It is probable that during the immense stretch of time which in Europe covered the growth of the various successive Palæolithic, and finally Neolithic, cultures — the "old-stone" ages during which man used stone implements which he merely chipped and flaked, and the "new-stone" age in which he ground and polished them — there happened time and again what has happened in the history and prehistory of man in Africa and North America. One of the incidents in this parallelism is the way in which the inhabitants accepted animals already trained and brought from elsewhere rather than attempt to train the similar beasts of their own forests. Doubtless the reason why the European bison is not a domestic animal is exactly the same as the reason why the American bison and African buffalo are not domestic animals. The northern European hunting savages were displaced or subjugated by, or received a higher culture from, tribes bringing from Asia or from the Mediterranean lands the cattle they had already tamed. The same things happened, in Africa south of the Sahara while it was still shrouded from civilized vision, and in America since the coming of the European.

These hunting savages existed for ages, for

hundreds of thousands of years, in Europe. During this period of time — immense by historic standards, yet geologically a mere moment — many different human types succeeded one another. The climate swung to and from glacial to subtropical; fauna succeeded fauna. One group of species of big beasts succeeded another as the climate and plant life changed; and then itself gave place to a third; and perhaps once more resumed its ancient place as the physical conditions again became what they once had been. At certain periods the musk-ox, the reindeer, the woolly rhinoceros, and the hairy mammoth, together with huge cave-bears, were found; at other periods southern forms of elephant and rhinoceros, and such tropical creatures as the hippopotamus, replaced the beasts of the snow land. Horses of different species were sometimes present in incredible numbers. There were species of wild cattle, including the European bison, and the urus or aurochs — spoken of by Cæsar, and kin to, and doubtless partly ancestral to, the tame ox. The cave-lion, perhaps indistinguishable from the modern African lion, was the most formidable beast of prey. I say "perhaps" indistinguishable, for we cannot be quite certain. Some of the races of cave-dwelling

PRIMEVAL MAN 219

men were good artists, and carved spirited figures of mammoth, rhinoceros, bison, horse, reindeer, and bear on ivory, or on the walls of caves. The big lion-like cats appear only rarely in these pictures.

In most cases the arctic and warm-temperate or near-tropical animals supplanted one another only incompletely as the waves of life advanced and receded when the climate changed. This seems a rather puzzling conjunction. The explanation is twofold. When the climate changes, when it becomes warmer, for instance, northern creatures that once were at home in the lowlands draw off into the neighboring highlands, leaving their old haunts to newcomers from the south, while nevertheless the two faunas may be only a few miles apart; just as in Montana and Alberta moose and caribou in certain places were found side by side with the prongbuck. Moreover, some species possess an adaptability which their close kin do not, and can thrive under widely different temperature conditions. A century ago the hippopotamus was found in the temperate Cape Colony, close to mountain ranges climatically fit for the typical beasts of north-temperate Eurasia. In Arizona at the present day mammals and birds of the Canadian fauna live on the mountain tops around the bases of which flourish animals characteristic of the tropical Mexican plateau; the former having been left stranded on high mountain islands when, with the retreat of the glaciers, the climate of the United States grew warmer and the tide of southern life-forms swept northward over the lowlands. Under such conditions the same river deposits might show a combination of utterly different faunas. Moreover, some modern animals are found from the arctics to the tropics. The American lynx extends, in closely connected forms, from the torrid deserts of Mexico to arctic Alaska; so does the mountain-sheep. The tiger flourishes in the steaming Malay forests and in snowy Manchuria. I have found the cougar breeding in the frozen, bitter midwinter among the high Rockies, in a country where snow covered the ground for six months, and where the caribou would be entirely at home; and again in Brazil under the equator, in the atmosphere of a hot-house. There were periods, during the ages before history dawned, but when man had long dwelt in Europe, in which herds of reindeer may have roamed the French and English uplands within sight of rivers wherein the hippopotamus dwelt as comfortably as he recently did at the Cape of Good Hope.

PRIMEVAL MAN

Some of the more recent of these European hunting savages — those who were perhaps in part our own forefathers, or who perhaps were of substantially the same ethnic type as the men of the older race strains in northeastern Asia, and even possibly of the American Indians — and many of their more remote predecessors were contemporaries of the lion, the horse, and the elephant. Different species of horse and elephant succeeded one another. The earlier ones were contemporaries of the hippopotamus and of not only the lion but the sabretooth. When the hairy elephant, the mammoth, was present, the fauna also often included the cave-lion, cave-hyena, cave-bear, wolf, boar, woolly rhinoceros, many species of deer (including the moose and that huge fallow deer, the Irish elk), horses, and the bison and the aurochs. The mammoth and woolly rhinoceros died out so recently that their carcasses are discovered preserved in the Siberian ice, and the undigested food in their stomachs shows that they ate northern plants of the kinds now common, and the twigs of the conifers and other trees which still flourish in the boreal realm of both hemispheres.

The lion was doubtless the most dreaded foe of the ancient European, just as he is to this day of certain African tribes. The Palæolithic hunters slaughtered myriads of wild horses, just as the ebony-hued hunters of Africa now slaughter the zebra and feast on its oily flesh. The spirited carvings and sketches of the hairy mammoth by the later Palæolithic cave-dwellers show that the elephant of the cold northlands had impressed their imaginations precisely as the hairless elephant of the hot south now impresses the imaginations of the tribes that dwell under the vertical African sun. The rhinoceros and wild cattle of the pine forests played in their lives the part played in the lives of our contemporaries, the hunting tribes of Africa, by the rhinoceros and the buffalo — the African wild ox — which dwell among open forests of acacias and drink from palm-bordered rivers. They saw no animal like that strange creature, the African giraffe; and several kinds of deer took the place of the varied species of bovine ruminants which, in popular parlance, we group together as antelopes.

Substantially the fauna of mighty beasts which furnished the means of livelihood, and also constantly offered the menace of death, to our European forefathers — or to the predecessors of our forefathers — was like that magnificent fauna which we who have travelled among

PRIMEVAL MAN

the savages of present-day Africa count it one of our greatest pleasures to have seen. During the ages when the successive races of hunter-savages dwelt in Europe a similar magnificent fauna of huge and strange beasts flourished on all the continents of the globe except in Australia. In Europe it vanished in prehistoric times, when man had long dwelt in the land. In Africa south of the Sahara, and partially in spots of Asia, it has persisted to this day. In North America it died out before, or perhaps, as regards the last stragglers, immediately after, the coming of man; in South America it seems clear that it survived, at least in places, until he was well established.

The three abundant and conspicuous beasts, all three typical of the great mammalian fauna which was contemporary with the prehistoric human hunters, and all three common to all the continents on which this great mammalian fauna was found, were the lion — using the name to cover several species of huge horse-killing and man-killing cats; the elephant, including several totally different species, among them the mammoth and mastodon; and the horse, including numerous widely different species. Together with these three universally distributed animals were many others belonging to types confined to certain of the continents. Rhinoceros were found in Europe, Asia, and Africa (they had once flourished in North America but had died out long before man appeared on the globe). Camels were found in Asia, in South America, and especially in North America, which was their centre of abundance and the place where they had developed. Wild oxen were found in all the continents except South America; deer everywhere except in true Africa, zoogeographical Africa, Africa south of the Sahara. The pigs of the Old World were replaced by the entirely different peccaries of the New World. Sheep, goats, and goat-antelopes lived in Eurasia and North America. Most of the groups of big ruminants commonly called "antelopes" are now confined to Africa; but it appears that formerly various representatives of them reached America. The giraffe through this period was purely African; the hippopotamus has retreated to Africa, although in the period we are considering its range extended to Eurasia. In South America were many extraordinary creatures totally different from one another, including ground-sloths as big as elephants. Two or three outlying representatives of the ground-sloths had wandered into North America; but elsewhere there were no animals

PRIMEVAL MAN

in any way resembling them. The horse, the lion, and the elephant were the three striking representatives of this vast and varied fauna which were common to all five continents.

The North American fauna of this type reached its height about the time — extending over many scores of thousands of years — when successive ice ages alternated with long stretches of temperate or subtropical climate throughout the northern hemisphere. During the period when this great North American fauna flourished hunter-savages of archaic type lived amid, and partly on, the great game of Europe. But, as far as we know, men did not come to America until after, or at the very end of, the time when these huge grass-eaters and twig-eaters, and the huge flesh-eaters which preyed on them, vanished from the earth, owing to causes which in most cases we cannot as yet even guess.

Much the most striking and interesting collection of the remains of this wonderful fauna is to be found near one of our big cities. On the outskirts of Los Angeles, in southern California, are asphalt deposits springing from petroleum beds in the shales below. The oil seeping up to the surface has formed shallow, spread-out pools and, occasionally, deep pits covered with water. In part of the area these pits and pools of tar have existed for scores of thousands or hundreds of thousands of years, since far back in the Pleistocene. They then acted as very dangerous and efficient mammal traps and bird traps — and now continue so to act, for the small mammals and the birds of the neighborhood still wander into them, get caught in the sticky substance, and die, as I have myself seen. Moreover the tar serves as a preservative of the bones of the creatures that thus perish. In consequence some of the ancient pits and pools are filled with immense masses of the well-preserved bones of the strange creatures that were smothered in them ages ago.

Nowhere else is there any such assemblage of remains giving such a nearly complete picture of the fauna of a given region at a given time. A striking peculiarity is that the skeletons of the flesh-eaters far surpass in number the skeletons of the plant-eaters. This is something almost unique, for of course predatory animals are of necessity much less numerous than the animals on which they prey. The reversal in this case of the usual proportions between the skeletal remains of herbivorous and carnivorous beasts and birds is due to the character of the

PRIMEVAL MAN 227

deposits. The tar round the edges of the pools or pits hardens, becomes covered with dust, and looks like solid earth; and water often stands in the tar pits after rain, while at night the shallow pools of fresh tar look like water. Evidently the big grazing or browsing beasts now and then wandered out on the hard asphalt next the solid ground, and suddenly became mired in the soft tar beyond. Probably the pits in which water stood served as traps year after year as the thirsty herds sought drink. Then each dead or dying animal became itself a lure for all kinds of flesh-eating beasts and birds, which in their turn were entrapped in the sticky mass. In similar manner, thirty years ago on the Little Missouri, I have known a grizzly bear, a couple of timber-wolves, and several coyotes to be attracted to the carcass of a steer which had bogged down in the springtime beside an alkali pool.

Another result of the peculiar conditions under which the skeletons accumulated is that an unusually large number of very old, very young, and maimed or crippled creatures were entrapped. Doubtless animals in full vigor were more apt to work themselves free at the moment when they found they were caught in the tar; and, moreover, a wolf or sabretooth which was weakened by age or by wounds received in encounter with its rivals, or with some formidable quarry, and which therefore found its usual prey difficult to catch, would be apt to hang around places where carcasses, or living creatures still feebly struggling, offered themselves to ravenous appetites.

The plant remains in these deposits show that the climate and vegetation were substantially those of California to-day, although in some respects indicating northern rather than southern California. There were cypress-trees of a kind still common farther north, manzanita, juniper, and oaks. Evidently the region was one of open, grassy plains varied with timber belts and groves. It has been said that to support such a fauna the vegetation must have been much more luxuriant than in this region at present. This is probably an error. The great game regions of Africa are those of scanty vegetation. Thick forest holds far less big animal life. Crossing the sunny Athi or Kapiti plains of East Africa, where the few trees are thorny, stunted acacias and the low grass is brown and brittle under the drought, the herds of zebra, hartebeest, wildebeest, and gazelle are a perpetual delight and wonder; and elephant, rhinoceros, and buffalo abounded

PRIMEVAL MAN

on them in the days before the white man came. On the Guaso Nyero of the north, and in the Sotik, the country was even drier at the time of my visit, and the character of the vegetation showed how light the normal rainfall was. The land was open, grassy plain, or was thinly covered with thorn scrub, with here and there acacia groves and narrow belts of thicker timber growth along the watercourses, and in the Sotik gnarled gray olives. Yet the game swarmed. We watched the teeming masses come down to drink at the shrunken rivers or at the dwindling ponds beside which our tents were pitched. As the line of the safari walked forward under the brazen sky, while we white men rode at the head with our rifles, the herds of strange and beautiful wild creatures watched us, with ears pricked forward, or stood heedless in the thin shade of the trees, their tails switching ceaselessly at the biting flies. In wealth of numbers, in rich variety and grandeur of species, the magnificent fauna we then saw was not substantially inferior to that which an age before dwelt on the California plains.

This Pleistocene California fauna included many beasts which persisted in the land until our own day. There were cougars, lynxes, timber-wolves, gray foxes, coyotes, bears, pronghorn antelopes and black-tail or white-tail deer nearly, or quite, identical with the modern forms. They were the same animals which I and my fellow ranchmen hunted when, in the early eighties of the last century, our branded cattle were first driven to the Little Missouri. They swarmed on the upper Missouri and the Yellowstone when Lewis and Clark found the bison and wapiti so tame that they would hardly move out of the way, while the grizzly bears slept on the open plains and fearlessly attacked the travellers. But in the Pleistocene, at the time we are considering, the day of these modern creatures had only begun. The contents of the tar-pits show that the animals named above were few in number, compared to the great beasts with which they were associated.

The giant among these Pleistocene giants of California, probably the largest mammal that ever walked the earth, was the huge imperial elephant. This mighty beast stood at least two feet higher than the colossal African elephant of to-day, which itself is bigger than the mammoth, and as big as any other extinct elephant. The curved tusks of the imperial elephant reached a length of sixteen feet. A herd of such mighty beasts must have been an awe-inspiring sight — had there been human

PRIMEVAL MAN 231

eyes to see it. Nor were they the only representatives of their family. A much more archaic type of elephant, the mastodon, flourished beside its gigantic cousin. The mastodon was a relatively squat creature, standing certainly four feet shorter than the imperial elephant, with comparatively small and slightly curved tusks and a flatter head. Enormous numbers of mastodons ranged over what is now the United States, and the adjacent parts of Canada and Mexico. The mastodons represented a stage farther back in the evolutionary line than the true elephants, and in the Old World they died out completely before the latter disappeared even from Europe and Siberia. But in North America, for unknown reasons, they outlasted their more highly developed kinsfolk and rivals, and there is some ground for believing that they did not completely disappear until after the arrival of man on this continent.

The elephant stock developed in the Old World, and it is probable that the true elephants were geologically recent immigrants to America, coming across the land bridge which then connected Alaska and Siberia. In California they encountered the big descendants of other big immigrants, which had reached North

America by another temporary land bridge, but from another continent, South America. These were the ground-sloths, giant edentates, which reached an extraordinary development in the southern half of our hemisphere, where distant and diminutive relatives — tree-sloths, ant-eaters, armadillos — still live. The most plentiful of these California ground-sloths, the mylodon, was about the size of a rhinoceros; an unwieldy, slow-moving creature, feeding on plants, and in appearance utterly unlike anything now living.

Together with these great beasts belonging to stocks that in recent geologic time had immigrated hither from the Old World and from the southern half of the New World was another huge beast of remote native ancestry. This was a giant camel, with a neck almost like that of a giraffe. Camels — including llamas — developed in North America. Their evolutionary history certainly stretched through a period of two or three million — perhaps four or five million — years on this continent, reaching back to a little Eocene ancestor no bigger than a jack-rabbit. Yet after living and developing in the land through these untold ages, over a period inconceivably long to our apprehension, the camels completely died out on this continent

PRIMEVAL MAN 233

of their birth, although not until they had sent branches to Asia and South America, where their descendants still survive.

Two other grass-eating beasts, of large size — although smaller than the above — were also plentiful. One, a bison, bigger, straighter-horned and less specialized than our modern bison, represented the cattle, which were among the animals that passed to America over the Alaskan land bridge in Pleistocene time.

The other was a big, coarse-headed horse, much larger than any modern wild horse, and kin to the then existing giant horse of Texas, which was the size of a percheron. The horses, like the camels, had gone through their developmental history on this continent, the earliest ancestor, the little four-toed "dawn horse" of the Eocene, being likewise the size of a jackrabbit. Through millions of years, while myriads of generations followed one another, the two families developed side by side, increasing in size and seemingly in adaptation to the environment. Each stock branched into many different species and genera. They spread into the Old World and into South America. Then, suddenly, — that is, suddenly in zoologic sense — both completely died out in their ancient home, and the horses in South America also, whereas half a dozen very distinct species are still found in Asia and Africa.

All these great creatures wandered in herds to and fro across the grassy Californian plains and among the reaches of open forest. Preying upon them were certain carnivores grimmer and more terrible than any now existing. The most distinctive and seemingly the most plentiful was the sabretooth. This was a huge, squat, short-tailed, heavily built cat with upper canines which had developed to an almost walrus-like length; only, instead of being round and blunt like walrus tusks, they were sharp, with a thin, cutting edge, so that they really were entitled to be called sabres or daggers. Whether the creature was colored like a lion or like a tiger or like neither, we do not know, for it had no connection with either save its remote kinship with all the cats. The sabretooth cats, like the true cats, had gone through an immensely long period of developmental history in North America, although they did not appear here as early as the little camels and horses. Far back across the ages, at or just after the close of the Eocene — the "dawn age" of mammalian life — certain moderate-sized or small cat-like creatures existed on this continent, doubtless ancestral to the sabretooth, but so

PRIMEVAL MAN

generalized in type that they display close affinities with the true cats, and even on certain points with the primitive dog creatures of the time. Age followed age — Oligocene, Miocene, Pliocene. The continents rose and sank and were connected and disconnected. Vast lakes appeared and disappeared. Mountain chains wore down and other mountain chains were thrust upward. Periods of heat, during which rich forests flourished north of the arctic circle, were followed by periods of cold, when the glacial ice-cap crept down half-way across the present temperate zone. Slowly, slowly, while the surface of the world thus changed, and through innumerable reaches of time, the sabretooth cats and true cats developed along many different lines in both the Old World and the New. One form of sabretooth was in Europe with the bestial near-human things who were the immediate predecessors of the first low but entirely human savages. It was in the two Americas, however, that the sabretooth line culminated, immediately before its final extinction, in its largest and most formidable forms. This California sabretooth was not taller than a big cougar or leopard, but was probably as heavy as a fair-sized lion. Its skeletal build is such that it cannot have been an agile creature, apt at the pursuit of light and swift prey. By rugged strength and by the development of its terrible stabbing and cutting dagger teeth, that is, by sheer fighting ability, it was fitted for attack upon and battle with the massive herbivores then so plentiful. It must indeed have been a fearsome beast in close grapple. Doubtless with its sharp, retractile claws it hung onto the huge bodies of elephant, camel, and ground-sloth, of horse and bison, while the sabres were driven again and again into the mortal parts of the prey and slashed the flesh as they withdrew. It seems possible that the mouth was opened wide and stabbing blows delivered, almost as a rattlesnake strikes with raised fangs. Vast numbers of sabretooth skeletons have been found in the asphalt; evidently the strange, formidable creature haunted any region which held attraction for the various kinds of heavy game on which it preyed.

The only other carnivore as abundant as the sabretooth was a giant wolf. This was heavier than any existing wolf, with head and teeth still larger in proportion. The legs were comparatively light. Evidently, like the sabretooth, this giant wolf had become specialized as a beast of battle, fitted to attack and master the bulky browsers and grazers, but not to overtake those that were smaller and swifter. The massive jaws and teeth could smash heavy bones and tear the toughest hide; and a hungry pack of these monsters, able to assail in open fight any quarry no matter how fierce or powerful, must have spread dire havoc and dismay among all things that could not escape by flight.

There were two still larger predatory species, which were much less plentiful than either the wolf or the sabretooth. One was a short-faced cave-bear, far larger than even the huge Alaskan bear of to-day. Doubtless it took toll of the herds; but bears are omnivorous beasts, and not purely predatory in the sense that is true of those finished killers, the wolves and big cats. Unlike the wolves and cats, bears were geologically recent immigrants to America.

The other was a true cat, a mighty beast; bigger than the African lion of to-day; indeed, perhaps the biggest and most powerful lion-like or tiger-like cat that ever existed. Seemingly it was much rarer than the sabretooth; but it is possible that this seeming rarity was due to its not lurking in the neighborhood of pools and licks but travelling more freely over the wastes, being of a build fit not only for combat but for an active and wandering life. It is usually spoken of as kin to the African lion, a decidedly smaller beast. It is possible that its real kinship lies with the tiger. The Manchurian form of the tiger is an enormous beast, and a careful comparison of the skulls and skeletons may show that it equals in size the huge western American cat of Pleistocene times. I have already spoken of the fact that in many cases it is almost impossible to distinguish the lion and tiger apart by the bones alone; and it may be that the exact affinities of these recently extinct species with living forms cannot be definitely determined. But during historic and prehistoric times the lion has been a beast of western Eurasia and of Africa. The tiger, on the contrary, is and has been a beast of eastern Asia, and apparently has been spreading westward and perhaps southward — that it was not as ancient an inhabitant of jungle-covered southern India as the elephant and leopard seems probable from the fact that it is not found in Ceylon, which island in all likelihood preserves most of the southern Indian fauna that existed prior to its separation from the mainland. Moreover, the finest form of tiger exists in cold northeastern Asia. In Pleistocene times this portion of Asia was connected by a broad land bridge with western America, where the mighty American cat then

PRIMEVAL MAN

roved and preyed on the herds of huge planteating beasts. We know that many Asiatic beasts crossed over this land bridge — the bears, bison, mountain-sheep, moose, caribou, and wapiti, which still live both in Asia and North America, and the mammoth and cave-bears, which have died out on both continents. It is at least possible — further investigation may or may not show it to be more than possible — that the huge Pleistocene cat of western America was the collateral ancestor of the Manchurian tiger. Whether it was another immigrant from Asia, or a developed form of some big American Pliocene cat, cannot with our present knowledge be determined.

Surely the thought of this vast and teeming, and utterly vanished wild life, must strongly appeal to every man of knowledge and love of nature, who is gifted with the imaginative power to visualize the past and to feel the keen delight known only to those who care intensely both for thought and for action, both for the rich experience acquired by toil and adventure, and for the rich experience obtained through books recording the studies of others.

Doubtless such capacity of imaginative appreciation is of no practical help to the hunter of big game to-day, any more than the power to visualize the long-vanished past in history helps a practical politican to do his ordinary work in the present workaday world. The governor of Gibraltar or of Aden, who cares merely to do his own intensely practical work, need know nothing whatever about any history more ancient than that of the last generation. But this is not true of the traveller. It is not even true of the politician who wishes to get full enjoyment out of life without shirking its duties. He certainly must not become a mere dreamer, or believe that his dreams will help him in practical action. But joy, just for joy's sake, has its place too, and need in no way interfere with work; and, of course, this is as true of the joy of the mind as of the joy of the body. As a man steams into the Mediterranean between the African coast and the "purple, painted headlands" of Spain, it is well for him if he can bring before his vision the galleys of the Greek and Carthaginian mercantile adventurers, and of the conquering Romans; the boats of the wolf-hearted Arabs; the long "snakes" of the Norse pirates, Odin's darlings; the stately and gorgeous war craft of Don John, the square-sailed ships of the fighting Dutch admirals, and the lofty three-deckers of Nelson, the greatest of all the masters of the sea. Aden is like a

PRIMEVAL MAN

furnace between the hot sea and the hot sand; but at the sight of the old rock cisterns, carved by forgotten hands, one realizes why on that coast of barren desolation every maritime people in turn, from the mists that shroud an immemorial antiquity to our own day of fevered materialistic civilization, has seized Aden Bay — Egyptian, Sabean, Byzantine, Turk, Persian, Portuguese, Englishman; and always, a few miles distant, in the thirsty sands, the changeless desert folk have waited until pride spent itself and failed, and the new power passed, as each old power had passed, and then the merciless men of the waste once more claimed their own.

Gibraltar and Aden cannot mean to the unimaginative what they mean to the men of vision, to the men stirred by the hero tales of the past, by the dim records of half-forgotten peoples. These men may or may not do their work as well as others, but their gifts count in the joy of living. Enjoyment the same in kind comes to the man who can clothe with flesh the dry bones of bygone ages, and can see before his eyes the great beasts, hunters and hunted, the beasts so long dead, which thronged the Californian land at a time when in all its physical features it had already become essentially what it still continues to be.

The beast life of this prehistoric California must be called ancient by a standard which would adjudge the Egyptian pyramids and the Mesopotamian palace mounds and the Maya forest temples to be modern. Yet when expressed in geologic terms it was but of yesterday. When it flourished the Eurasian hunting savages were in substantially the same stage of progress as the African hunting savages who now live surrounded by a similar fauna. On the whole, taking into account the number, variety, and size of the great beasts, the fauna which surrounded Palæolithic man in Europe was inferior to that amid which dwell the black-skinned savages of equatorial Africa. Even Africa, however, although unmatched in its wealth of antelopes, cannot quite parallel, with its lion, elephant, and zebras, the lordlier elephant, the great horse, and the huge cat of the earlier Californian fauna; and the giraffe, the hyena, the rhinoceros, and the hippopotamus do not quite offset the sabretooth, the giant wolf, the mastodon, the various species of enormous ground-sloths, and the huge camel; the bison and buffalo about balance each other.

There were no human eyes to see nor human ears to hear what went on in southern California when it held an animal life as fierce and

PRIMEVAL MAN

strange and formidable as mid-Africa to-day. The towering imperial elephants and the burly mastodons trumpeted their approach one to the other. The great camels, striding noiselessly on their padded feet, passed the clumsy ground-sloths on their way to water. The herds of huge horses and bison drank together in pools where the edges were trodden into mire by innumerable hoofs. All these creatures grew alertly on guard when the shadows lengthened and the long-drawn baying of the wolf pack heralded the night of slaughter and of fear; and the dusk thrilled with the ominous questing yawns of sabretooth and giant tiger, as the beasts of havoc prowled abroad from their day lairs among the manzanitas, or under cypress and live-oak.

The tar-pools caught birds as well as beasts. Most of these birds were modern — vultures, eagles, geese, herons. But there were condor-like birds twice the size of any living condor, the biggest birds, so far as we know, that ever flew. There were also, instead of wild turkeys, great quantities of wild peacocks — at least they have been identified as peacocks or similar big, pheasant-like birds. If the identification is correct, this is an unexpected discovery and a fresh proof of how this extinct American fauna at so many points resembled that of Asia. It was natural that a collateral ancestor of the present Asiatic pheasant-like birds should dwell beside a collateral ancestor of the present Asiatic tiger.[1]

Moreover, the tar-pools hold human bones. These, however, are probably of much later date than the magnificent fauna above described, perhaps only a few thousand years old. They belong to a rather advanced type of man. It is probable that before man came to America at all, the earlier types had died out in Eurasia, or had been absorbed and developed, or else had been thrust southward into Africa, Tasmania, Australia, and remote forest tracts of Indo-Malaysia, where, being such backward savages, they never developed anything remotely resembling a civilization. It was probably people kin to some of the later cave-

---

[1] Professor J. C. Merriam, of the University of California, first studied this fauna. The excavations are now being carried on by Director Frank S. Daggett, of the capital Museum of Los Angeles County. I have spoken above of the vast herds of game encountered over a century ago by Lewis and Clark on the upper Missouri. The journals of these two explorers form an American classic, and they have found a worthy editor in Reuben Gold Thwaites; there could not be an edition more satisfactory from every standpoint — including that of good taste. In anthropology I follow the views of Fairfield Osborne and Ales Hrdlicka; I am not competent to decide as to the points where they differ; and they would be the first to say that some of the hypotheses they advance must be accepted as provisional until our knowledge is greater.

PRIMEVAL MAN 245

dwellers who furnished the first (and perhaps until the advent of the white man the only important) immigration to America. These immigrants, the ancestors of all the tribes of Indians, spread from Alaska to Terra del Fuego. Over most of the territory in both Americas they remained at the hunting stage of savage life, although they generally supplemented their hunting by a certain amount of cultivation of the soil, and although in places they developed into advanced and very peculiar culture communities.

When these savages reached North America it is likely, from our present knowledge, that the terrible and magnificent Pleistocene fauna had vanished, although in places the last survivors of the mastodon, and perhaps of one or two other forms, may still have lingered. What were the causes of this wide-spread, and complete, and — geologically speaking — sudden extermination of so many and so varied types of great herbivorous creatures, we cannot say. It may be we can never do more than guess at them. It is certainly an extraordinary thing that complete destruction should have suddenly fallen on all, literally all, of the species. Camels and horses, after they had dwelt on this continent for millions of years, since almost the dawn of mammalian life, developing from little beasts the size of woodchucks into the largest and most stately creatures of their kind that ever trod the earth's surface, all at once disappeared to the very last individual. Ground-sloths and elephants vanished likewise. The bigger forms of bison also died out, although one species remained. Many causes of extinction have been suggested. Perhaps all of them were more or less operative. Perhaps others of which we know nothing were operative. We cannot say.

But as regards certain of the formidable, but heavy rather than active, beasts of prey it is possible to hazard a guess. Compared to agile destroyers like the cougar and the timber-wolf, the sabretooth and the big-headed, small-legged giant wolf were strong, heavy, rather clumsy creatures. Predatory animals of their kind were beasts of battle rather than beasts of the chase. They were fitted to overcome by downright fighting strength a big, slow, self-confident quarry, rather than to run down a swift and timid quarry by speed or creep up to a wary and timid quarry by sinuous stealth. So long as the heavy herbivores were the most numerous these fighting carnivores were dominant over their sly, swift, slinking brethren. But when the great mass of plant-eaters grew

PRIMEVAL MAN

to trust to speed and vigilance for their safety there was no longer room for preying beasts of mere prowess.

In South America it is probable that the heavy fauna died out much later than in North America and northern Eurasia; that is, it died out much later than in what zoogeographers call the holarctic realm. During most of the Tertiary period or age of mammals, the period intervening between the close of the age of great reptiles and the time when man in human form appeared on the planet, South America was an island, and its faunal history was as distinct and peculiar as that of Australia. Aside from marsupials and New World monkeys, its most characteristic animals were edentates and very queer ungulates with no resemblance to those of any other continent. Toward the close of the Tertiary land bridges connected the two Americas, and an interchange of faunas followed. The South American fauna was immensely enriched by the incoming of elephants, horses, sabretooth cats, true cats, camels, bears, tapirs, peccaries, deer, and dogs, all of which developed along new and individual lines. A few of these species, llamas and tapirs for instance, still persist in South America although they have died out in the land from which they came.

But in the end, and also for unknown causes, this great fauna died out in South America likewise, leaving a continent faunistically even more impoverished than North America. The great autochthonous forms shared the extinction of the big creatures of the immigrant fauna; for under stress of competition with the newcomers, the ancient ungulates and edentates had developed giants of their own.

Recent discoveries have shown that the extinction was not complete when the ancestors of the Indians of to-day reached the southern Andes and the Argentine plains. An age previously the forefathers of these newcomers had lived in a land with the wild horse, the wild elephant, and the lion; and now, at the opposite end of the world, they had themselves reached such a land. The elephants were mastodons of peculiar type; the horses were of several kinds, some resembling modern horses, others differing from them in leg and skull formation more than any of the existing species of ass, horse, or zebra differ from one another; the huge cats probably resembled some other big modern feline more than they did the lion. Associated with them were many great beasts, whose like does not now exist on earth. The sabretooth was there, as formidable as his brother of the north, and, like this brother, bigger and more specialized than any of his Old World kin, which were probably already extinct. Among the ungulates of native origin was the long-necked, high-standing macrauchenia, shaped something like a huge, humpless camel or giraffe, and with a short proboscis. This animal doubtless browsed among the trees. Another native ungulate, the toxodon, as big and heavily made as a rhinoceros, was probably amphibious, and had teeth superficially resembling those of a rodent. The edentates not only included various ground-sloths, among them the megatherium, which was the size of an elephant, and the somewhat smaller mylodon, but also creatures as fantastic as those of a nightmare. These were the glyptodons, which were bulkier than oxen and were clad in defensive plate-armor more complete than that of an armadillo; in one species the long, armored tail terminated in a huge spiked knob, like that of some forms of mediæval mace.

The glyptodons doubtless trusted for protection to their mailed coats. The ground-sloths had no armor. Like the terrestrial ant-bear of Brazil they walked slowly on the outer edges of their fore feet, which were armed with long and powerful digging claws. They could neither flee nor hide; and it seems a marvel that they could have held their own in the land against the big cats and sabretooth. Yet they persisted for ages, and spread northward from South America. It is hard to account for this. But it is just as hard to account for certain phenomena that are occurring before our very eyes. While journeying through the interior of Brazil I not infrequently came across the big tamandua, the ant-bear or ant-eater. We found it not only in the forests but out on the marshes and prairies. It is almost as big as a small black bear. In its native haunts it is very conspicuous, both because of its size and its coloration, and as it never attempts to hide it is always easily seen. It is so slow that a man can run it down on foot. It has no teeth, and its long, curved snout gives its small head an almost bird-like look. Its fore paws, armed with long, digging claws, are turned in, and it walks on their sides. It is long-haired and thick-hided, colored black and white, and with a long, bushy tail held aloft; and as it retreats at a wabbly canter, its brush shaking above its back, it looks anything but formidable. Yet it is a gallant fighter, and can inflict severe wounds with its claws, as well as hugging with its powerful fore legs; and if menaced it will

PRIMEVAL MAN

itself fearlessly assail man or dog. When chased by hounds, in the open, I have seen one instantly throw itself on its back, in which position it was much more dangerous to the hounds than they were to it. Doubtless if attacked by a jaguar — and we killed jaguars in the immediate neighborhood — it would, if given a moment's warning, have defended itself in the same fashion. I suppose that this defense would be successful; for otherwise it seems incredible that such a conspicuous, slow-moving beast can exist at all in exactly the places where jaguars, able to kill a cow or horse, are plentiful. But, even so, it is difficult to understand how it has been able to persist for ages in company with the great spotted cat, the tyrant of the Brazilian wilderness. At any rate, with this example before us, we need not wonder overmuch at the ability of megatherium and mylodon to hold their own in the presence of the sabretooth.

In the late fall of 1913, as previously decribed, I motored north from the beautiful Andean lake, Nahuel Huapi, through the stony Patagonian plains to the Rio Negro. The only wild things of any size that we saw were the rheas, or South American ostriches, and a couple of guanacos, or wild llamas, small, swift, humpless camels, of which the ancestral forms were abundant in the North American Miocene. But one of my companions, the distinguished Argentine explorer, educator, and man of science, Francisco Moreno, had some years previously made a discovery which showed that not many thousand years back, when the Indians had already come into the land, the huge and varied fauna of the Pleistocene still lingered at the foot of the Andes. He had found a cave in which savage men had dwelt; and in the cave were the remains of the animals which they had killed, or which had entered the cave at times when its human tenants were absent. Besides the weapons and utensils of the savages, he had found the grass which they had used for beds, and enclosures walled with stones for purposes of which he could not be sure. It will be remembered that in the cave-home of the 'Ndorobo which Kermit found there were beds of grass, and enclosures walled with brush, in which their dogs were kept. Whether these early Patagonian Indians had dogs I do not know; but many African tribes build low stone walls as foundations for sheds used for different purposes; and sometimes, among savages, it is absolutely impossible to guess the use to which a given structure is put unless it is actually seen

PRIMEVAL MAN

in use — exactly as sometimes it is wholly impossible to divine what a particular specimen of savage pictorial art indicates unless the savage is there to explain it to his civilized brother.

Among the signs of human occupation Doctor Moreno found, well preserved in the cold cave, not only the almost fresh bones, but even pieces of the skin, of certain extinct animals. Among the species whose bones were found were the macrauchenia, tiger, horse, and mylodon. When Doctor Moreno said tiger, I asked if he did not mean jaguar; but he said no, that he meant a huge cat like an Old World lion or tiger; I do not know with what modern feline its affinities were closest. The discovery of the comparatively fresh remains of the horse gave rise in some quarters to the belief that it was possible this species of horse survived to the day the Spaniards came to the Argentine and was partly ancestral to the modern Argentine horse; but the supposition is untenable, for the horse in question represents a very archaic and peculiar type, with specialized legs and an extraordinary skull, and could not possibly have had anything to do with the production of the wild, or rather feral, horses of the pampas and the Patagonian plains. Of the mylodon Doctor Moreno found not only comparatively fresh bones, with bits of sinew, but dried dung — almost as large as that of an elephant — and some big pieces of skin. The skin was clothed with long, coarse hair, and small ossicles were set into it, making minute bony plates. Doctor Moreno gave me a fragment of the skin, and also bones and dung; they are now in the American Museum of Natural History. The discovery gave rise to much fanciful conjecture; it was even said that the mylodon had been domesticated and kept tame in the caves; but Doctor Moreno laughed at the supposition and said that it lacked any foundation in fact. He also said that, contrary to what has sometimes been asserted, the age of the remains must be estimated in thousands, possibly ten thousands, and certainly not hundreds, of years.

There is no need of fanciful guesswork in order to enhance the startling character of the discovery. It seems to show beyond question that the early hunting savages of southernmost South America lived among the representatives of a huge fauna, now wholly extinct, just as was true of the earlier, and far more primitive, hunting savages of Europe.

Save in tropical Africa and in portions of hither and farther India this giant fauna has

PRIMEVAL MAN

now everywhere died out. In most regions, and in the earlier stages, man had little or nothing to do with its destruction. But during the last few thousand years he has been, the chief factor in the extermination of the great creatures wherever he has established an industrial or agricultural civilization or semi-civilization. The big cat he has warred against in self-defense. The elephant in India has been kept tame or half tame. The Old World horse has been tamed and transplanted to every portion of the temperate zones, and to the dry or treeless portions of the torrid zone.

Around the Mediterranean, the cradle of the ancient culture of our race, we have historic record of the process. Over three thousand years ago the Egyptian and Mesopotamian kings hunted the elephant in Syria. A thousand years later the elephant was a beast of war in the armies of the Greeks, the Carthaginians, and the Romans. Twenty-five hundred years ago the lion was a dreaded beast of ravin in the Balkan Peninsula and Palestine, as he was a hundred years ago in North Africa; now he is to be found south of the Atlas, or, nearing extinction, east of the Euphrates. Seemingly the horse was tamed long after the more homely beasts, the cattle, swine, goats, and sheep. He was not a beast for peaceful uses; he was the war-horse, whose neck was clothed with thunder, who pawed the earth when he heard the shouting of the captains. At first he was used not for riding, but to draw the war chariots. Rameses and the Hittites decided their great battles by chariot charges; the mighty and cruel Assyrian kings rode to war and hunting in chariots; the Homeric Greeks fought in chariots; Sisera ruled the land with his chariots of iron; and long after they had been abandoned elsewhere war chariots were used by the champions of Erin. Cavalry did not begin to supersede them until less than a thousand years before our era; and from that time until gunpowder marked the beginning of the modern era the horse decided half the great battles of history.

But with this process primitive man had nothing to do. He was and, in the few remote spots where he still exists unchanged, he is wholly unable even to conceive of systematic war against the lion, or of trying to tame the horse or elephant. These three, alone among the big beasts of the giant fauna in which the age of mammals had culminated, once throve in vast numbers from the Cape of Good Hope and the valley of the Nile northward to the Rhone and the Danube, eastward across India

PRIMEVAL MAN 257

and Siberia, and from Hudson Bay to the Straits of Magellan. They were dominant figures in the life of all the five continents when primitive man had struggled upward from the plane of his ape-like ancestors and had become clearly human. For ages he was too feeble to be as much of a factor in their lives as they were in the lives of one another; and in North America he never became such a factor. The great man-killing cat was his dreaded enemy, to be fought only under the strain of direst need. The horse became a favorite prey when he grew cunning enough to devise snares and weapons. The elephant he feared and respected for its power and occasional truculence, and endeavored to destroy on the infrequent occasions when chance gave an opening to his own crafty ferocity.

All this is true, at the present day, in portions of mid-Africa. I have been with tribes whom only fear or imminent starvation could drive to attack the lion; and I have seen the naked warriors of the Nandi kill the great, maned manslayer with their spears. Again and again, as an offering of peace and goodwill, I have shot zebras for natives who greedily longed for its flesh. My son and I killed a rogue elephant bull at the earnest petition of a small Uganda tribe whose crops he had destroyed, whose field watchers he had killed, and whose village he menaced with destruction.

Of all the wonderful great beasts with which primitive man in his most primitive forms has been associated, the three with which on the whole this association was most wide-spread in time and space, were the horse, the lion, and the elephant.

CHAPTER IX

BOOKS FOR HOLIDAYS IN THE OPEN

I AM sometimes asked what books I advise men or women to take on holidays in the open. With the reservation of long trips, where bulk is of prime consequence, I can only answer: The same books one would read at home. Such an answer generally invites the further question as to what books I read when at home. To this question I am afraid my answer cannot be so instructive as it ought to be, for I have never followed any plan in reading which would apply to all persons under all circumstances; and indeed it seems to me that no plan can be laid down that will be generally applicable. If a man is not fond of books, to him reading of any kind will be drudgery. I most sincerely commiserate such a person, but I do not know how to help him. If a man or a woman is fond of books he or she will naturally seek the books that the mind and soul demand. Suggestions of a possibly helpful character can be made by outsiders, but only suggestions;

and they will probably be helpful about in proportion to the outsider's knowledge of the mind and soul of the person to be helped.

Of course, if any one finds that he never reads serious literature, if all his reading is frothy and trashy, he would do well to try to train himself to like books that the general agreement of cultivated and sound-thinking persons has placed among the classics. It is as discreditable to the mind to be unfit for sustained mental effort as it is to the body of a young man to be unfit for sustained physical effort. Let man or woman, young man or girl, read some good author, say Gibbon or Macaulay, until sustained mental effort brings power to enjoy the books worth enjoying. When this has been achieved the man can soon trust himself to pick out for himself the particular good books which appeal to him.

The equation of personal taste is as powerful in reading as in eating; and within certain broad limits the matter is merely one of individual preference, having nothing to do with the quality either of the book or of the reader's mind. I like apples, pears, oranges, pineapples, and peaches. I dislike bananas, alligator-pears, and prunes. The first fact is certainly not to my credit, although it is to my advantage;

and the second at least does not show moral turpitude. At times in the tropics I have been exceedingly sorry I could not learn to like bananas, and on round-ups, in the cow country in the old days, it was even more unfortunate not to like prunes; but I simply could not make myself like either, and that was all there was to it.

In the same way I read over and over again "Guy Mannering," "The Antiquary," "Pendennis," "Vanity Fair," "Our Mutual Friend," and the "Pickwick Papers"; whereas I make heavy weather of most parts of the "Fortunes of Nigel," "Esmond," and the "Old Curiosity Shop"— to mention only books I have tried to read during the last month. I have no question that the latter three books are as good as the first six; doubtless for some people they are better; but I do not like them, any more than I like prunes or bananas.

In the same way I read and reread "Macbeth" and "Othello"; but not "King Lear" nor "Hamlet." I know perfectly well that the latter are as wonderful as the former — I wouldn't venture to admit my shortcomings regarding them if I couldn't proudly express my appreciation of the other two! But at my age I might as well own up, at least to myself.

to my limitations, and read the books I thoroughly enjoy.

But this does not mean permitting oneself to like what is vicious or even simply worthless. If any man finds that he cares to read "Bel Ami," he will do well to keep a watch on the reflex centres of his moral nature, and to brace himself with a course of Eugene Brieux or Henry Bordeaux. If he does not care for "Anna Karenina," "War and Peace," "Sebastopol," and "The Cossacks" he misses much; but if he cares for the "Kreutzer Sonata" he had better make up his mind that for pathological reasons he will be wise thereafter to avoid Tolstoy entirely. Tolstoy is an interesting and stimulating writer, but an exceedingly unsafe moral adviser.

It is clear that the reading of vicious books for pleasure should be eliminated. It is no less clear that trivial and vulgar books do more damage than can possibly be offset by any entertainment they yield. There remain enormous masses of books, of which no one man can read more than a limited number, and among which each reader should choose those which meet his own particular needs. There is no such thing as a list of "the hundred best books," or the "best five-foot library."

BOOKS FOR HOLIDAYS

Dozens of series of excellent books, one hundred to each series, can be named, all of reasonably equal merit and each better for many readers than any of the others; and probably not more than half a dozen books would appear in all these lists. As for a "five-foot library," scores can readily be devised, each of which at some given time, for some given man, under certain conditions, will be best. But to attempt to create such a library that shall be of universal value is foreordained to futility.

Within broad limits, therefore, the reader's personal and individual taste must be the guiding factor. I like hunting books and books of exploration and adventure. I do not ask any one else to like them. I distinctly do not hold my own preferences as anything whatever but individual preferences; and this chapter is to be accepted as confessional rather than didactic. With this understanding I admit a liking for novels where something happens; and even among these novels I can neither explain nor justify why I like some and do not like others; why, among the novels of Sienkiewicz, I cannot stand "Quo Vadis," and never tire of "With Fire and Sword," "Pan Michael," the "Deluge" and the "Knights of the Cross."

Of course, I know that the best critics scorn

the demand among novel readers for "the happy ending." Now, in really great books — in an epic like Milton's, in dramas like those of Æschylus and Sophocles — I am entirely willing to accept and even demand tragedy, and also in some poetry that cannot be called great, but not in good, readable novels, of sufficient length to enable me to get interested in the hero and heroine!

There is enough of horror and grimness and sordid squalor in real life with which an active man has to grapple; and when I turn to the world of literature — of books considered as books, and not as instruments of my profession — I do not care to study suffering unless for some sufficient purpose. It is only a very exceptional novel which I will read if He does not marry Her; and even in exceptional novels I much prefer this consummation. I am not defending my attitude. I am merely stating it.

Therefore it would be quite useless for me to try to explain why I read certain books. As to how and when, my answers must be only less vague. I almost always read a good deal in the evening; and if the rest of the evening is occupied I can at least get half an hour before going to bed. But all kinds of odd moments turn up during even a busy day, in which it is

BOOKS FOR HOLIDAYS

possible to enjoy a book; and then there are rainy afternoons in the country in autumn, and stormy days in winter, when one's work outdoors is finished and after wet clothes have been changed for dry, the rocking-chair in front of the open wood-fire simply demands an accompanying book.

Railway and steamboat journeys were, of course, predestined through the ages as aids to the enjoyment of reading. I have always taken books with me when on hunting and exploring trips. In such cases the literature should be reasonably heavy, in order that it may last. You can under these conditions read Herbert Spencer, for example, or the writings of Turgot, or a German study of the Mongols, or even a German edition of Aristophanes, with erudite explanations of the jokes, as you never would if surrounded by less formidable authors in your own library; and when you do reach the journey's end you grasp with eager appetite at old magazines, or at the lightest of literature.

Then, if one is worried by all kinds of men and events — during critical periods in administrative office, or at national conventions, or during congressional investigations, or in hard-fought political campaigns — it is the greatest relief and unalloyed delight to take up some really good, some really enthralling book — Tacitus, Thucydides, Herodotus, Polybius, or Goethe, Keats, Gray, or Lowell — and lose all memory of everything grimy, and of the baseness that must be parried or conquered.

Like every one else, I am apt to read in streaks. If I get interested in any subject I read different books connected with it, and probably also read books on subjects suggested by it. Having read Carlyle's "Frederick the Great"— with its splendid description of the battles, and of the unyielding courage and thrifty resourcefulness of the iron-tempered King; and with its screaming deification of able brutality in the name of morality, and its practise of the suppression and falsification of the truth under the pretense of preaching veracity — I turned to Macaulay's essay on this subject, and found that the historian whom it has been the fashion of the intellectuals to patronize or deride showed a much sounder philosophy and an infinitely greater appreciation of and devotion to truth than was shown by the loquacious apostle of the doctrine of reticence.

Then I took up Waddington's "Guerre de Sept Ans"; then I read all I could about Gustavus Adolphus; and, gradually dropping everything but the military side, I got hold of quaint

BOOKS FOR HOLIDAYS 267

little old histories of Eugene of Savoy and Turenne. In similar fashion my study of and delight in Mahan sent me further afield, to read queer old volumes about De Ruyter and the daring warrior-merchants of the Hansa, and to study, as well as I could, the feats of Suffren and Tegethoff. I did not need to study Farragut.

Mahaffy's books started me to reread — in translation, alas! — the post-Athenian Greek authors. After Ferrero I did the same thing as regards the Latin authors, and then industriously read all kinds of modern writers on the same period, finishing with Oman's capital essay on "Seven Roman Statesmen." Gilbert Murray brought me back from Greek history to Greek literature, and thence by a natural suggestion to parts of the Old Testament, to the Nibelungenlied, to the Roland lay and the *chansons de gestes*, to Beowulf, and finally to the great Japanese hero-tale, the story of the Forty-Nine Ronins.

I read Burroughs too often to have him suggest anything save himself; but I am exceedingly glad that Charles Sheldon has arisen to show what a hunter-naturalist, who adds the ability of the writer to the ability of the trained observer and outdoor adventurer, can do for our last great wilderness, Alaska. From Sheldon I turned to Stewart Edward White, and then began to wander afar, with Herbert Ward's "Voice from the Congo," and Mary Kingsley's writings, and Hudson's "El Ombu," and Cunningham Grahame's sketches of South America. A re-reading of *The Federalist* led me to Burke, to Trevelyan's history of Fox and of our own Revolution, to Lecky; and finally by way of Malthus and Adam Smith and Lord Acton and Bagehot to my own contemporaries, to Ross and George Alger.

Even in pure literature, having nothing to do with history, philosophy, sociology, or economy, one book will often suggest another, so that one finds one has unconsciously followed a regular course of reading. Once I travelled steadily from Montaigne through Addison, Swift, Steele, Lamb, Irving, and Lowell to Crothers and Kenneth Grahame — and if it be objected that some of these *could* not have suggested the others I can only answer that they *did* suggest them.

I suppose that every one passes through periods during which he reads no poetry; and some people, of whom I am one, also pass through periods during which they voraciously devour poets of widely different kinds. Now it will be Horace and Pope; now Schiller, Scott,

Longfellow, Körner; now Bret Harte or Kipling; now Shelley or Herrick or Tennyson; now Poe and Coleridge; and again Emerson or Browning or Whitman. Sometimes one wishes to read for the sake of contrast. To me Owen Wister is the writer I wish when I am hungry with the memories of lonely mountains, of vast sunny plains with seas of wind-rippled grass, of springing wild creatures, and lithe, sun-tanned men who ride with utter ease on ungroomed, half-broken horses. But when I lived much in cow camps I often carried a volume of Swinburne, as a kind of antiseptic to alkali dust, tepid, muddy water, frying-pan bread, sow-belly bacon, and the too-infrequent washing of sweat-drenched clothing.

Fathers and mothers who are wise can train their children first to practise, and soon to like, the sustained mental application necessary to enjoy good books. They will do well also to give each boy or girl the mastery of at least some one foreign language, so that at least one other great literature, in addition to our own noble English literature, shall be open to him or her. Modern languages are taught so easily and readily that whoever really desires to learn one of them can soon achieve sufficient command of it to read ordinary books with reasonable ease; and then it is a mere matter of practise for any one to become able thoroughly to enjoy the beauty and wisdom which knowledge of the new tongue brings.

Now and then one's soul thirsts for laughter. I cannot imagine any one's taking a course in humorous writers, but just as little can I sympathize with the man who does not enjoy them at times — from Sydney Smith to John Phœnix and Artemus Ward, and from these to Stephen Leacock. Mark Twain at his best stands a little apart, almost as much so as Joel Chandler Harris. Oliver Wendell Holmes, of course, is the laughing philosopher, the humorist at his very highest, even if we use the word "humor" only in its most modern and narrow sense.

A man with a real fondness for books of various kinds will find that his varying moods determine which of these books he at the moment needs. On the afternoon when Stevenson represents the luxury of enjoyment it may safely be assumed that Gibbon will not. The mood that is met by Napier's "Peninsular War," or Marbot's memoirs, will certainly not be met by Hawthorne or Jane Austen. Parkman's "Montcalm and Wolfe," Motley's histories of the Dutch Republic, will hardly fill the soul on a day when one turns naturally to the "Heimskringla"; and there is a sense of disconnection if after the "Heimskringla" one takes up the "Oxford Book of French Verse."

Another matter which within certain rather wide limits each reader must settle for himself is the dividing line between (1) not knowing anything about current books, and (2) swamping one's soul in the sea of vapidity which overwhelms him who reads *only* "the last new books." To me the heading employed by some reviewers when they speak of "books of the week" comprehensively damns both the books themselves and the reviewer who is willing to notice them. I would much rather see the heading "books of the year before last." A book of the year before last which is still worth noticing would probably be worth reading; but one only entitled to be called a book of the week had better be tossed into the wastebasket at once. Still, there are plenty of new books which are not of permanent value but which nevertheless are worth more or less careful reading; partly because it is well to know something of what especially interests the mass of our fellows, and partly because these books, although of ephemeral worth, may really set forth something genuine in a fashion which for the moment stirs the hearts of all of us.

Books of more permanent value may, because of the very fact that they possess literary interest, also yield consolation of a non-literary kind. If any executive grows exasperated over the shortcomings of the legislative body with which he deals, let him study Macaulay's account of the way William was treated by his parliaments as soon as the latter found that, thanks to his efforts, they were no longer in immediate danger from foreign foes; it is illuminating. If any man feels too gloomy about the degeneracy of our people from the standards of their forefathers, let him read "Martin Chuzzlewit"; it will be consoling.

If the attitude of this nation toward foreign affairs and military preparedness at the present day seems disheartening, a study of the first fifteen years of the nineteenth century will at any rate give us whatever comfort we can extract from the fact that our great-grandfathers were no less foolish than we are.

Nor need any one confine himself solely to the affairs of the United States. If he becomes tempted to idealize the past, if sentimentalists seek to persuade him that the "ages of faith," the twelfth and thirteenth centuries, for instance, were better than our own, let him read any trustworthy book on the subject — Lea's

BOOKS FOR HOLIDAYS

"History of the Inquisition," for instance, or Coulton's abridgment of Salimbene's memoirs. He will be undeceived and will be devoutly thankful that his lot has been cast in the present age, in spite of all its faults.

It would be hopeless to try to enumerate all the books I read, or even all the kinds. The foregoing is a very imperfect answer to a question which admits of only such an answer.

CHAPTER X

BIRD RESERVES AT THE MOUTH OF THE MISSISSIPPI

ON June 7, 1915, I was the guest of my friend John M. Parker, of New Orleans, at his house at Pass Christian, Mississippi. For many miles west, and especially east, of Pass Christian, there are small towns where the low, comfortable, singularly picturesque and attractive houses are owned, some by Mississippi planters, some by city folk who come hither from the great Southern cities, and more and more in winter-time from the great Northern cities also, to pass a few months. The houses, those that are isolated and those in the little towns, stand in what is really one long row; a row broken by vacant reaches, but as a whole stretching for sixty miles, with the bright waters of the Gulf lapping the beach in front of them, and behind them leagues of pine forest. Between the Gulf and the waters lies a low ridge or beach of white sand. It is hard to make anything grow in this

THE MISSISSIPPI RESERVES 275

sand; but the owners of the houses have succeeded, using dead leaves and what manure is available; and in this leaf-mould the trees and grasses and flowers grow in profusion. Long, flimsy wooden docks stretch out into the waters of the Gulf; there is not much bad weather, as a rule, but every few years there comes a terrible storm which wrecks buildings and bridges, destroys human lives by the thousand, washes the small Gulf sailing craft ashore, and sweeps away all the docks.

Our host's house was cool and airy, with broad, covered verandas, and mosquito screens on the doors and the big windows. The trees in front were live-oaks, and others of his own planting — magnolias, pecans, palms, and a beautiful mimosa. The blooming oleanders and hydrangeas were a delight to the eye. Behind, the place stretched like a long ribbon to the edge of the fragrant pine forest, where the long-leaved and loblolly pines rose like tall columns out of the needle-covered sand. Five pairs of mocking-birds and one pair of thrashers had just finished nesting; at dawn, when the crescent of the dying moon had risen above the growing light in the east, the mockers sang wonderfully, and after a while the thrasher chimed in. Only the singing of nightingales where they are plentiful, as in some Italian woods, can compare in strength and ecstasy and passion, in volume and intricate change and continuity, with the challenging love-songs of many mockers, rivalling one another, as they perch and balance and spring upward and float downward through the branches of live-oak or magnolia, after sunset and before sunrise, and in the warm, still, brilliant moonlight of spring and early summer.

There were other birds. The soldierly looking red-headed woodpeckers, in their striking black, red, and white uniform, were much in evidence. Gaudy painted finches, or "nonpareils," were less conspicuous only because of their small size. Blue jays had raised their young in front of the house, and, as I was informed, had been successfully beaten off by the mockers and thrashers when they attempted assaults on the eggs and nestlings of the latter. Purple martins darted through the air. Kingbirds chased the big grackles and the numerous small fish-crows — not so very much bigger than the grackles — which uttered queer, hoarse croakings. A pair of crested flycatchers had their nest in a hollow in a tree; the five boldly marked eggs rested, as usual, partly on a shed snake skin. How, I wonder, through the immemorial ages, and why, did this particular bird develop its strange determination always, where possible, to use a snake's cast-off skin in building its nest? Every season, I was told, this flycatcher nested in the same hollow; and every season the hollow was previously nested in by a tufted titmouse. Loggerhead shrikes were plentiful. Insects were their usual food, but they also pounced on small birds, mice, and lizards, and once on a little chicken. They empale their prey on locust thorns and on the spines of other trees and bushes; and I have known a barbed-wire fence to be decorated with the remains of their victims. There were red cardinal-birds; and we saw another red bird also, a summer tanager.

But the most interesting birds on the place were not wild, being nothing more nor less than ordinary fowls engaged in what to me were most unordinary occupations. Parker had several hundred fowls, and had by trial discovered the truth of the statement that capons make far better mothers than do hens, especially for very young chicks. We saw dozens of broods of chickens, and one or two of young guinea-fowl, being taken care of by caponized bantams, game-cocks, and cochin-chinas. These improvised mothers looked almost precisely as they did before being caponized, the differences, chiefly in the color of the comb, being insignificant, for they were full-grown birds when operated on. But their natures had suffered the most extraordinary change, for they had developed not only the habits but the voices of unusually exemplary mother hens. They never crowed; they clucked precisely like hens; and they protected, covered, fed, and led about their broods just like hens. They were timid, except in defense of the chicks; but on their behalf they were really formidable fighters. The change in habits takes place with extraordinary rapidity. In a few hours the cock has completely changed and can be placed with a brood which he promptly adopts. In perhaps one case in ten he does not take readily to his duties as an *ex-officio* hen; and in such case the further measure adopted seems as incredible as the rest of the performance, for he is made drunk with whiskey, acts as if he were intoxicated, and then promptly develops maternal feelings, and zealously enters on his new career.

We saw game-cocks clucking and calling to their broods of little chicks, to get them to the crumbs we tossed to them, and then sitting with the chicks not only under their wings but on their backs. They kept the broods with them until the young were nearly as large as they were; in one case the brood consisted of guinea-fowl. Moreover, they welcomed any brood, no matter how large. One big rooster was leading around so many chickens — all, by what seemed a sardonic jest, his own progeny, the progeny of the days when he was a mere unregenerate father — that when they took shelter under him he had to spread his wings; "like a buzzard," said my host, to whom soaring buzzards were familiar sights. Of course, the extraordinary part of all this was not the loss of the male qualities but the immediate and complete acquirement of those of the female. It was as if steers invariably took to mothering calves, or geldings to adopting foals.

These capon-mothers, with their weight and long spurs, fought formidably for their chicks. In one case a Cooper's hawk swooped on a half-grown chick, whereupon the game-cock who was officiating as hen flew at the aggressor, striking it so hard as to injure the top of the wing. The hawk was unable to fly, and the cock pressed it too close to let it escape. Although the rooster could not kill the hawk, for the latter threw itself on its back with extended talons, he had rendered it unable to escape, and one of the men about the place came up and killed it, having been attracted by the noise of the fight. Another cock killed a big blacksnake which tried to carry off one of the chicks. The cock darted to and fro over the snake, striking it continually until it succumbed.

Pass Christian is an ideal place for a man to go who wishes to get away from the Northern cold for a few weeks, and be where climate, people, and surroundings are all delightful, and the fishing and shooting excellent. There is a good chance, too, that the fish and game will be preserved for use, instead of recklessly exterminated; for during the last dozen years Louisiana and Mississippi, like the rest of the Union, have waked to the criminality of marring and ruining a beautiful heritage which should be left, and through wise use (not nonuse) can be left, undiminished, to the generations that are to come after us. As yet the Gulf in front of the houses swarms with fish of many kinds up to the great tarpon, the mailed and leaping giant of the warm seas; and with the rapid growth of wisdom in dealing with nature we may hope that there will soon be action looking toward the regulation of seining and to protection of the fish at certain seasons. On land the quail have increased in the neigh-

THE MISSISSIPPI RESERVES

borhood of Pass Christian during the last few years. This is largely due to the activity of my host and his two sons as hunters. They have a pack of beagles, trained to night work, and this pack has to its credit nearly four hundred coons and possums — together with an occasional skunk! — and, moreover, has chivied the gray foxes almost out of the country; and all these animals are the inveterate enemies of all small game, and especially of ground-nesting birds. To save interesting creatures, it is often necessary not merely to refrain from killing them but also to war on their enemies.

One of the sons runs the Parker stock-farm in upper Louisiana, beside the Mississippi. There are about four thousand acres, half of it highland, the other half subject to flood if the levees break. Five years ago such a break absolutely destroyed the Parker plantations, then exclusively on low land. Now, in event of flood, the stock can be driven, and the human beings escape, to the higher ground. Young Parker, now twenty-two years old, has run the plantation since he was sixteen. The horses, cattle, and sheep are all of the highest grade; the improvement in the stock of Louisiana and Mississippi during the last two decades has been really noteworthy. Game, and wild things generally, have increased in numbers on this big stock-farm. There is no wanton molestation of any animal permitted, no plundering of nests, no shooting save within strictly defined limits, and so far as possible all rare things are given every chance to increase. As an example, when, in clearing a tract of swamp land, a heron's nest was discovered, the bushes round about were left undisturbed, and the heron family was reared in safety. Wild turkeys have somewhat, and quail very markedly, increased. The great horned owls, which destroyed the ducks, have to be warred against, and the beasts of prey likewise. Surely it will ultimately again be recognized in our country that life on a plantation, on a great stock-farm or ranch, is one of the most interesting, and, from the standpoint of both body and soul, one of the most healthy, of all ways of earning a living.

At four on the morning of the 8th our party started from the wharf in front of Pass Christian. We were in two boats. One, good-sized and comfortable, under the command of Captain Lewis Young, was the property of the State Conservation Commission of Louisiana, the commission having most courteously placed it at our disposal. On this boat were my host,

THE MISSISSIPPI RESERVES 283

his two sons, John, Jr., and Tom, myself, and a photographer, Mr. Coquille, of New Orleans. The other boat, named the *Royal Tern*, was the property of the Audubon Society, being allotted to the work of cruising among and protecting the bird colonies on those islands set apart as bird refuges by the National and State Governments. On this boat — which had a wretched engine, almost worthless — went Mr. Herbert K. Job and Mr. Frank M. Miller. Mr. Miller was at one time president of the Louisiana Conservation Commission, and the founder of the Louisiana State Audubon Society, and is one of the group of men to whom she owes it that she, the home state of Audubon, of our first great naturalist, is now thoroughly awake to the danger of reckless waste and destruction of all the natural resources of the State, including the birds. Mr. Herbert K. Job is known to all who care for bird study and bird preservation. He is a naturalist who has made of bird-photography a sport, a science, and an art. His pictures, and his books in which these pictures appear, are fascinating both to the scientific ornithologist and to all lovers of the wild creatures of the open. Like the other field naturalists I have known, like the men who were with me in Africa and South America,

Mr. Job is an exceptionally hardy, resolute, and resourceful man, following his wilderness work with single-minded devotion, and continually, and in matter-of-fact manner, facing and overcoming hardship, wearing toil, and risk which worthy stay-at-home people have no means whatever of even gauging. I owed the pleasure of Mr. Job's company to Mr. Frank M. Chapman, at whose suggestion he was sent with me by the National Audubon Society.

The State Conservation Commission owes its existence to the wise public spirit and far-sightedness of the Louisiana Legislature. The Audubon Society, which has done far more than any other single agency in creating and fostering an enlightened public sentiment for the preservation of our useful and attractive birds, is a purely voluntary organization, consisting of men and women who in these matters look further ahead than their fellows, and who have the precious gift of sympathetic imagination, so that they are able to see, and to wish to preserve for their children's children, the beauty and wonder of nature. (During the year preceding this trip, by the way, the society enrolled one hundred and fifty-one thousand boys and girls in its junior bird clubs, all of which give systematic instruction in the value of bird life.) It was the Audubon Society which started the movement for the establishment of bird refuges. The society now protects and polices about one hundred of these refuges, which, of course, are worthless unless thus protected.

The *Royal Tern* is commanded by Captain William Sprinkle, born and bred on this Gulf coast, who knows the sea-fowl, and the islands where they breed and dwell, as he knows the winds and the lovely, smiling, treacherous Gulf waters. He is game warden, and he and the *Royal Tern* are the police force for over five hundred square miles of sand-bars, shallow waters, and intricate channels. The man and the boat are two of the chief obstacles in the way of the poachers, the plume-hunters, and eggers, who always threaten these bird sanctuaries.

Many of these poachers are at heart good men, who follow their fathers' business, just as respectable men on the seacoast once followed the business of wrecking. But when times change and a once acknowledged trade comes under the ban of the law the character of those following it also changes for the worse. Wreckers are no longer respectable, and plume-hunters and eggers are sinking to the same level. The illegal business of killing breeding birds, of leaving nestlings to starve wholesale, and of general ruthless extermination, more and more tends to attract men of the same moral category as those who sell whiskey to Indians and combine the running of "blind pigs" with highway robbery and murder for hire.

In Florida one of the best game wardens of the Audubon Society was killed by these sordid bird-butchers. A fearless man and a good boat are needed to keep such gentry in awe. Captain Sprinkle meets the first requirement, the hull of the *Royal Tern* the second. But the engines of the *Tern* are worthless; she can catch no freebooter; she is safe only in the mildest weather. Is there not some bird-lover of means and imagination who will put a good engine in her? Such a service would be very real. As for Captain Sprinkle, his services are, of course, underpaid, his salary bearing no relation to their value. The Biological Survey does its best with its limited means; the Audubon Society adds something extra; but this very efficient and disinterested laborer is worth a good deal more than the hire he receives. The government pays many of its servants, usually those with rather easy jobs, too much; but the best men, who do the hardest work, the men in the life-sav-

THE MISSISSIPPI RESERVES 287

ing and lighthouse service, the forest-rangers, and those who patrol and protect the reserves of wild life, are almost always underpaid.

Yet, in spite of all the disadvantages, much has been accomplished. This particular reservation was set apart by presidential proclamation in 1905. Captain Sprinkle was at once put in charge. Of the five chief birds, the royal terns, Caspian terns, Cabot's terns, laughing gulls, and skimmers, there were that season about one thousand nests. This season, ten years later, there are about thirty-five thousand nests. The brown pelicans and Louisiana herons also show a marked increase. The least tern, which had been completely exterminated or driven away, has returned and is breeding in fair numbers.

As we steamed away from the Pass Christian dock dawn was turning to daylight under the still brilliant crescent moon. Soon we saw the red disk of the sun rising behind the pine forest. We left Mississippi Sound, and then were on the Gulf itself. The Gulf was calm, and the still water teemed with life. Each school of mullets or sardines could be told by the queer effect on the water, as of a cloud shadow. Continually we caught glimpses of other fish; and always they were fleeing from death or ravenously seeking to inflict death on the weak. Nature is ruthless, and where her sway is uncontested there is no peace save the peace of death; and the fecund stream of life, especially of life on the lower levels, flows like an immense torrent out of non-existence for but the briefest moment before the enormous majority of the beings composing it are engulfed in the jaws of death, and again go out into the shadow.

Huge rays sprang out of the water and fell back with a resounding splash. Devil-fish, which made the rays look like dwarfs, swam slowly near the surface; some had their mouths wide open as they followed their prey. Globular jellyfish, as big as pumpkins, with translucent bodies, pulsed through the waters; little fishes and crabs swam among their short, thick tentacles and in between the waving walls into which the body was divided. Once we saw the head of a turtle above water; it was a loggerhead turtle, and the head was as large as the head of a man; when I first saw it, above the still water, I had no idea what it was.

By noon we were among the islands of the reservation. We had already passed other and larger islands, for the most part well wooded. On these there were great numbers of coons

THE MISSISSIPPI RESERVES

and minks, and therefore none of the sea-birds which rest on the ground or in low bushes. The coons are more common than the minks and muskrats. In the inundations they are continually being carried out to sea on logs; a planter informed me that on one occasion in a flood he met a log sailing down the swollen Mississippi with no less than eleven coons aboard. Sooner or later castaway coons land on every considerable island off the coast, and if there is fresh water, and even sometimes if there is none, they thrive; and where there are many coons, the gulls, terns, skimmers, and other such birds have very little chance to bring up their young. Coons are fond of rambling along beaches; at low tide they devour shell-fish; and they explore the grass tufts and bushes, and eat nestlings, eggs, and even the sitting birds. If on any island we found numerous coon tracks there were usually few nesting sea-fowl, save possibly on some isolated point. The birds breed most plentifully in the numberless smaller islands — some of considerable size — where there is no water, and usually not a tree. Some of these islands are nothing but sand, with banks and ramparts of shells, while others are fringed with marsh-grass and covered with scrub mangrove. But the occasional fierce tropical storms not only change the channels and alter the shape of many of the islands, but may even break up some very big island. In such case an island with trees and water may for years be entirely uninhabited by coons, and the birds may form huge rookeries thereon. The government should exterminate the coons and minks on all the large islands, so as to enable the birds to breed on them; for on the small islands the storms and tides work huge havoc with the nests.

Captain Young proved himself not only a first-class captain but a first-class pilot through the shifting and tangled maze of channels and islands. The *Royal Tern*, her engines breaking down intermittently, fell so far in the rear that in the early afternoon we anchored, to wait for her, off an island to which a band of pelicans resorted — they had nested, earlier in the year, on another island some leagues distant. The big birds, forty or thereabouts in number, were sitting on a sand-spit which projected into the water, enjoying a noontide rest. As we approached they rose and flapped lazily out to sea for a few hundred yards before again lighting. Later in the afternoon they began to fly to the fishing-grounds, and back and forth, singly and in small groups. In flying they

THE MISSISSIPPI RESERVES

usually gave a dozen rapid wing-beats, and then sailed for a few seconds. If several were together the leader gave the "time" to the others; they all flapped together, and then all glided together. The neck was carried in a curve, like a heron's; it was only stretched out straight like a stork's or bustard's when the bird was diving. Some of the fishing was done, singly or in parties, in the water, the pelicans surrounding shoals of sardines and shrimps, and scooping them up in their capacious bags. But, although such a large, heavy bird, the brown pelican is an expert wing-fisherman also. A pair would soar round in circles, the bill perhaps pointing downward, instead of, as usual, being held horizontally. Then, when the fish was spied the bird plunged down, almost perpendicularly, the neck stretched straight and rigid, and disappeared below the surface of the water with a thump and splash, and in a couple of seconds emerged, rose with some labor, and flew off with its prey. At this point the pelicans had finished breeding before my arrival — although a fortnight later Mr. Job found thousands of fresh eggs in their great rookeries west of the mouth of the Mississippi. The herons had well-grown nestlings, whereas the terns and gulls were in the midst of the breeding, and the skimmers had only just begun. The pelicans often flew only a few yards, or even feet, above the water, but also at times soared or wheeled twenty or thirty rods in the air, or higher. They are handsome, interesting birds, and add immensely, by their presence, to the pleasure of being out on these waters; they should be completely protected everywhere — as, indeed, should most of these sea-birds.

The two Parker boys — the elder of whom had for years been doing a man's work in the best fashion, and the younger of whom had just received an appointment to Annapolis — kept us supplied with fish, caught with the hook and rod, except the flounders, which were harpooned. The two boys were untiring; nothing impaired their energy, and no chance of fatigue and exertion, at any time of the day or night, appealed to them save as an exhilarating piece of good fortune. At a time when so large a section of our people, including especially those who claim in a special sense to be the guardians of cultivation, philanthropy, and religion, deliberately make a cult of pacifism, poltroonery, sentimentality, and neurotic emotionalism, it was refreshing to see the fine, healthy, manly young fellows who were emphatically neither "too proud to fight" nor too proud to work, and with whom hard work, and gentle regard for the rights of others, and the joy of life, all went hand in hand.

Toward evening of our first day the weather changed for the worse; the fishers among the party were recalled, and just before nightfall we ran off, and after much groping in the dark we made a reasonably safe anchorage. By midnight the wind fell, dense swarms of mosquitoes came aboard, and, as our mosquito-nets were not well up (thanks partly to our own improvidence, and partly to the violence of the wind, for we were sleeping on deck because of the great heat), we lived in torment until morning. On the subsequent nights we fixed our mosquito-bars so carefully that there was no trouble. Mosquitoes and huge, green-headed horse-flies swarm on most of the islands. I witnessed one curious incident in connection with one of these big, biting horse-flies. A kind of wasp preys on them, and is locally known as the "horse-guard," or "sheriff-fly," accordingly. These horse-guards are formidable-looking things and at first rather alarm strangers, hovering round them and their horses; but they never assail beast or man unless themselves molested, when they are ready enough to use their powerful sting. The horses and cattle speedily recognize these big, humming, hornet-like horse-guards as the foes of their tormentors. As we walked over the islands, and the green-headed flies followed us, horse-guards also joined us; and many greenheads and some horse-guards came on board. Usually when the horse-guard secured the greenhead it was pounced on from behind, and there was practically no struggle — the absence of struggle being usual in the world of invertebrates, where the automaton-like actions of both preyer and prey tend to make each case resemble all others in its details. But on one occasion the greenhead managed to turn, so that he fronted his assailant and promptly grappled with him, sinking his evil lancet into the wasp's body and holding the wasp so tight that the latter could not thrust with its sting. They grappled thus for several minutes. The horse-guard at last succeeded in stabbing its antagonist, and promptly dropped the dead body. Evidently it had suffered much, for it vigorously rubbed the wounded spot with its third pair of legs, walked hunched up, and was altogether a very sick creature.

On the following day we visited two or three islands which the man-of-war birds were using as roosts. These birds are the most wonderful fliers in the world. No other bird has such an

THE MISSISSIPPI RESERVES 295

expanse of wing in proportion to the body weight. No other bird of its size seems so absolutely at home in the air. Frigate-birds — as they are also called — hardly ever light on the water, yet they are sometimes seen in mid-ocean. But they like to live in companies, near some coast. They have very long tails, usually carried closed, looking like a marlin-spike, but at times open, like a great pair of scissors, in the course of their indescribably graceful aerial evolutions. We saw them soaring for hours at a time, sometimes to all seeming absolutely motionless as they faced the wind. They sometimes caught fish for themselves, just rippling the water to seize surface swimmers, or pouncing with startling speed on any fish which for a moment leaped into the air to avoid another shape of ravenous death below. If the frigate-bird caught the fish transversely, it rose, dropped its prey, and seized it again by the head before it struck the water. But it also obtained its food in less honorable fashion —by robbing other birds. The pelicans were plundered by *all* their fish-eating neighbors, even the big terns; but the man-of-war bird robbed the robbers. We saw three chase a royal tern, a very strong flier; the tern towered, ascending so high we could hardly see it, but in great spirals its pursuers rose still faster, until one was above it; and then the tern dropped the fish, which was snatched in midair by one of the bandits. Captain Sprinkle had found these frigate-birds breeding on one of the islands the previous year, each nest being placed in a bush and containing two eggs. We visited the island; the big birds — the old males jet black, the females with white breasts, the young males with white heads — were there in numbers, perched on the bushes, and rising at our approach. But there were no nests, and, although we found one fresh egg, it was evidently a case of sporadic laying, having nothing to do with home-building.

On another island, where we also found a big colony of frigate-birds roosting on the mangrove and Gulf tamarisk scrub, there was a small heronry of the Louisiana heron. The characteristic flimsy heron nests were placed in the thick brush, which was rather taller than a man's head. The young ones had left the nests, but were still too young for anything in the nature of sustained flight. They were, like all young herons, the pictures of forlorn and unlovely inefficiency, as they flapped a few feet away and strove with ungainly awkwardness to balance themselves on the yielding bush

THE MISSISSIPPI RESERVES

tops. The small birds we found on the islands were red-winged blackbirds, Louisiana seaside sparrows, and long-billed marsh-wrens — which last had built their domed houses among the bushes, in default of tall reeds. On one island Job discovered a night-hawk on her nest. She fluttered off, doing the wounded-bird trick, leaving behind her an egg and a newly hatched chick. He went off to get his umbrella-house, and when he returned the other egg was hatching, and another little chick, much distressed by the heat, appeared. He stood up a clam-shell to give it shade, and then, after patient waiting, the mother returned, and he secured motion-pictures of her and her little family. These birds offer very striking examples of real protective coloration.

The warm shallows, of course, teem with mollusks as well as with fish — not to mention the shrimps, which go in immense silver schools, and which we found delicious eating. The occasional violent storms, when they do not destroy islands, throw up on them huge dikes or ramparts of shells, which makes the walking hard on the feet.

There are more formidable things than shells in the warm shallows. The fishermen as they waded near shore had to be careful lest they should step on a sting-ray. When a swim was proposed as our boat swung at anchor in mid-channel, under the burning midday sun, Captain Sprinkle warned us against it because he had just seen a large shark. He said that sharks rarely attacked men, but that he had known of two instances of their doing so in Mississippi Sound, one ending fatally. In this case the man was loading a sand schooner. He was standing on a scaffolding, the water half-way up his thighs, and the shark seized him and carried him into deep water. Boats went to his assistance at once, scaring off the shark; but the man's leg had been bitten nearly in two; he sank, and was dead when he was finally found.

The following two days we continued our cruise. We steamed across vast reaches of open Gulf, the water changing from blue to yellow as it shoaled. Now and then we sighted or passed low islands of bare sand and scrub. The sky was sapphire, the sun splendid and pitiless, the heat sweltering. We came across only too plain evidence of the disasters always hanging over the wilderness folk. A fortnight previously a high tide and a heavy blow had occurred coincidentally. On the islands where the royal terns especially loved to nest the high water spelled destruction. The terns nest close together, in bird cities, so to speak, and generally rather low on the beaches. On island after island the waves had washed over the nests and destroyed them by the ten thousand. The beautiful royal terns were the chief sufferers. On one island there was a space perhaps nearly an acre in extent where the ground was covered with their eggs, which had been washed thither by the tide; most of them had then been eaten by those smart-looking highwaymen, the trim, slate-headed laughing gulls. The terns had completely deserted the island and had gone in their thousands to another; but some skimmers remained and were nesting. The westernmost island, we visited was outside the national reservation, and that very morning it had been visited and plundered by a party of eggers. The eggs had been completely cleared from most of the island, gulls and terns had been shot, and the survivors were in a frantic state of excitement. It was a good object-lesson in the need of having reserves, and laws protecting wild life, and a sufficient number of efficient officers to enforce the laws and protect the reserves. Defenders of the short-sighted men who in their greed and selfishness will, if permitted, rob our country of half its charm by their reckless extermination of all useful and beautiful wild things sometimes seek to champion them by saying that "the game belongs to the people." So it does; and not merely to the people now alive, but to the unborn people. The "greatest good of the greatest number" applies to the number within the womb of time, compared to which those now alive form but an insignificant fraction. Our duty to the whole, including the unborn generations, bids us restrain an unprincipled present-day minority from wasting the heritage of these unborn generations. The movement for the conservation of wild life, and the larger movement for the conservation of all our natural resources, are essentially democratic in spirit, purpose, and method.

On some of the islands we found where green turtles had crawled up the beaches to bury their eggs in the sand. We came across two such nests. One of them I dug up myself. The eggs we took to the boat, where they were used in making delicious pancakes, which went well with fresh shrimp, flounder, weakfish, mackerel, and mullet.

The laughing gulls and the black skimmers were often found with their nests intermingled, and they hovered over our heads with the same noisy protest against our presence. Although they often — not always — nested so close together, the nests were in no way alike. The gulls' dark-green eggs, heavily blotched with brown, two or three in number, lay on a rude platform of marsh-grass, which was usually partially sheltered by some bush or tuft of reeds, or, if on wet ground, was on a low pile of driftwood. The skimmers' eggs, light whitish green and less heavily marked with brown, were, when the clutch was full, four to six in number. There was no nest at all, nothing but a slight hollow in the sand, or gravel or shell débris. In the gravel or among the shell débris it was at first hard to pick out the eggs; but as our eyes grew accustomed to them we found them without difficulty. Sometimes we found the nests of gull and skimmer within a couple of feet of one another, one often under or in a bush, the other always out on the absolutely bare open. Considering the fact that the gull stood ready, with cannibal cheerfulness, to eat the skimmer's eggs if opportunity offered, I should have thought that to the latter bird such association would have seemed rather grewsome; but, as a matter of fact, there seemed to be no feeling of constraint whatever on either side, and the only fighting I saw, and this of a very mild type, was among the gulls themselves.

As we approached their nesting-places all these birds rose, and clamored loudly as they hovered over us, lighting not far off, and returning to their nests as we moved away.

The skimmers are odd, interesting birds, and on the whole were, if anything, rather tamer even than the royal terns and laughing gulls, their constant associates. They came close behind these two in point of abundance. They flew round and round us, and to and fro, continually uttering their loud single note, the bill being held half open as they did so. The lower mandible, so much longer than the upper, gives them a curious look. Ordinarily the bill is held horizontally and closed; but when after the small fish on which they feed the lower mandible is dropped to an angle of forty-five degrees, ploughing lightly the surface of the water and scooping up the prey. They fly easily, with at ordinary times rather deliberate strokes of their long wings, wheeling and circling, and continually crying if roused from their nests. When flying the white of their plumage is very conspicuous, and as they flapped around every detail of form and coloration, of bill and plumage, could be observed.

When sitting they appear almost black, and, in consequence, when on their nests, on the beaches or on the white-shell dikes, they are visible half a mile off, and stand out as distinctly as a crow on a snow-bank.[1] They are perfectly aware of this, and make no attempt to elude observation, any more than the gulls and terns do. The fledglings are concealingly colored, and crouch motionless, so as to escape notice from possible enemies; and the eggs, while they do not in color harmonize with the surroundings to the extent that they might artificially be made to do, yet easily escape the eye when laid on a beach composed of broken sea-shells. But the coloration of the adults is of a strikingly advertising character, under all circumstances, and especially when they are sitting on their nests. Among all the vagaries of the fetichistic school of concealing-colorationists none is more amusing than the belief that the coloration of the adult skimmer is ever, under any conditions, of a concealing quality. Sometimes the brooding skimmer attempted to draw us away from the nest by fluttering off across the sand like a wounded bird. Like the gulls, the skimmers moved about much more freely on the ground than did the terns.

[1] An expression borrowed from Stewart Edward White's capital "Rediscovered Country."

The handsome little laughing gull was found everywhere, and often in numerous colonies, although these colonies were not larger than those of the skimmer, and in no way approached the great breeding assemblages of the royal terns on the two or three islands where the latter especially congregated. They were noisy birds, continually uttering a single loud note, but only occasionally the queer laughter which gives them their name. They looked very trim and handsome, both on the wing and when swimming or walking; and their white breasts and dark heads made them very conspicuous on their nests, no matter whether these were on open ground or partially concealed in a bush or reed cluster. Like the skimmers, although perhaps not quite so markedly, their coloration was strongly advertising at all times, including when on their nests. Their relations with their two constant associates and victims, the skimmer and the royal tern — the three being about the same size — seemed to me very curious. The gull never molested the eggs of either of the other birds if the parents were sitting on them or were close by. But gulls continually broke and devoured eggs, especially terns' eggs, which had been temporarily abandoned. Nor was this all. When a colony of nesting royal terns flew off at our approach, the hesitating advent of the returning parents was always accompanied by the presence of a few gulls. Commonly the birds lit a few yards away from the eggs, on the opposite side from the observer, and then by degrees moved forward among the temporarily forsaken eggs. The gulls were usually among the foremost ranks, and each, as it walked or ran to and fro, would now and then break or carry off an egg; yet I never saw a tern interfere or seem either alarmed or angered. These big terns are swifter and better fliers than the gulls, and the depredations take place all the time before their eyes. Yet they pay no attention that I could discern to the depredation. Compare this with the conduct of king-birds to those other egg-robbers, the crows. Imagine a king-bird, or, for that matter, a mocking-bird or thrasher, submitting with weak good humor to such treatment! If these big terns had even a fraction of the intelligence and spirit of king-birds, no gull would venture within a half-mile of their nesting-grounds.

It is one of the innumerable puzzles of biology that the number of eggs a bird lays seems to have such small influence on the abundance of the species. A royal tern lays one egg, rarely two; a gull three; a skimmer four to six. The gull eats the eggs of the other two, especially of the tern; as far as we know, all have the same foes; yet the abundance of the birds is in inverse ratio to the number of their eggs. Of course, there is an explanation; but we cannot even guess at it as yet. With this, as with so many other scientific questions, all we can say is, with Huxley, that we are not afraid to announce that we do not know.

The beautiful royal terns were common enough, flying in the air and diving boldly after little fish. We listened with interest to their cry, which was a kind of creaking bleat. We admired the silver of their plumage as they flew overhead. But we did not come across vast numbers of them assembled for breeding until the fourth day. Then we found them on an island on which Captain Sprinkle told us he had never before found them, although both skimmers and gulls had always nested on it. The previous fall he had waged war with traps against the coons, which, although there was no fresh water, had begun to be plentiful on the island. He had caught a number, two escaping, one with the loss of a hind foot, and one with the loss of a fore foot. The island was seven miles long, curved, with occasional stretches of salt marsh, and with reaches of

THE MISSISSIPPI RESERVES 307

scrub, but no trees. Most of it was bare sand. We saw three coon tracks, two being those of the three-footed animals; evidently the damaged leg was now completely healed and was used like the others, punching a round hole in the sand. We saw one coon, at dusk, hunting for oysters at the water's edge.

The gulls and skimmers were nesting on this island in great numbers, but the terns were many times more plentiful. There were thousands upon thousands of them. Their breeding-places were strung in a nearly straight line for a couple of miles along the sand flats. A mile off, from our boat, we were attracted by their myriad forms, glittering in the brilliant sunlight as they rose and fell and crossed and circled over the nesting-places. The day was bright and hot, and the sight was one of real fascination. As we approached a breeding colony the birds would fly up, hover about, and resettle when we drew back a sufficient distance. The eggs, singly, or rarely in pairs, were placed on the bare sand, with no attempt at a nest, the brooding bird being sometimes but a few inches, sometimes two or three feet, from the nearest of its surrounding neighbors. The colonies of breeders were scattered along the shore for a couple of miles, each one being one or two hundred yards, or over, from the next. In one such breeding colony I counted a little over a thousand eggs; there were several of smaller size, and a few that were larger, one having perhaps three times as many. A number of the eggs, perhaps ten per cent, had been destroyed by the gulls; the coons had ravaged some of the gulls' nests, which were in or beside the scrub. The eggs of the terns, being so close together and on the bare sand, were very conspicuous; they were visible to a casual inspection at a distance of two or three hundred yards, and it was quite impossible for any bird or beast to overlook them near by. These gregarious nesters, whose eggs are gathered in a big nursery, cannot profit by any concealing coloration of the eggs. The eggs of the royal and Cabot's terns were perhaps a shade less conspicuous than the darker eggs of the Caspian tern, all of them lying together; but on that sand, and crowded into such a regular nursery, none of them could have escaped the vision of any foe with eyes. As I have said, the eggs of the skimmer, as the clutches were more scattered, were much more difficult to make out, on the shell beaches. Concealing coloration has been a survival factor only as regards a minority, and is responsible for the precise coloration of only a small

THE MISSISSIPPI RESERVES

minority, of adult birds and mammals; how much and what part it plays, and in what percentage of cases, in producing the coloration of eggs, is a subject which is well worth serious study. As regards most of these seabirds which nest gregariously, their one instinct for safety at nesting time seems to be to choose a lonely island. This is their only, and sufficient, method of outwitting their foes at the crucial period of their lives.

We found only eggs in the nurseries, not young birds. In each nursery there were always a number of terns brooding their eggs, and the air above was filled with a ceaseless flutter and flashing of birds leaving their nests and returning to them — or eggs, rather, for, speaking accurately, there were no nests. The sky above was alive with the graceful, long-winged things. As we approached the nurseries the birds would begin to leave. If we halted before the alarm became universal, those that stayed always served as lures to bring back those that had left. If we came too near, the whole party rose in a tumult of flapping wings; and when all had thus left it was some time before any returned. With patience it was quite possible to get close to the sitting birds; I noticed that in the heat many had their bills open. Those that were on the wing flew round and round us, creaking and bleating, and often so near that every detail of form and color was vivid in our eyes. The immense majority were royal terns, big birds with orange beaks. With them were a very few Caspian terns, still bigger, and with bright-red beaks, and quite a number of Cabot's terns, smaller birds with yellow-tipped black beaks. These were all nesting together, in the same nurseries.

It has been said on excellent authority that terns can always be told from gulls because, whereas the latter carry their beaks horizontally, the terns carry their bills pointing downward, "like a mosquito." My own observations do not agree with this statement. When hovering over water where there are fish, and while watching for their prey, terns point the bill downward, just as pelicans do in similar circumstances; just as gulls often do when they are seeking to spy food below them. But normally, on the great majority of the occasions when I saw them, the terns, like the gulls, carried the bill in the same plane as the body.

On another island we found a small colony of Forster's tern; and we saw sooty terns, and a few of the diminutive least terns. But I was much more surprised to find on, or rather

THE MISSISSIPPI RESERVES 311

over, one island a party of black terns. As these are inland birds, most of which at this season are breeding around the lakes of our Northwestern country, I was puzzled by their presence. Still more puzzling was it to come across a party of turnstones, with males in full, brightly varied nuptial dress, for turnstones during the breeding season live north of the arctic circle, in the perpetual sunlight of the long polar day. On the other hand, a couple of big oyster-catchers seemed, and were, entirely in place; they are striking birds and attract attention at a great distance. We saw dainty Wilson's plover with their chicks, and also semipalmated sandpipers.

On the morning of the 12th we returned to Pass Christian. I was very glad to have seen this bird refuge. With care and protection the birds will increase and grow tamer and tamer, until it will be possible for any one to make trips among these reserves and refuges, and to see as much as we saw, at even closer quarters. No sight more beautiful and more interesting could be imagined.

I am far from disparaging the work of the collector who is also a field naturalist. On the contrary, I fully agree with Mr. Joseph Grinnell's recent plea for him. His work is indispensable. It is far more important to protect his rights than to protect those of the sportsman; for the serious work of the collector is necessary in order to prevent the scientific study of ornithology from lapsing into mere dilettanteism indulged in as a hobby by men and women with opera-glasses. Moreover, sportsmen also have their rights, and it is folly to sacrifice these rights to mere sentimentality — for, of course, sentimentality is as much the antithesis and bane of healthy sentiment as bathos is of pathos. If thoroughly protected, any bird or mammal would speedily increase in numbers to such a degree as to drive man from the planet; and of recent years this has been signally proved by actual experience as regards certain creatures, notably as regards the wapiti in the Yellowstone (where the prime need now is to provide for the annual killing of at least five thousand), and to a less extent as regards deer in Vermont.

But as yet these cases are rare exceptions. As yet with the great majority of our most interesting and important wild birds and beasts the prime need is to protect them, not only by laws limiting the open season and the size of the individual bag, but especially by the creation of sanctuaries and refuges. And, while

THE MISSISSIPPI RESERVES 313

the work of the collector is still necessary, the work of the trained faunal naturalist, who is primarily an observer of the life histories of the wild things, is even more necessary. The progress made in the United States, of recent years, in creating and policing bird refuges,[1] has been of capital importance.

At nightfall of the third day of our trip, when we were within sight of Fort Jackson and of the brush and low trees which here grow alongside the Mississippi, we were joined by Mr. M. L. Alexander, the president of the Conservation Commission, on the commission's boat *Louisiana*. He was more than kind and courteous, as were all my Louisiana friends. He and Mr. Miller told me much of the work of the commission; work not only of the utmost use to Louisiana, but of almost equal consequence to the rest of the country, if only for the example set.

The commission was not founded until 1912, yet it has already accomplished a remarkable amount along many different lines. The work of reforestation of great stretches of denuded, and at present worthless, pine land has begun; work which will turn lumbering into a permanent Louisiana industry by making lumber a

[1] See Appendix B.

permanent crop asset, like corn or wheat, only taking longer to mature — an asset which it is equally important not to destroy. In taking care of the mineral resources a stop has been put to waste as foolish as it was criminal; for example, a gas-well which had flowed to waste until six million dollars' worth of gas had been lost was stopped and stored at the cost of five thousand one hundred dollars. The oysters are now farmed and husbanded, the beds being leased in such fashion that there is a steady improvement of the product. Louisiana is peculiarly rich in fish, and a policy has been inaugurated which, if persevered in, will make the paddle-fish industry as important as the sturgeon fishery is in Russia. Not only do the waters of Louisiana now belong to the State, but also the land under the water, this last proving in practise an admirable provision. Some three hundred thousand acres of game reserves and wild-life refuges (mostly uninhabitable by man) have now been established. These have largely been gifts to the State by wise and generous private individuals and corporations, the chief donors being Messrs. Edward A. McIlhenny and Charles Willis Ward, Mrs. Russell Sage, and the Rockefeller Foundation. The Conservation Commission has ac-

THE MISSISSIPPI RESERVES 315

cepted the gifts, and is taking care of the reserves and refuges through its State wardens, with the result that wild birds of many kinds, including even the wary geese, which come down as winter visitants by the hundred thousand, have become very tame, and many beautiful birds which were on the verge of extinction are now re-established and increasing in numbers. These reserves, which lie for the most part in the low country along the coast, are west of the Mississippi.

Job had just come from a visit to the private reserve of Edward A. McIlhenny on Avery Island. It is the most noteworthy reserve in the country. It includes four thousand acres, and is near the Ward-McIlhenny reserve, which they have given to the State — a king's gift! Avery's Island is very beautiful. A great, shallow, artificial lake, surrounded by dwellings, fields, lawns, a railroad, and ox-wagon road, does not seem an ideal home for herons; but it has proved such under the care of Mr. McIlhenny. He started the reserve twenty years ago with eight snowy herons. Now it contains about forty thousand herons of several species. Complete freedom from molestation has rendered the birds extraordinarily tame. The beautiful snow-white lesser egret, which had been almost exterminated by the plume-hunters, flourishes by the thousand; the greater egret has been bothered so by the smaller one that it has retired before it; its heronries are now to be found mainly in other parts of the protected region. Many other kinds of heron, and many waterfowl, literally throng the place. Ducks winter by the thousand, and, most unexpectedly, some even of the northern kinds, like the gadwall, now stay to breed. Most of these birds are so tame that there is little difficulty in taking photographs of them.

The Audubon societies, and all similar organizations, are doing a great work for the future of our country. Birds should be saved because of utilitarian reasons; and, moreover, they should be saved because of reasons unconnected with any return in dollars and cents. A grove of giant redwoods or sequoias should be kept just as we keep a great and beautiful cathedral. The extermination of the passenger-pigeon meant that mankind was just so much poorer; exactly as in the case of the destruction of the cathedral at Rheims. And to lose the chance to see frigate-birds soaring in circles above the storm, or a file of pelicans winging their way homeward across the crimson afterglow of the sunset, or a myriad terns flashing in the bright light of midday as they hover in a shifting maze above the beach — why, the loss is like the loss of a gallery of the masterpieces of the artists of old time.

CHAPTER XI

A CURIOUS EXPERIENCE

IN 1915 I spent a little over a fortnight on a private game reserve in the province of Quebec. I had expected to enjoy the great northern woods, and the sight of beaver, moose, and caribou; but I had not expected any hunting experience worth mentioning. Nevertheless, toward the end of my trip, there befell me one of the most curious and interesting adventures with big game that have ever befallen me during the forty years since I first began to know the life of the wilderness.

In both Canada and the United States the theory and indeed the practise of preserving wild life on protected areas of land have made astonishing headway since the closing years of the nineteenth century. These protected areas, some of very large size, come in two classes. First, there are those which are public property, where the protection is given by the State. Secondly, there are those where the ownership and the protection are private.

By far the most important, of course, are the

A CURIOUS EXPERIENCE

public preserves. These by their very existence afford a certain measure of the extent to which democratic government can justify itself. If in a given community unchecked popular rule means unlimited waste and destruction of the natural resources — soil, fertility, waterpower, forests, game, wild-life generally — which by right belong as much to subsequent generations as to the present generation, then it is sure proof that the present generation is not yet really fit for self-control, that it is not yet really fit to exercise the high and responsible privilege of a rule which shall be both by the people and for the people. The term "for the people" must always include the people unborn as well as the people now alive, or the democratic ideal is not realized. The only way to secure the chance for hunting, for the enjoyment of vigorous field-sports, to the average man of small means, is to secure such enforced game laws as will prevent anybody and everybody from killing game to a point which means its diminution and therefore ultimate extinction. Only in this way will the average man be able to secure for himself and his children the opportunity of occasionally spending his yearly holiday in that school of hardihood and self-reliance—the chase. New Brunswick, Maine, and Vermont during the last generation have waked up to this fact. Moose and deer in New Brunswick and Maine, deer in Vermont, are so much more plentiful than they were a generation ago that young men of sufficient address and skill can at small cost spend a holiday in the woods, or on the edge of the rough backwoods farm land, and be reasonably sure of a moose or a deer. To all three commonwealths the game is now a real asset because each moose or deer alive in the woods brings in, from the outside, men who spend among the inhabitants much more than the money value of the dead animal; and to the lover of nature the presence of these embodiments of the wild vigor of life adds immensely to the vast majesty of the forests.

In Canada there are many great national reserves; and much — by no means all — of the wilderness wherein shooting is allowed, is intelligently and faithfully protected, so that the game does not diminish. In the summer of 1915 we caught a glimpse of one of these great reserves, that including the wonderful mountains on the line of the Canadian Pacific, from Banff to Lake Louise, and for many leagues around them. The naked or snow-clad peaks, the lakes, the glaciers, the evergreen forest

A CURIOUS EXPERIENCE

shrouding the mountainsides and valleys, the clear brooks, the wealth of wild flowers, make up a landscape as lovely as it is varied. Here the game — bighorn and white goat-antelope, moose, wapiti, and black-tail deer and white-tail deer — flourish unmolested. The flora and fauna are boreal, but boreal in the sense that the Rocky Mountains are boreal as far south as Arizona; the crimson paint-brush that colors the hillsides, the water-ousel in the rapid torrents — these and most of the trees and flowers and birds suggest those of the mountains which are riven asunder by the profound gorges of the Colorado rather than those which dwell among the lower and more rounded Eastern hill-masses from which the springs find their way into the rivers that flow down to the North Atlantic. Around these and similar great nurseries of game, the hunting is still good in places; although there has been a mistaken lenity shown in permitting the Indians to butcher mountain-sheep and deer to the point of local extermination, and although, as is probably inevitable in all new communities, the game laws are enforced chiefly at the expense of visiting sportsmen, rather than at the expense of the real enemies of the game, the professional meat and hide hunters who slaughter for the profit.

In Eastern Canada, as in the Eastern United States, there has been far less chance than in the West to create huge governmental game reserves. But there has been a positive increase of the big game during the last two or three decades. This is partly due to the creation and enforcement of wise game laws — although here also it must be admitted that in some of the Provinces, as in some of the States, the alien sportsman is judged with Rhadamanthine severity, while the home offenders, and even the home Indians, are but little interfered with. It would be well if in this matter other communities copied the excellent example of Maine and New Brunswick. In addition to the game laws, a large part is played in Canadian game preservation by the hunting and fishing clubs. These clubs have policed, and now police many thousands of square miles of wooded wilderness, worthless for agriculture; and in consequence of this policing the wild creatures of the wilderness have thriven, and in some cases have multiplied to an extraordinary degree, on these club lands.

In September, 1915, I visited the Tourilli Club, as the guest of an old friend, Doctor Alexander Lambert, a companion of previous hunting trips in the Louisiana cane-brakes, in

A CURIOUS EXPERIENCE 323

the Rockies, on the plains bordering the Red River of the south, and among the Bad Lands through which the Little Missouri flows. The Tourilli Club is an association of Canadian and American sportsmen and lovers of the wilderness. The land, leased from the government by the club, lies northwest of the attractive Old World city of Quebec — the most distinctive city north of the Mexican border, now that the creole element in New Orleans has been almost swamped. The club holds about two hundred and fifty square miles along the main branches and the small tributaries of the Saint Anne River, just north of the line that separates the last bleak farming land from the forest. It is a hilly, almost mountainous region, studded with numerous lakes, threaded by rapid, brawling brooks, and covered with an unbroken forest growth of spruce, balsam, birch and maple.

On the evening of the day I left Quebec I camped in a neat log cabin by the edge of a little lake. I had come in on foot over a rough forest trail with my two guides or porters. They were strapping, good-humored French Canadians, self-respecting and courteous, whose attitude toward their employer was so much like that of Old World guides as to be rather interesting to a man accustomed to the absolute and unconscious democracy of the Western cow camps and hunting trails. One vital fact impressed me in connection with them as in connection with my Spanish-speaking and Portuguese-speaking friends in South America. They were always fathers of big families as well as sons of parents with big families; the big family was normal to their kind, just as it was normal among the men and women I met in Brazil, Argentina, Chile, Uruguay, and Paraguay, to a degree far surpassing what is true of native Americans, Australians, and English-speaking Canadians. If the tendencies thus made evident continue to work unchanged, the end of the twentieth century will witness a reversal in the present positions of relative dominance, in the new and newest worlds, held respectively by the people who speak English, and the people who speak the three Latin tongues. Darwin, in the account of his famous voyage, in speaking of the backwardness of the countries bordering the Plate River, dwells on the way they lag behind, in population and material development, compared to the English settlers in Australia and North America. Were he alive now, the development of the countries around Buenos Ayres and Montevideo would make him revise his judgment. And, whatever may be the case in the future, so far this material development has not, as in the English-speaking world and in old France, been accompanied by a moral change which threatens complete loss of race supremacy because of sheer dwindling in the birth-rate. The men and women of Quebec, Brazil, and Argentina are still primarily fathers and mothers; and unless this is true of a race it neither can nor ought to permanently prosper. The atrophy of the healthy sexual instinct is in its effects equally destructive whether it be due to licentiousness, asceticism, coldness, or timidity; whether it be due to calculated self-indulgence, love of ease and comfort, or absorption in worldly success on the part of the man, or, on the part of the woman, to that kind of shrieking "feminism," the antithesis of all worth calling womanly, which gives fine names to shirking of duty, and to the fear of danger and discomfort, and actually exalts as praiseworthy the abandonment or subordination by women of the most sacred and vitally important of the functions of womanhood. It is not enough that a race shall be composed of good fighters, good workers, and good breeders; but, unless the qualities thus indicated are present in the race foundation, then the superstructure, however seemingly imposing, will topple. As I watched my French guides prepare supper I felt that they offered fine stuff out of which to make a nation.

Beside the lake an eagle-owl was hooting from the depths of the spruce forest; hoohoo — h-o-o-o — hoohoo. From the lake itself a loon, floating high on the water, greeted me with eerie laughter. A sweetheart-sparrow sang a few plaintive bars among the alders. I felt as if again among old friends.

Next day we tramped to the comfortable camp of the president of the club, Mr. Glen Ford McKinney. Half-way there Lambert met me; and for most of the distance he, or one of the guides, carried a canoe, as the route consisted of lakes connected by portages, sometimes a couple of miles long. When we reached the roomy comfortable log houses on Lake McKinney, at nightfall, we were quite ready for our supper of delicious moose venison. Lambert, while fishing in his canoe, a couple of days previously, had killed a young bull as it stood feeding in a lake, and for some days moose meat was our staple food. After that it was replaced by messes of freshly caught trout, and once or twice by a birch-partridge. Mrs. Lambert was at the camp, and Mr. and Mrs.

A CURIOUS EXPERIENCE

McKinney joined us there. A club reserve such as this, with weather-proof cabins scattered here and there beside the lakes, offers the chance for women of the outdoors type, no less than for men no longer in their first youth, to enjoy the life of the wonderful northern wilderness, and yet to enjoy also such substantial comforts as warmth, dry clothes, and good food at night, after a hard day in the open.

Such a reserve offers a fine field for observation of the life histories of the more shy and rare wild creatures practically unaffected by man. Many persons do not realize how completely on these reserves the wild life is led under natural conditions, wholly unlike those on small artificial reserves. Most wild beasts in the true wilderness lead lives that are artificial in so far as they are primarily conditioned by fear of man. In wilderness reserves like this, on the contrary, there is so much less dread of human persecution that the lives led by such beasts as the moose, caribou, and beaver more closely resemble life in the woods before the appearance of man. As an example, on the Tourilli game reserve wolves, which did not appear until within a decade, have been much more destructive since then than men, and have more profoundly influenced for evil the lives of the other wild creatures.

The beavers are among the most interesting of all woodland beasts. They had been so trapped out that fifteen years ago there were probably not a dozen individuals left on the reserve. Then they were rigidly protected. After ten years they had increased literally a hundredfold. At the end of that time trapping was permitted for a year; hundreds of skins were taken, and then trapping was again prohibited.

The beaver on the reserve at present number between one and two thousand. We saw their houses and dams everywhere. One dam was six feet high; another dam was built to the height of about a foot and a half, near one of our camping places, in a week's time. The architects were a family of beavers; some of the branches bore the big marks of the teeth of the parent beavers, some the marks of the small teeth of the young ones. It was interesting to see the dams grow, stones being heaped on the up-current side to keep the branches in place. Frequently we came across the animals themselves, swimming a stream or lake, and not much bothered by our presence. When left unmolested they are quite as much diurnal

A CURIOUS EXPERIENCE

as nocturnal. Again and again, as I sat hidden on the lake banks, beaver swam to and fro close beside me, even at high noon. One, which was swimming across a lake at sunset, would not dive until we paddled the canoe straight for it as hard as we could; whereupon it finally disappeared with a slap of its tail. Once at evening Lambert pulled his canoe across the approach to a house, barring the way to the owner—a very big beaver. It did not like to dive under the canoe, and swam close up on the surface, literally gritting its teeth, and now and then it would slap the water with its tail, whereupon the heads of other beaver would pop up above the waters of the lake.

By damming the outlets of some of the lakes and killing the trees and young stuff around the edges, the beaver on this reserve had destroyed some of the favorite haunts of the moose. We saw the old and new houses on the shores of the lakes and beside the streams; some of them were very large, taller than a man, and twice as much across. Some of the old dams, at the pond outlets and across the streams, had become firm causeways, grown-up with trees. The beaver is a fecund animal, its habits are such that few of the beasts of ravin can kill it more than occasionally, and when not too murderously persecuted by man it increases with extraordinary rapidity.

This is primarily due to the character of its food. The forest trees themselves furnish what it eats. This means that its food supply is practically limitless. It has very few food rivals. The trunks of full-grown trees offer what is edible to a most narrowly limited number of vertebrates, and therefore — a fact often lost sight of — until man appears on the scene forests do not support anything like the same number and variety of large beasts as open, grassy plains. There are tree-browsing creatures, but these can only get at the young growth; the great majority of beasts prefer prairies or open scrub to thick forest. The open plains of central North America were thronged with big game to a degree that was never true of the vast American forests, whether subarctic, temperate, or tropical. The great game regions of Africa were the endless dry plains of South and East Africa, and not the steaming West African forests. There are, of course, some big mammals that live exclusively on low plants and bushes that only grow in the forest, and some trees at certain seasons yield fruits and nuts which fall to the ground; but, speaking generally, an ordinary full-grown

A CURIOUS EXPERIENCE

tree of average size yields food only to beasts of exceptional type, of which the most conspicuous in North America are the tree-porcupine and the beaver. Even these eat only the bark; no vertebrate, so far as I know, eats the actual wood of the trunk.

These bark-eaters, therefore, have almost no food rivals, and the forest furnishes them food in limitless quantities. The beaver has developed habits more interesting and extraordinary than those of any other rodent — indeed as interesting as those of any other beast — and its ways of life are such as to enable it to protect itself from its enemies, and to insure itself against failure of food, to a degree very unusual among animals. It is no wonder that, when protected against man, it literally swarms in its native forests. Its dams, houses, and canals are all wonderful, and on the Tourilli they were easily studied. The height at which many of the tree trunks had been severed showed that the cutting must have been done in winter when the snow was deep and crusted. One tree which had not fallen showed a deep spiral groove going twice round the trunk. Evidently the snow had melted faster than the beavers worked; they were never able to make a complete ring, although they had gnawed twice around the tree, and finally the rising temperature beat the teeth, and the task was perforce abandoned.

I was surprised at the complete absence from the Tourilli of the other northern tree-eater — bark-eater — the porcupine. Inquiry developed the fact that porcupines had been exceedingly numerous until within a score of years or less. Then a mysterious disease smote the slow, clumsy, sluggish creatures, and in the course of two or three years they were absolutely exterminated. In similar fashion from some mysterious disease (or aggregation of diseases, which sometimes all work with virulence when animals become too crowded) almost all the rabbits in the reserve died off some six years ago. In each case it was a universally, or well-nigh universally, fatal epidemic, following a period during which the smitten animals had possessed good health and had flourished and increased greatly in spite of the flesh-eaters that preyed on them. In some vital details the cases differed. Hares, compared to porcupines, are far more prolific, far more active, and with far more numerous foes; and they also seem to be much more liable to these epidemics, although this may be merely because they so much more quickly increase to

A CURIOUS EXPERIENCE 333

the point that seems to invite the disease. The porcupines are rather unsocial, and are so lethargic in their movements that the infection took longer to do its full work. But this work was done so thoroughly that evidently the entire race of porcupines over a large tract of country was exterminated. Porcupines have few foes that habitually prey on them, although it is said that there is an exception in the shape of the pekan — the big, savage sable, inappropriately called fisher by the English-speaking woodsmen. But they breed so slowly (for rodents) and move about so little that when exterminated from a district many years elapse before they again begin to spread throughout it. The rabbits, on the contrary, move about so much that infectious diseases spread with extraordinary rapidity and they are the habitual food of every fair-sized bird and beast of prey, but their extraordinary fecundity enables them rapidly to recover lost ground. As regards these northern wood-rabbits, and doubtless other species of hares, it is evident that their beast and bird foes, who prey so freely on their helplessness, nevertheless are incompetent to restrain the overdevelopment of the species. Their real foes, their only real foes, are the minute organisms that produce the diseases which at intervals sweep off their swarming numbers. The devastation of these diseases, whether the agents spreading them are insects or still smaller, microscopic creatures, is clearly proved in the case of these North American rabbits and porcupines; probably it explains the temporary and local extermination of the Labrador meadow-mice after they have risen to the culminating crest of one of those "waves of life" described by Doctor Cabot. It has ravaged among big African ruminants on an even more extensive scale than among these North American rodents. Doubtless such disease-devastation has been responsible for the extinction of many, many species in the past; and where for any cause species and individuals became crowded together, or there was an increase in moisture and change in temperature, so that the insect carriers of disease became more numerous, the extinction might easily befall more than one species.

Of course, such epidemic disease is only one of many causes that may produce such extermination or reduction in numbers. More efficient food rivals may be a factor; just as sheep drive out cattle from the same pasturage, and as, in Australia, rabbits drive out sheep. Or animal foes may be a cause. Fifteen years

A CURIOUS EXPERIENCE

ago, in the Tourilli, caribou were far more plentiful than moose. Moose have steadily increased in numbers. But some seven years ago wolves, of which none had been seen in these woods for half a century, made their appearance. They did not seriously molest the full-grown moose (nor the black bears), although they occasionally killed moose calves, and very rarely, when in a pack, an adult, but they warred on all the other animals, including the lucivees when they could catch them on the ice in winter. They followed the caribou unceasingly, killing many, and in consequence the caribou are now far less common. Barthelmy Lirette, the most experienced hunter and best observer among the guides — even better than his brother Arthur — told me that the wolves usually made no effort to assail the moose, and that never but once had he heard of their killing a grown moose. But they followed any caribou they came across, big or little. Once on snow-shoes he had tracked such a chase all day long. A single wolf had followed a caribou for twenty-five miles before killing it. Evidently the wolf deliberately set about tiring his victim so that it could not resist. In the snow the caribou sank deep. The wolf ran lightly. His tracks showed that he had galloped whenever the caribou had galloped, and walked behind it when it became too tired to run, and then galloped again when under the terror of his approach the hunted thing once more flailed its fading strength into flight. Its strength was utterly gone when its grim follower at last sprang on it and tore out its life.

An arctic explorer once told me that on a part of the eastern coast of Greenland he found on one visit plenty of caribou and arctic foxes. A few years later he returned. Musk-oxen had just come into the district, and wolves followed them. The musk-ox is helpless in the presence of human hunters, much more helpless than caribou, and can exist only in the appalling solitudes where even arctic man cannot live; but against wolves, its only other foes, its habits of gregarious and truculent self-defense enable it to hold its own as the caribou cannot. The wolves which were hangers-on of the musk-ox herds speedily killed or drove out both the foxes and the caribou on this stretch of Greenland coast, and as a result two once plentiful species were completely replaced by two other species, which change also doubtless resulted in other changes in the smaller wild life.

Here we can explain the reason for the change

as regards three of the animals, inasmuch as this change was ultimately conditioned by the movements of the fourth, the musk-ox. But we know nothing of the cause which produced the musk-ox migration, which migration resulted in such unsettling of life conditions for the wolves, caribous, and foxes of this one locality. Neither can we with our present knowledge explain the causes which in Maine and New Brunswick during the last thirty or forty years have brought about a diminution of the caribou, although there has been an increase in the number of moose and deer; wolves cannot have produced this change, for they kill the deer easier than the caribou. Field naturalists have in such questions an ample opportunity for work of the utmost interest. Doubtless they can in the future give us complete or partial explanations of many of these problems which are at present insoluble. In any event these continuous shiftings of faunas at the present day enable us to form some idea of the changes which must have occurred on innumerable occasions during man's history on this planet. Beyond question many of the faunas which seem to us contemporary when their remains are found associated with those of prehistoric man were really successive and may have alternated again and again before one or both finally disappeared. Life is rarely static, rarely in a state of stable equilibrium. Often it is in a condition of unstable equilibrium, with continual oscillations one way and the other. More often still, while there are many shifts to and fro, the general tendency of change is with slow steadiness in one direction.

After a few days the Lamberts and I shifted to Lambert's home camp; an easy two days' journey, tramping along the portage trails and paddling across the many lakes. It was a very comfortable camp, by a beautiful lake. There were four log cabins, each water-tight and with a stove; and the largest was in effect a sitting-room, with comfortable chairs and shelves of books. They stood in a sunny clearing. The wet, dense forest was all around, the deep mossy ground spangled with bright-red partridge-berries. Behind the cabins was a small potato patch. Wild raspberries were always encroaching on this patch, and attracted the birds of the neighborhood, including hermit and olive-back thrushes, both now silent. Chickadees were in the woods, and woodpeckers — the arctic, the hairy, and the big log-cock — drummed on the dead trees. One mid-afternoon a great gray

A CURIOUS EXPERIENCE

owl called repeatedly, uttering a short loud sound like that of some big wild beast. In front of the main cabin were four graceful mountain ashes, brilliant with scarlet berry clusters. On a neighboring lake Coleman Drayton had a camp; the view from it across the lake was very beautiful. He killed a moose on the lake next to his and came over to dinner with us the same evening.

On the way to Lambert's camp I went off by myself for twenty-four hours, with my two guides, Arthur Lirette, one of the game wardens of the club, and Odilon Genest. Arthur was an experienced woodsman, intelligent and responsible, and with the really charming manners that are so much more common among men of French or Spanish blood than among ourselves. Odilon was a strong young fellow, a good paddler and willing worker. I wished to visit a lake which moose were said to frequent. We carried our canoe thither.

After circling the lake in the canoe without seeing anything, we drew it ashore among some bushes and sat down under a clump of big spruces to watch. Although only partially concealed, we were quiet; and it is movement that attracts the eyes of wild things. A beaver house was near by and the inmates swam about not thirty feet from us; and scaup-ducks and once a grown brood of dusky mallard drifted and swam by only a little farther off. The beaver kept slapping the water with their broad trowel-tails, evidently in play; where they are wary they often dive without slapping the water. No bull appeared, but a cow moose with two calves came down to the lake, directly opposite us, at one in the afternoon and spent two hours in the water. Near where the three of them entered the lake was a bed of tall, coarse reed-grass standing well above the water. Earlier in the season this had been grazed by moose, but these three did not touch it. The cow, having entered the water, did not leave. She fed exclusively with her head under water. Wading out until only the ridge of her back was above the surface, and at times finding that the mud bothered even her long legs, she plunged her huge homely head to the bottom, coming up with between her jaws big tufts of dripping bottom-grass — the moose grass — or the roots and stems of other plants. After a time she decided to change her station, and, striking off into deep water, she swam half a mile farther down the lake. She swam well and powerfully, but sunk rather deep in the water, only her head and the ridge of her withers

A CURIOUS EXPERIENCE

above it. She continued to feed, usually broadside to me, some three hundred and fifty yards off; her big ears flopped forward and back, and her long snout, with the protuberant nostrils, was thrust out as she turned from time to time to look or smell for her calves. The latter had separated at once from the mother, and spent only a little time in the water, appearing and disappearing among the alders, and among the berry-bushes on a yielding bog of pink and gray moss. Once they played together for a moment, and then one of them cantered off for a few rods.

When moose calves go at speed they usually canter. By the time they are yearlings, however, they have adopted the trot as their usual gait. When grown they walk, trot when at speed, and sometimes pace; but they gallop so rarely that many good observers say that they never gallop or canter. This is too sweeping, however. I have myself, as will be related, seen a heavy old bull gallop for fifty yards when excited, and I have seen the tracks where a full-grown cow or young bull galloped for a longer distance. Lambert came on one close up in a shallow lake, and in its fright it galloped ashore, churning through the mud and water. In very deep snow one will sometimes gallop or bound for a dozen leaps, and under sudden fright from an enemy near by even the biggest moose will sometimes break into a gallop which may last for several rods. More often, even under such circumstances, the animal trots off; and the trot is its habitual, and, save in exceptional circumstances, its only, rapid gait, even when charging.

As the cow and her young ones stood in the water or on the bank it was impossible not to be struck by the conspicuously advertising character of the coloration. The moose is one of the few animals of which the body is inversely countershaded, being black save for the brownish or grayish of the back. The huge black mass at once attracts the eye, and the whitish or grayish legs are also strikingly visible. The bright-red summer coat of the white-tail deer is, if anything, of even more advertising quality; but the huge bulk of a moose, added to its blackness, makes it the most conspicuous of all our beasts.

Moose are naturally just as much diurnal as nocturnal. We found them visiting the lakes at every hour of the day. They are so fond of water as to be almost amphibious. In the winter they feed on the buds and twig tips of young spruce and birch and swamp-maple; and

A CURIOUS EXPERIENCE

when there is no snow they feed freely on various ground plants in the forest; but for over half the year they prefer to eat the grasses and other plants which grow either above or under the water in the lakes. They easily wade through mud not more than four feet deep, and take delight in swimming. But until this trip I did not know that moose, while swimming, dived to get grass from the bottom. Mr. McKinney told me of having seen this feat himself. The moose was swimming to and fro in a small lake. He plunged his head beneath water, and then at once raised it, looking around, evidently to see if any enemy were taking advantage of his head being concealed to approach him. Then he plunged his head down again, threw his rump above water, and dived completely below the surface, coming up with tufts of bottom-grass in his mouth. He repeated this several times, once staying down and out of sight for nearly half a minute.

After the cow moose left the water she spent an hour close to the bank, near the inlet. We came quite near to her in the canoe before she fled; her calves were farther in the woods. It was late when we started to make our last portage; a heavy rain-storm beat on us, speedily drenching us, and the darkness and the driving downpour made our walk over the rough forest trail one of no small difficulty. Next day we went to Lambert's camp.

Some ten miles northeast of Lambert's camp lies a stretch of wild and mountainous country, containing many lakes, which has been but seldom visited. A good cabin has been built on one of the lakes. A couple of years ago Lambert went thither, but saw nothing, and Coleman Drayton was there the same summer; Arthur, my guide, visited the cabin last spring to see if it was in repair; otherwise the country had been wholly undisturbed. I determined to make a three days' trip to it, with Arthur and Odilon. We were out of meat and I desired to shoot something for the table. My license permitted me to kill one bull moose. It also permitted me to kill two caribou, of either sex; but Lambert felt, and I heartily agreed with him, that no cow ought to be shot.

We left after breakfast one morning. Before we had been gone twenty-five minutes I was able to obtain the wished-for fresh meat. Our course, as usual, lay along a succession of lakes connected by carries, or portages. We were almost at the end of the first portage when we caught a glimpse of a caribou feeding in the thick woods some fifty yards to the right of our trail. It was eating the streamers of gray-green moss which hung from the dead lower branches of the spruces. It was a yearling bull. At first I could merely make out a small patch of its flank between two tree trunks, and I missed it — fortunately, for, if wounded, it would probably have escaped. At the report, instead of running, the foolish young bull shifted his position to look at us; and with the next shot I killed him. While Arthur dressed him Odilon returned to camp and brought out a couple of men. We took a shoulder with us for our provision and sent the rest back to camp. Hour after hour we went forward. We paddled across the lakes. Between them the trails sometimes led up to and down from high divides; at other times they followed the courses of rapid brooks which brawled over smooth stones under the swaying, bending branches of the alders. Off the trail fallen logs and bowlders covered the ground, and the moss covered everything ankle-deep or knee-deep.

Early in the afternoon we reached the cabin. The lake, like most of the lakes thereabouts, was surrounded by low, steep mountains, shrouded in unbroken forest. The light-green domes of the birches rose among the sombre spruce spires; on the mountain crests the pointed spruces made a serrated line against the sky. Arthur and I paddled off across the lake in the light canoe we had been carrying. We had hardly shoved off from shore before we saw a caribou swimming in the middle of the lake. It was a young cow, and doubtless had never before seen a man. The canoe much excited its curiosity. A caribou, thanks probably to its peculiar pelage, is a very buoyant swimmer. Unlike the moose, this caribou had its whole back, and especially its rump, well out of water; the short tail was held erect, and the white under-surface glinted whenever the swimmer turned away from us. At first, however, it did not swim away, being too much absorbed in the spectacle of the canoe. It kept gazing toward us with its ears thrown forward, wheeling to look at us as lightly and readily as a duck. We passed it at a distance of some seventy-five yards, whereupon it took fright and made off, leaving a wake like a paddle-wheel steamer and, when it landed, bouncing up the bank with a great splashing of water and cracking of bushes. A caribou swims even better than a moose, but whereas a moose not only feeds by preference in the water, but half the time has its head under water, the caribou

A CURIOUS EXPERIENCE

feeds on land, although occasionally cropping water-grass that stands above the surface.

We portaged beside a swampy little stream to the next lake and circled it in the canoe. Silently we went round every point, alert to find what the bay beyond might hold. But we saw nothing; it was night when we returned. As we paddled across the lake the stars were glorious overhead and the mysterious landscape shimmered in the white radiance of the moonlight. Loons called to one another, not only uttering their goblin laughter, but also those long-drawn, wailing cries, which seem to hold all the fierce and mournful loneliness of the northern wastes. Then we reached camp, and feasted on caribou venison, and slept soundly on our beds of fragrant balsam boughs.

Next morning, on September 19, we started eastward, across a short portage, perhaps a quarter of a mile long, beside which ran a stream, a little shallow river. At the farther end of the portage we launched the canoe in a large lake hemmed in by mountains. The lake twisted and turned, and was indented by many bays. A strong breeze was blowing. Arthur was steersman, Odilon bowsman, while I sat in the middle with my Springfield rifle. We skirted the shores, examining each bay.

Half an hour after starting, as we rounded a point, we saw the huge black body and white shovel antlers of a bull moose. He was close to the alders, wading in the shallow water and deep mud and grazing on a patch of fairly tall water-grass. So absorbed was he that he did not notice us until Arthur had skilfully brought the canoe to within eighty yards of him. Then he saw us, tossed his great antlered head aloft, and for a moment stared at us, a picture of burly majesty. He stood broadside on, and a splendid creature he was, of towering stature, the lord of all the deer tribe, as stately a beast of the chase as walks the round world.

The waves were high, and the canoe danced so on the ripple that my first bullet went wild, but with the second I slew the mighty bull.

We had our work cut out to get the bull out of the mud and on the edge of the dry land. The antlers spread fifty-two inches. Some hours were spent in fixing the head, taking off the hide, and cutting up the carcass. Our canoe was loaded to its full capacity with moose meat when we started toward the beginning of the portage leading from the southeastern corner of the lake toward the Lamberts' camp. Here we landed the meat, putting cool

From a photograph by Alexander Lambert, M.D.

Colonel Roosevelt and Arthur Lirette with antlers of moose shot September 19, 1915.

moss over it, and left it to be called for on our way back, on the morrow.

It was shortly after three when we again pushed off in the canoe, and headed for the western end of the lake, for the landing from which the portage led to our cabin. It had been a red-letter day, of the ordinary hunting red-letter type. I had no conception that the real adventure still lay in front of us.

When half a mile from the landing we saw another big bull moose on the edge of the shore ahead of us. It looked and was — if anything — even bigger-bodied than the one I had shot in the morning, with antlers almost as large and rather more palmated. We paddled up to within a hundred yards of it, laughing and talking, and remarking how eager we would have been if we had not already got our moose. At first it did not seem to notice us. Then it looked at us but paid us no further heed. We were rather surprised at this but paddled on past it, and it then walked along the shore after us. We still supposed that it did not realize what we were. But another hundred yards put us to windward of it. Instead of turning into the forest when it got our wind, it merely bristled up the hair on its withers, shook its head, and continued to walk after the canoe, along the shore. I had heard of bull moose, during the rut, attacking men unprovoked, if the men were close up, but never of anything as wanton and deliberate as this action, and I could hardly believe the moose meant mischief, but Arthur said it did; and obviously we could not land with the big, evil-looking beast coming for us — and, of course, I was most anxious not to have to shoot it. So we turned the canoe round and paddled on our back track. But the moose promptly turned and followed us along the shore. We yelled at him, and Odilon struck the canoe with his paddle, but with no effect. After going a few hundred yards we again turned and resumed our former course; and as promptly the moose turned and followed us, shaking his head and threatening us. He seemed to be getting more angry, and evidently meant mischief. We now continued our course until we were opposite the portage landing, and about a hundred yards away from it; the water was shallow and we did not wish to venture closer, lest the moose might catch us if he charged. When he came to the portage trail he turned up it, sniffing at our footsteps of the morning, and walked along it into the woods; and we hoped that now he would become uneasy and go off. After waiting a few minutes we paddled slowly toward the landing, but before reaching it we caught his loom in the shadow, as he stood facing us some distance down the trail. As soon as we stopped he rushed down the trail toward us, coming in to the lake; and we backed hastily into deep water. He vented his rage on a small tree, which he wrecked with his antlers. We continued to paddle round the head of the bay, and he followed us; we still hoped we might get him away from the portage, and that he would go into the woods. But when we turned he followed us back, and thus went to and fro with us. Where the water was deep near shore we pushed the canoe close in to him, and he promptly rushed down to the water's edge, shaking his head, and striking the earth with his fore hoofs. We shouted at him, but with no effect. As he paraded along the shore he opened his mouth, lolling out his tongue; and now and then when he faced us he ran out his tongue and licked the end of his muzzle with it. Once, with head down, he bounded or galloped round in a half circle; and from time to time he grunted or uttered a low, menacing roar. Altogether the huge black beast looked like a formidable customer, and was evidently in a most evil rage and bent on man-killing.

For over an hour he thus kept us from the shore, running to meet us wherever we tried to go. The afternoon was waning, a cold wind began to blow, shifting as it blew. He was not a pleasant-looking beast to meet in the woods in the dusk. We were at our wits' ends what to do. At last he turned, shook his head, and with a flourish of his heels galloped — not trotted — for fifty yards up beside the little river which paralleled the portage trail. I called Arthur's attention to this, as he had been telling me that a big bull never galloped. Then the moose disappeared at a trot round the bend. We waited a few minutes, cautiously landed, and started along the trail, watching to see if the bull was lying in wait for us; Arthur telling me that if he now attacked us I must shoot him at once or he would kill somebody.

A couple of hundred yards on the trail led within a few yards of the little river. As we reached this point a smashing in the brush beyond the opposite bank caused us to wheel; and the great bull came headlong for us, while Arthur called to me to shoot. With a last hope of frightening him I fired over his head, without the slightest effect. At a slashing trot he crossed the river, shaking his head, his ears back, the hair on his withers bristling. "Tirez, m'sieu, tirez; vite, vite!" called Arthur, and when the bull was not thirty feet off I put a bullet into his chest, in the sticking point. It was a mortal wound, and stopped him short; I fired into his chest again, and this wound, too, would by itself have been fatal. He turned and recrossed the stream, falling to a third shot, but as we approached he struggled to his feet, grunting savagely, and I killed him as he came toward us.

I was sorry to have to kill him, but there was no alternative. As it was, I only stopped him in the nick of time, and had I not shot straight at least one of us would have paid forfeit with his life in another second. Even in Africa I have never known anything but a rogue elephant or buffalo, or an occasional rhinoceros, to attack so viciously or with such premeditation when itself neither wounded nor threatened.

Gentle-voiced Arthur, in his delightful habitant's French, said that the incident was "pas mal curieux." He used "pas mal" as a superlative. The first time he used it I was completely bewildered. It was hot and sultry, and Arthur remarked that the day was "pas mal mort." How the day could be "not badly dead" I could not imagine, but the proper translation turned out to be "a very lifeless day," which was true.

On reaching Lambert's camp, Arthur and Odilon made affidavit to the facts as above set forth, and this affidavit I submitted to the secretary of mines and fisheries of Quebec, who approved what I had done.

On the day following that on which we killed the two bulls we went back to Lambert's home camp. While crossing one lake, about the middle of the forenoon, a bull moose challenged twice from the forest-clad mountain on our right. We found a pawing-place, a pit where one — possibly more than one — bull had pawed up the earth and thrashed the saplings roundabout with its antlers. The place smelled strongly of urine. The whole of the next day was spent in getting in the meat, skins, and antlers.

I do not believe that this vicious bull moose had ever seen a man. I have never heard of another moose acting with the same determination and perseverance in ferocious malice; it behaved, as I have said, like some of the rare vicious rogues among African elephants, buffaloes, and rhinoceroses. Bull moose during the rut are fierce animals, however, and, although there

A CURIOUS EXPERIENCE

is ordinarily no danger whatever in shooting them, several of my friends have been resolutely charged by wounded moose, and I know of, and have elsewhere described, one authentic case where the hunter was killed. A boy carrying mail through the woods to the camp of a friend of mine was forced to climb a tree by a bull which threatened him. My friend Pride, of Island Falls, Maine, was charged while in a canoe at night, by a bull moose which he had incautiously approached too near, and the canoe was upset. If followed on snow-shoes in the deep snow, or too closely approached in its winter yard, it is not uncommon for a moose to charge when its pursuer is within a few yards. Once Arthur was charged by a bull which was in company with a cow. He was in a canoe, at dusk, in a stream, and the bull rushed into the water after him, while he paddled hard to get away; but the cow left, and the bull promptly followed her. In none of these cases, however, did the bull act with the malice and cold-blooded purposefulness shown by the bull I was forced to kill.

Two or three days later I left the woods. The weather had grown colder. The loons had begun to gather on the larger lakes in preparation for their southward flight. The nights

356   A BOOK-LOVER'S HOLIDAYS

were frosty. Fall was in the air. Once there was a flurry of snow. Birch and maple were donning the bravery with which they greet the oncoming north; crimson and gold their banners flaunted in the eyes of the dying year.

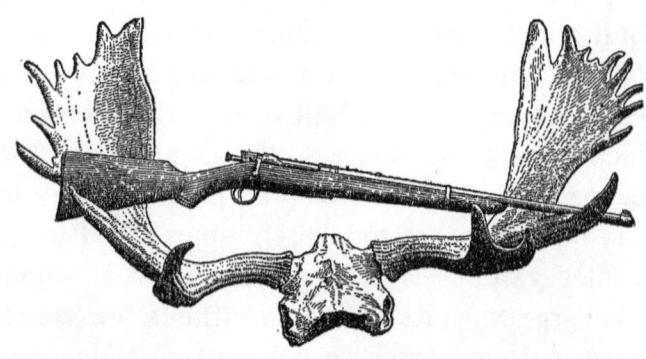

Antlers of moose shot September 19, 1915, with Springfield rifle No. 6000, Model 1903.

This rifle, now a retired veteran, is not heavy enough for steady use on heavy game; but it is so handy and accurate, has such penetration, and keeps in such good order that it has been my chief hunting-rifle for the last dozen years on three continents, and has repeatedly killed heavy game. With it I have shot some three hundred head of all kinds, including the following:

Lion, hyena, elephant, rhinoceros (square-mouthed and hook-nosed), hippopotamus, zebras of two kinds, wart-hog, giraffe, giant eland, common eland, roan antelope, oryx, wildebeest, topi, white-withered lechwe, waterbucks, hartebeests, kobs, impalla, gerenuk, gazelles, reedbucks, bushbucks, klipspringer, oribis, duikers, steinbok, dikdik, monkeys.

Jaguar, tapir, big peccary, giant ant-eater, capybara, wood-deer, monkey.

Cougar, black bear, moose, caribou, white-tail deer.

Crocodile, cayman, python.

Ostrich, bustard, wild turkey, crane, pelican, maribou, ibis, whale-head stork, jabiru stork, guinea-fowl, francolin.

APPENDICES

APPENDIX A

The frontispiece I owe to the courtesy of Mr. Theodore Pitman, a fellow Harvard student of Archie's, whom we met on Buckskin Mountain; being both a hunter and a lover of the picturesque, he was as much impressed as we were by the scene when a cougar stood in a pine, with the Grand Canyon as a background. The photograph at the end of the book is by Doctor Alexander Lambert, and the tail-piece is from a photograph by him.

I had been told by old hunters that black bears would sometimes attack moose calves, and in one instance, in the Rockies, my informant described to me how a big grizzly, but a few weeks out of its den in spring, attacked and slew full-grown moose. I was not surprised at the latter statement, having myself come across cattle-killing grizzlies; but I wondered at a black bear, which is not much of a beast of prey, venturing to meddle with the young of so formidable a fighter as a moose. However, it is true. Recently my nephew Hall Roosevelt, who was working at Dawson City, went on a moose hunt in the valley of the Yukon. One night a moose cow passed by the camp, having first swum a stream in front of the camp. She was followed at some little distance by a calf. The latter halted near the camp. Suddenly a black bear, with a tremendous crashing of branches, came with a rush through the bushes, and seized the calf; although it was driven off, it had with its teeth so injured the spine of the calf that they were obliged to shoot the latter.

On a hunt in the Northern Rockies, Archie met a man who had two dogs, an ordinary track-hound and a Russian wolfhound. One day they came across a white goat, and before the slow creature could reach the precipice the dogs overtook and bayed it. The track-hound merely jumped to and fro, baying; but the wolfhound rushed straight in and caught the goat by the neck on one side; whereupon the track-hound seized the other side of the neck. Immediately, with two wicked backward thrusts of its horns, first to one side, then to the other, the goat killed both its assailants; the stiletto-like horns were driven to the hilt with a single jab.

The attack by the moose upon us, mentioned in the final chapter, was so unusual that I give the deposition of the two guides who were with me, and also the report of the senior of the two, the game warden, in reference to the occurrence. They are as follows:

CANADA
Province of Quebec,
District of Quebec,

I, Theodore Roosevelt, residing at Oyster-Bay in the United States of America, do solemnly declare as follows:

That I have just returned from a trip in the Tourilli Club limits as a Guest of Dr. Alexander Lambert, I had the ordinary game license No. 25 issued to me on the 6th day of september instant. On september the nineteenth, on Lake Croche, having with me as guides, Arthur Lirette and Odilon Genest, I killed an old bull moose as authorized by the license, which only permitted to me to kill one moose. That afternoon, shortly after three o'clock, we were returning in our canoe to the West end of the Lake, where a portage trail led to our camp; a small stream runs besides the portage trail; when half a mile from our proposed landing place, we saw an old bull moose on the shore. We paddled up to within a

APPENDIX A

hundred yards of it. We supposed that when it saw us, it would take to the woods. It however walked along the edge of the water parallel to our canoe, looking at us. We passed it, and gave it our wind, thinking this would surely cause it to run. But it merely raised its hair on its withers and shook its horns and followed after the canoe. We shouted, but it paid no heed to us; we then reversed our canoe and paddled in the opposite direction; but following us and threatening us, the bull moose turned and walked the same way we did, we renewed our former course, and thereupon so did the moose, where the water was shallow, we did not venture near it, but where the water was deep, we went within fifty yards; and it then thrashed the branches of a young tree with its antlers, and pawed the earth and advanced a little way into the water towards us, walking parallel to our canoe, it reached the portage trail, it turned and walked up this trail and sniffed at our morning's tracks, and we supposed it had fled; but on nearing the landing place, we saw it standing in the trail, and it rushed down towards us and we had to back quickly into deep water; we paddled on round the shore, hoping it would get tired and go; we shouted and tried to frighten it, but it merely shook its head and stamped on the ground and bounded in a circle; then it swaggered along grunting, it kept its mouth open, and lolled out its tongue and when it turned towards us, it ran its tongue over its muzzle, thus it accompanied us to and for an hour, cutting us off whenever we tried to land; then it turned, and went up the little stream, shaking its head, and galloping or bounding not trotting, for fifty yards, it disappeared around a bend of a stream, we waited a few minutes, and landed, and started along the portage trail for camp, after about ten minutes, the trail approached the little stream; then the moose suddenly appeared rushing

APPENDIX A

towards us at a slashing trot, its hair ruffled and tossing his head.

Arthur Lirette, who is one of the game wardens of the Tourilli Club, called out to me to shoot, or the moose would do us mischief, in a last effort to frighten it, I fired over its head, but it paid no heed to this and rushed over the stream at us; Arthur again called: "Tirez, monsieur, tirez, vite, vite, vite," and I fired into the moose's chest, when he was less than twenty feet away, coming full tilt at us, grunting, shaking his head, his ears back and his hair brindled; the shot stopped him; I fired into him again; both shots were fatal; he recrossed the little stream and fell to a third shot; but when we approached, he rose, grunting and started towards us. I killed him. If I had not stopped him, he would have certainly killed one or more of our party; and at twenty feet I had to shoot as straight as I knew how, or he would have reached us. I had done everything possible in my power to scare him away for an hour and a quarter, and I solemnly declare that I killed him only when it was imperatively necessary, in order to prevent the loss of one or more of our own lives, and I make this solemn declaration conscientiously, believing it to be true, and knowing that it is of the same force and effect as if made under oath, and by virtue of the Canada EVIDENCE ACT, 1893.

(*Signed*) THEODORE ROOSEVELT,

Declared before me, this 24th day of september 1915.
(*Signed*) E. A. PANET, *N. P. & J. P.*

TRUE COPY,

S. DUFAULT
Deputy-Minister, Department Colonization,
Mines and Fisheries, Quebec.

APPENDIX A

CANADA,
Province de Québec,
District de Québec.

Je, Arthur Lirette, du village de St-Raymond, gardien du Club de Pêche et de Chasse Tourilli, et Je, Odilon, Genest, du même lieu, en ma qualité de guide, déclare sollennellement que les faits relatés ci-hauts par la déclaration de M. Théodore Roosevelt, laquelle nous a été lue et traduite en francais par le Notaire E. A. Panet, de St-Raymond, que cette déclaration contient la vérité dans toute son étendue, et que si le dit Th. Roosevelt n'avait pas tué l'orignal mentionné par lui, que nos vies étaient en danger.

Et je fais cette déclaration solennelle consciencieusement la croyant vraie, et sachant qu'elle a la même force et l'effet, comme si elle avait été faite sous serment, en vertu de "The CANADA EVIDENCE ACT, 1893.

Déclaré devant moi, à St-Raymond, ce 24 ème jour de septembre, 1915.

   (*Signe*) "Arthur Lirette"
     " "Odilon Genest,"
     " "E. A. Panet, *N. P. & J. Paix*.

VRAIE COPIE,

S. Dufault

Sous-Ministre, Département de la Colonisation, des Mines et des Pêcheries, Québec.

COPY

St. Raymond, 7 Octobre 1915

Cher Messieur
   Rapport

Le 19 Septembre 1915 Mons. Col. Teodore Rosevelt partant pour faire la chasse a l'orignal dans le club Tourilli accompagne d'Arthur Lirette et Odilion Genest comme guides vers 9 heures du matin au lac Croche du Bras du Nord le Col Rosevelt tua un original dans l'apres midi voulant sen revenir du camp du lac a l'ile avec la tete et le panage dans le canot vers les 3 heures ½ nous apercumes un autre original sur le bord du lac nous avons arreter notre canot nous l'avons regarder et l'orignal nous regardait bien ferocement nous etions a peu pres un arpent de distance l'on se mit a ramer pour aller au portage du lac a l'ile et l'animal se mis a suive sur la meme directions de nous nous avons retourner sur nos pas une couple d'arpent et l'orignal fit la meme chose et l'on pouvait voir qu'il etait bien enrager alors l'on se mit a crier et frapper sur le canot avec les avirons afin de pouvoir l'effayer au contraire il se mit a corné les arbres du bord du lac avec le poil bien droit sur le dos et il grattait avec ses pattes dans la terre ensuite il a pris le portage nous avons rester pour 10 minute ensuit nous avon ramer pour se rendre au portage le pensant disparu mais l'on ne pu se rendre que l'animal revenait de nouveau sur nous avons reculer de nouveau sur le lac et l'orignal est rendu dans l'eau jusquau genoux ensuite se mit de galopper et sauter et a traverser la petite Riviere et se mit a piocher et Beugler et se battre avec les arbres il a rester 5 minutes a peu pres et nous avons essayer a rapprocher encore sur terre mais imposible car l'animal est revenus de nouveau sur le bord du lac faire la meme chose ensuite il pris la petite Riviere en trottant a peu pres 200 pieds et il disparu nous avons laisser faire pour quelques instant ensuite nous avons approcher sur terre au petit portage cela faisait que n'on avait eté gardé par cet animal pour une heure a une heure ½ ensuite j'ai dis a Monsier et Odilion que l'on faisait mieux de se suivre et mener autant de bruit possible afin de l'effrayer mais l'orseque n'on eut fait deux arpents dans le portage j'ai apercus l'animal qui semblait nous attendre dans le petit ruisseau et la voyant qu'il y avait bien du danger pour nous tous nous etions a une distance le 30 verges de lui j'ai avertit Monsier de tirer et Mons. a pris sa carabine et a tirer en l'air afin de lui faire bien peur et de pouvoir le chasser mais au contraire en entendant le coup du fusil il foncé sur nous j'ai dit a Monsieur Col. tirer bien vite et il a tiré de nouveau l'animal qui etait a 18 pieds de nous a peu pres et il la blessé a mort il a fait deux sault en s'eloignant de nous mais il s'est retourner encore sur nous et j'ai dis au Colonel de tiré afin de le mettre à terre cela faisait une heure et demi que cet animal nous gardait.

Arthur Lirette,
Gardien.

APPENDIX B

On the initiative of the Audubon Society the National Government, when I was President, began the work of creating and policing bird refuges by establishing the following refuges:

March 14, 1903. Pelican Island Reservation. Pelican Island in Indian River, Florida.

October 4, 1904. Breton Island Reservation. Breton, Old Harbor, and Free Mason Islands, Louisiana.

March 9, 1905. Stump Lake Reservation. Stump Lake in North Dakota.

October 10, 1905. Siskiwit Islands Reservation. Unsurveyed islands of the Siskiwit group on the south side of Isle Royal in Lake Superior, Michigan.

October 10, 1905. Huron Islands Reservation. Unsurveyed islands of the Huron Islands group, Lake Superior, Michigan.

October 10, 1905. Passage Key Reservation. An island near the mouth of Tampa Bay, Florida.

February 10, 1906. Indian Key Reservation. An island in Tampa Bay, Florida.

August 8, 1907. Tern Islands Reservation. All the small islets commonly called mud lumps in or near the mouths of the Mississippi River, Louisiana.

August 17, 1907. Shell Keys Reservation. Unsurveyed islets in the Gulf of Mexico about three and one-half miles south of Marsh Island, Louisiana.

October 14, 1907. Three Arch Rocks Reservation. Unsurveyed islands known as Three Arch Rocks in the Pacific Ocean off the coast of Oregon.

APPENDIX B 367

October 23, 1907. Flattery Rocks Reservation. Islands lying off the coast of Washington.

October 23, 1907. Copalis Rock Reservation. Islands lying off the coast of the State of Washington in the Pacific Ocean.

October 23, 1907. Quillayute Needles Reservation. Islands lying off the coast of Washington in the Pacific Ocean.

December 7, 1907. East Timbalier Island Reservation. Small, marshy islands commonly known as East Timbalier Island in the Gulf of Mexico, south of Louisiana.

February 24, 1908. Mosquito Inlet Reservation. Small mangrove and salt-grass islets, shoals, sand-bars, and sand-spits in and near the mouths of the Halifax and Hillsboro Rivers, Florida.

April 6, 1908. Tortugas Keys Reservation. Group known as Dry Tortugas in the Gulf of Mexico, south of Florida.

August 8, 1908. Key West Reservation. Keys and islands of the Florida Keys group near Key West, Florida.

August 8, 1908. Klamath Lake Reservation. Islands situated in Lower Klamath Lake and the marsh and swamp lands unsuitable for agricultural purposes in townships thirty-nine, forty, and forty-one south, Oregon, and in townships forty-seven and forty-eight north, California.

August 18, 1908. Lake Malheur Reservation. Shore lines of Lakes Malheur and Harney and the streams and waters connecting these lakes, Oregon.

August 28, 1908. Chase Lake Reservation. Public lands about Chase Lake, North Dakota.

September 15, 1908. Pine Island Reservation. Bird Island and Middle Island in Pine Island Sound on the west coast of Florida.

APPENDIX B

September 26, 1908. Matlacha Pass Reservation. Three small islands located in Matlacha Pass, west coast of Florida.

September 26, 1908. Palma Sola Reservation. Small, unsurveyed island in Palma Bay, Florida.

October 23, 1908. Island Bay Reservation. Unsurveyed mangrove and other islands in township forty-two south, west coast of Florida.

October 26, 1908. Loch-Katrine Reservation. Lands about reservoir site in Oregon Basin, Wyoming.

January 26, 1909. Pelican Island Reservation. Enlarged to include several other adjacent islands.

February 3, 1909. Hawaiian Islands Reservation. Islets and reefs situated in the Pacific Ocean, near the western extension of the Hawaiian archipelago.

February 25, 1909. Salt River Reservation. Parts of townships four and five north, Gila and Salt River Meridian, Arizona.

February 25, 1909. East Park Reservation. Parts of townships seventeen and eighteen north in California.

February 25, 1909. Deer Flat Reservation. Embracing parts of townships two and three, Boise Meridian, Idaho.

February 25, 1909. Willow Creek Reservation. Embracing part of township twenty-one, Montana Meridian, Montana.

February 25, 1909. Carlsbad Reservation. Embracing two reservoir sites along Pecos River in townships eighteen, nineteen, twenty, and twenty-one south, New Mexico.

February 25, 1909. Rio Grande Reservation. Embracing parts of townships seven, eight, nine, ten, eleven, twelve, and thirteen south, Principal Meridian, New Mexico.

February 25, 1909. Cold Springs Reservation. Em-

APPENDIX B 369

bracing parts of townships four and five north, Willamette Meridian, Oregon.

February 25, 1909. Belle Fourche Reservation. Embracing parts of townships eight, nine, and ten north, Black Hills Meridian, South Dakota.

February 25, 1909. Strawberry Valley Reservation. Embracing parts of townships three and four south, Uinta Meridian, Utah.

February 25, 1909. Keechelus Reservation. Embracing parts of townships twenty-one and twenty-two north, Willamette Meridian, Washington.

February 25, 1909. Kachess Reservation. Embracing Kachess Lakes reservoir site, Washington.

February 25, 1909. Clealum Reservation. Embracing parts of townships twenty, twenty-one, and twenty-two north, Willamette Meridian, Washington.

February 25, 1909. Bumping Lake Reservation. Embracing the Bumping Lake reservoir site, Washington.

February 25, 1909. Conconully Reservation. Embracing part of township thirty-five north, Willamette Meridian, Washington.

February 25, 1909. Pathfinder Reservation. Embracing parts of townships twenty-six, twenty-seven, twenty-eight, twenty-nine, and thirty north, Wyoming.

February 25, 1909. Shoshone Reservation. Embracing part of township fifty-two north, Wyoming.

February 25, 1909. Minidoka Reservation. Embracing parts of townships eight and nine south, Boise Meridian, Idaho.

February 27, 1909. Tuxedni Reservation. Embracing Chisik Island and Egg Island entrance to Tuxedni Harbor in Cook Inlet, Alaska.

February 27, 1909. Saint Lazaria Reservation. Embracing the Island of Saint Lazaria, entrance to Sitka Sound, Alaska.

APPENDIX B

February 27, 1909. Yukon Delta Reservation. Embracing all the treeless tundra of the delta of the Yukon River west of longitude one hundred and sixty-two degrees and twenty minutes west from Greenwich and south of the Yukon River, Alaska.

February 27, 1909. Culebra Reservation. Embracing the islands of the Culebra group, Porto Rico, excepting Culebra Island, which is a naval and lighthouse reservation.

February 27, 1909. Farallon Reservation. Embracing the middle and north Farallon Islands and other rocks northwest of the same, located on the coast of California near San Francisco.

February 27, 1909. Behring Sea Reservation. Embracing Saint Matthew Island, Hall Island, and Pinnacle Islet, approximately in latitude sixty degrees and thirty minutes north, longitude one hundred and seventy-two degrees and thirty minutes west, in Behring Sea, Alaska.

February 27, 1909. Pribilof Reservation. Embracing Walrus Island and Otter Island of the Pribilof group, in Behring Sea, Alaska.

March 2, 1909. Bogoslof Reservation. Embracing volcanic islands commonly known as the Bogoslof group, approximately in latitude fifty-three degrees and fifty-eight minutes north, longitude one hundred and sixty-seven degrees and fifty-three minutes west from Greenwich, Behring Sea, Alaska.

Since then these have been added:

April 11, 1911. Clear Lake Reservation. Embracing the Clear Lake reservoir site, California. Modified by executive order of January 13, 1912, by eliminating, for administrative purposes, three hundred and twenty acres surrounding the Reclamation dam.

APPENDIX B 371

January 11, 1912. Hazy Islands Reservation. Embracing Hazy Island group, approximately in latitude fifty-five degrees and fifty-four minutes north, longitude one hundred and thirty-four degrees and thirty-six minutes west from Greenwich, Alaska.

January 11, 1912. Forrester Island Reservation. Embracing Forrester Island and Wolf Rock, approximately in latitude fifty-four degrees and forty-eight minutes north, longitude one hundred and thirty-three degrees and thirty-two minutes west from Greenwich, Alaska.

January 11, 1912. Niobrara Reservation. Embracing parts of townships thirty-three and thirty-four north, ranges twenty-six and twenty-seven west, Sixth Principal Meridian, Nebraska, the same being a part of the abandoned Fort Niobrara Military Reservation. This reservation was enlarged by executive order of November 14, 1912, adding approximately nine hundred acres, which included the building and old parade-grounds of the military reservation.

February 21, 1912. Green Bay Reservation. Embraces Hog Island at the entrance to Green Bay, within township thirty-three north, range thirty east, of the Fourth Principal Meridian, Wisconsin.

December 7, 1912. Chamisso Island Reservation. Embraces Chamisso Island and Puffin and other rocky islets in its vicinity, approximately in latitude sixty-six degrees and thirteen minutes north, longitude one hundred and sixty-one degrees and fifty-two minutes west from Greenwich, at the eastern end of Kotzebue Sound, Alaska.

December 17, 1912. Pishkin Reservation. Embraces Pishkin reservoir site in townships twenty-two and twenty-three north, range seven west, Montana Principal Meridian, Montana.

APPENDIX B

December 19, 1912. Desecheo Island Reservation. Embraces Desecheo Island in Mona Passage, Porto Rico, but is subject to naval and lighthouse purposes.

January 9, 1913. Gravel Island Reservation. Embraces Gravel Island and Spider Island, approximately in latitude forty-five degrees and fifteen minutes north, longitude eighty-six degrees and fifty-eight minutes west from Greenwich, in Lake Michigan, Wisconsin.

March 3, 1913. Aleutian Islands Reservation. Embraces all of the islands of the Aleutian chain, Alaska, including Unimak and Sannak Islands on the east and Otter Island on the west, reserved for preserve and breeding-ground for native birds, and in addition thereto for the propagation of reindeer and fur-bearing animals and encouragement and development of the fisheries.

April 21, 1913. Walker Lake Reservation. Embraces 9.68 acres of land in section one, township fifteen north, range twelve east, and five acres in township sixteen north, range twelve east, of the Fifth Principal Meridian, Arkansas.

May 6, 1913. Petit Bois Island Reservation. Embraces all of the public land upon Petit Bois Island located in the Gulf of Mexico about ten miles off the coast of Alabama and Mississippi, in townships nine and ten south, ranges three and four west of Saint Stephens Meridian.

September 4, 1913. Anaho Island Reservation. Embraces Anaho Island in Pyramid Lake, Nevada.

June 6, 1914. Smith Island Reservation. Embraces Smith and Minor Islands, situated in the Straits of Juan de Fuca, about fourteen miles north by west from Port Townsend, Washington.

January 20, 1915. Ediz Hook Reservation. Embraces an arm of land extending into the Straits of Juan de Fuca, in township thirty-one north, range six west of Willamette Meridian, Washington.

APPENDIX B 373

January 20, 1915. Dungeness Spit Reservation. Embraces an arm of land extending into the Straits of Juan de Fuca, in township thirty-one north, ranges three and four west of Willamette Meridian, Washington.

By executive order of March 19, 1913, the protection of native birds within the Panama Canal Zone was established, the jurisdiction over same to lie with the Isthmian Canal Commission and its successor, the governor of the Canal Zone, and on January 27, 1914, an amendatory executive order was issued prohibiting night hunting, the use of spring-guns and traps, etc., with additional penalties therefor.

www.ingramcontent.com/pod-product-compliance
Lightning Source LLC
Chambersburg PA
CBHW022008300426
44117CB00005B/75